THE FIFTEENTH MONTH

THE FIFTEENTH MONTH

AZTEC HISTORY IN THE RITUALS OF PANQUETZALIZTLI

JOHN F. SCHWALLER

UNIVERSITY OF OKLAHOMA PRESS : NORMAN

Publication of this book is made possible through
the generosity of Edith Kinney Gaylord.

Cover stamp: Detail of drawing by Emily Umberger of Tlalteuctli, Hackmack Box, Museum fur Volkerkunde, Hamburg. See fig. 16 on p. 186.

Title page: Detail of drawing by Emily Umberger of Teocalli de la Guerra Sagrada, Museo Nacional de Anthropologia, Mexico. See fig. 10 on p. 180.

Library of Congress Cataloging-in-Publication Data

Names: Schwaller, John Frederick, author.
Title: The fifteenth month : Aztec history in the rituals of Panquetzaliztli / John F. Schwaller.
Description: Norman : University of Oklahoma Press, [2019] | Includes bibliographical references and index.
Identifiers: LCCN 2018037550 | ISBN 978-0-8061-6276-8 (hardcover : alk. paper)
Subjects: LCSH: Aztecs—Rites and ceremonies. | Aztec calendar.
Classification: LCC F1219.76.R57 S39 2019 | DDC 529/.32978452—dc23
LC record available at https://lccn.loc.gov/2018037550

The paper in this book meets the guidelines for permanence and durability of the Committee on Production Guidelines for Book Longevity of the Council on Library Resources, Inc. ∞

1 2 3 4 5 6 7 8 9 10

CONTENTS

ILLUSTRATIONS

Plates

Figures

Maps

PREFACE

This book has some similarities to the Aztec god Huitzilopochtli. According to legend, he emerged fully formed and armed from his mother, Coatlicue, in a manner not unlike the birth of the Greek goddess Athena, who also emerged formed and armed from the head of her father, Zeus. So this book emerged almost fully formed from a conference paper I gave in February 2014 at a Nahuatl gathering at the University of Maryland, College Park. As I presented the paper, I began to see layer upon layer of meaning in the rituals I was describing. The question-and-answer period took those ideas and expanded them many times over until I left the meeting with the outline for a book. I cannot begin to thank the other participants in that meeting, and especially James Maffie, for having been midwives in the birth of this book.

Leading up to that meeting, when presented with the opportunity to present at the Nahuatl meeting organized by Maffie, I had wanted something fun and simple. I have always been very fond of an article by Susan Schroeder, "The First American Valentine: Nahua Courtship and Other Aspects of Family Structuring in Mesoamerica." I have always held that it is one of the most elegant, sophisticated, and fascinating studies of Nahua culture. Using an adorable anecdote about the birth of the Mexica *huey tlahtoani*, Huitzilihuitl, Schroeder paints a delightful and rich portrait of the Nahua family. I had always wanted to come upon some small incident, ritual, or anecdote that I could use similarly. In thinking of a paper topic for the Maryland conference, I discovered the central ritual of Panquetzaliztli, "the Swiftness of Huitzilopochtli," wherein a priest runs a circuit of more than twenty miles carrying an amaranth-dough image of the god Huitzilopochtli. I was dumbstruck and told my wife immediately of the "Mexica marathon." That would be the topic of my one-off paper for the upcoming conference. Yet it was not to be a one-off. The more I studied the month, the more layers of meaning I encountered, the deeper I had to probe, and the more layers of meaning emerged.

My interest in the Aztecs, as we universally knew them in my youth, began when I was a wee little boy vacationing in Mexico with my parents. Our annual trips to Mexico gave me an opportunity to learn more about the country and its people. The monumental ruins of Teotihuacan and Monte Alban, neither of them Aztec, were my playgrounds. I fondly remember clambering over temples, crawling in tunnels, and romping through ball courts with my big brother. While trips to museums usually filled me with dread, I really enjoyed the old Museum of Anthropology in the Presidential Palace off the Zócalo and was thrilled and impressed when the collection was moved to the wonderful and awe-inspiring facility in which it currently sits in Chapultepec Park. Aztec gods and place-names were not uncommon topics of conversation at our dinner table when I was growing up.

As a graduate student, I had the opportunity to study Nahuatl with R. Joe Campbell at Indiana University thanks to a National Defense Foreign Language Fellowship. In this I owe a deep debt of gratitude to the Navaho code talkers of the Second World War for having used their skills to help our forces in the Pacific Theater and for raising awareness in the United States about less-spoken and endangered languages. Nahuatl is an endangered language, but thanks to the work of many native speakers, significant effort is being put into protecting and expanding its influence. Although it will embarrass him, I want to recognize the efforts of John Sullivan of the University of Zacatecas for his tireless efforts at assisting native speakers to reclaim their language and its cultural heritage. Through the Zacatecas Institute for Teaching and Research in Ethnology (IDIEZ), Sullivan and his team have launched many efforts to reinvigorate the use of Nahuatl in Mexico. I am honored to know him.

As noted above, there are specific persons whose contributions I need to acknowledge. James Maffie provided the forum where my ideas were first presented. I also want to thank the participants in the Northeast Group of Nahuatl Scholars meetings at Yale who have also assisted me tremendously in developing this book, especially Louise Burkhart, Caterina Pizzigoni, and John Sullivan, who organize it with me annually. My thanks go to Rebecca Duffendach for her guidance in helping me through the intricacies of the various manuscripts included in the Sahagún corpus of Tlatelolco materials. The participants in the New York Latin American History Workshop and the Department of History of the University at Albany were kind in allowing me the opportunity to present parts of this work for their criticism. Among individuals, I need to single out my colleague here in Albany, Louise Burkhart. She and I offer a weekly Nahuatl seminar for anyone interested in joining us. Over the last three years, we have had the pleasure of working with about twenty students. It keeps us on our toes, and there is never a meeting from which I do not gain some new insight.

My work on this project has relied heavily on the assistance of my mentor and friend R. Joe Campbell. His massive data set of all the morphemes in the various Molina dictionaries and the *Florentine Codex* is a wonder. He has always been kind and gracious in making this database freely available. Likewise, my dear friend Frances Karttunen has also been liberal in helping me with the finer points of Nahuatl grammar, morphology, and other linguistic issues. Anne and I look forward to our annual visits to Nantucket to enjoy her company and gracious hospitality. Art historians have been especially helpful both through personal communication and via their works. At various points, Elizabeth H. Boone, Barbara Mundy, Kay Read, Susan Milbrath, Patrick Thomas Hajovsky, and Emily Umberger have given me important insights and helped me understand images in a new way to provide for a richer interpretation. Of course, we all stand on the shoulders of giants. One person in particular, who did not directly assist me in this research but who has been a friend and mentor, although he did not know it, has been don Miguel León-Portilla. I met don Miguel when I was a young scholar working on my dissertation. In the ensuing years, he has always been kind and generous toward me. For this, I thank him. I need to also recall the memory of don Antonio Pompa y Pompa. When I was a graduate student, I was supported through a Benito Juárez–Abraham Lincoln Fellowship, funded bilaterally by the U.S. and Mexican governments. For the purposes of this fellowship, I needed to have a Mexican adviser. Don Antonio graciously accepted that responsibility. His office was in the "new" Museum of Anthropology, which gave me an excuse to visit both the library and the collection.

Most recently, I had the great pleasure of being a summer fellow at Dumbarton Oaks, where I had the opportunity to spend almost two months doing nothing but work on this book. The timing was perfect since I had received the anonymous readers' reports, and I could set about making necessary changes in an uninterrupted environment. But the real joy was being on the campus of such a lovely place, surrounded by gardens, brilliant colleagues, and an excellent staff. The highlight of each day was sitting down to a fantastic lunch prepared in the Refectory. I am deeply in debt to Dumbarton Oaks; Dr. Jan Ziolkowski, the director; and Dr. Colin McEwan, the director for Pre-Columbian Studies. I must also thank Dr. Joanne Pillsbury of the Metropolitan Museum of Art, who as former director of Pre-Columbian Studies at Dumbarton Oaks first encouraged me to apply to be a fellow. I also offer deep thanks to the anonymous readers of this book for Oklahoma. Their insights have only helped to improve it.

Of course, all the insights that I might have I owe to the help and formation of these wonderful scholars. Any errors and blunders are completely my own, and I am sure their name is legion.

Lastly, my family has provided me with more love and support than I probably deserve. My career as an academic administrator meant that we never lived in any place more than six or seven years. My sons were born in Florida; lived in California, Montana, and Minnesota; and went to college in Iowa as I went on to New York. Our family home, wherever it was, became home to them, not because of the building or the neighborhood, but because of the people and furnishings in it. The constants in their lives were my family home in Cuernavaca, Mexico, and my wife's family's vacation home in Minnesota. I cannot be more proud of my sons. They have, against all odds, followed me in the academy. Robert is an associate professor at the University of Kansas, and William is pursuing a doctorate at Temple. Robert is a historian of early-colonial Mexico, William an art historian of contemporary Argentina and the United States. My wonderful wife, Anne, has joined me in all these adventures, has come to love Mexico and Spain as much as I do, and has kept me grounded in the reality of a loving home and family. But our pride and joy are the youngest members of our family, Joseph Frederick Beckley Schwaller and his new little sister Aurelia Mercedes Beckley Schwaller, the fifth generation of our family to live in Lawrence, Kansas. Although it is too soon to know, perhaps the Aztecs will interest them, too.

THE FIFTEENTH MONTH

INTRODUCTION

A Mexica priest, richly arrayed in the costume of the god Huitzilopochtli, emerged from the sanctuary on the top of the Templo Mayor of Tenochtitlan as the sun rose over the eastern mountain peaks. The Templo Mayor was the very tall pyramid in the center of the ancient city, atop which were the twin sanctuaries of Huitzilopochtli (Hummingbird on the Left), the Mexica's own god, and Tlaloc, the all-important god of rain. It was a cool and crisp winter morning. The sun was near its farthest point south as it rose that morning. The priest, called the Topiltzin Quetzalcoatl, held a dough image of Huitzilopochtli in his arms. For today, that god was known as Painal (the Swiftness/the Messenger). In front of him, another priest carried a long, streaming paper banner in the form of the powerful *xiuhcoatl,* the fire snake associated with meteors, which was the special weapon of Huitzilopochtli. They formed a small entourage with a few other priests to perform one of the most important rituals of the solar calendar, "the Swiftness of Huitzilopochtli." The priest was about to run a course of some twenty-three miles through the city and beyond in the western and southern parts of the Central Basin of Mexico. Four sacrifices were made along the way, victims killed to give power to the deity. Crowds thronged along the route. Some people tried to grab pieces of the divine image. Warriors and merchants witnessed the events of the day and later took center stage in leading sacrifices. At the end of the run, the Topiltzin Quetzalcoatl returned to the Templo Mayor and strode up its 113 steps, placing his precious cargo back in the sanctuary. Exhausted, he was revived by his fellow priests who made small cuts on his ears. Returning to his duties, he presided over more sacrifices, several score captured warriors and slaves who had been purchased by the merchants for the celebration.

This running ceremony was the culmination of a series of rituals and celebrations dedicated to Huitzilopochtli, the principal god of the Mexica, in the month of Panquetzaliztli. It was considered one of four preeminent celebrations, if not the singular event of the year. Thousands of people participated directly in the preparations for and execution of the rituals of this month. Each small ritual, each action within the month, had a symbolic message for participants and for observers. This book will analyze these ceremonies and rituals in the period prior to Spanish arrival. While religion is certainly an important component, this study focuses more closely on the historical and political importance of these elements.

Some of the earliest modern scholars working on the "Aztecs" noted that the running of the Swiftness seemed to be a symbolic re-creation of that people's migration myth and of the birth of Huitzilopochtli. But other than this observation, little further research attempted to encompass the intricate set of ceremonies and rituals that marked that month's celebration. This book will dig a little deeper and look at the historical memory embedded in these ritual performances.

In this endeavor, terminology is an important consideration. The people on whom most of this work focuses have traditionally been known in the West as the Aztecs. This term served well until the 1970s, when we became more aware that it carried several biases and was not particularly accurate. Since that time, a more accurate system of names has evolved among scholars and the descendants of the people themselves. In this book, I will seek to use the naming system that seems to be more accurate in distinguishing between several related groups.

This book explores the practices of natives who lived in Tenochtitlan, which is modern-day Mexico City. They called themselves the Mexica. The term "Mexico" comes from that name and means "the place of the Mexica." Originally, the Mexica founded two *altepeme* (city-states),[1] in what is now Mexico City: Tenochtitlan and Tlatelolco. For greater accuracy, we can discuss the Tenochca Mexica and the Tlatelolca Mexica to distinguish between the peoples of these two cities. The Mexica were members of a larger cultural group that was linked by the use of a common language, Nahuatl (also known as the Aztec language). As a consequence, in order to refer to the larger cultural group generally, the term "Nahua" will be used. Thus, residents of any number of preconquest city-states who spoke Nahuatl were Nahuas. Lastly, from about 1430 onward, the Mexica allied themselves with two other Nahua city-states: Tetzcoco (modern Texcoco) and Tlacopan (modern Tacuba). Convention holds that this Triple Alliance might accurately be known as the Aztec Empire. The term "Aztec" is vague in that it refers to any one of several groups who claim a common origin in the mythical place known as Aztlan. Cognizant of this, I will use the term "Aztec" rarely; it will generally refer to the Triple Alliance and to persons associated with it.

This book is replete with Nahuatl terms. I have attempted to write them using a common orthographic system known as the ACK system. J. Richard Andrews wrote the definitive grammar of the language; R. Joe Campbell has taught a generation of scholars and created a massive database of Nahuatl morphemes; and Frances Karttunen wrote the mostly widely accepted modern analytical dictionary of Classical Nahuatl based on colonial sources that attested two important features of the language: vowel length and the glottal stop. In this book, a modified ACK orthography will be used. Where possible, I will use traditional spellings, but when important features such as the glottal stop are needed, I will insert it using the ACK system.

Using a modified ACK system, some common names will appear odd. For example, the person we know as Montezuma is spelled "Moteuczoma" (He Who Scowls Like a Lord).[2] Readers familiar with publications in Spanish that contain Nahuatl terms will notice the absence of the graphic accent. By convention in Mexico, the name of the language is rendered as "Náhuatl," emphasizing that in Nahuatl, the stress would naturally fall on the first syllable;[3] the actual Nahuatl rule is that the stress always falls on the penultimate (next-to-last) syllable. Since this differs from Spanish in some respects, Spanish-language writers frequently insert accents where Nahuatl diverges from Spanish. Since we do not use graphic accents in English and since Nahuatl is absolutely regular in its placement of stress, there really is no reason to add a graphic accent to a Nahuatl word when writing in English.

Much of the action of this book takes place in the Central Basin of Mexico, what in an earlier era was called the Valley of Mexico, or Anahuac using its Nahuatl name. The Central Basin is a high-altitude valley at approximately 2,250 meters above sea level (7,380 feet) and is surrounded by mountains, including snow-capped peaks in the southeast. Because it is surrounded by mountains and hills, the basin collects water from rainfall, snowmelt, and natural springs. But there is no gap through which the water can escape. Consequently, the lake that formed became increasingly saline in the shallow flats in the northern part of the basin while the deeper sections in the south continued to be fresh. The Spanish considered the two parts to be a single body of water, but the Nahua of the valley saw it as five distinct parts, ranging in salinity and consequently having distinct flora and fauna.

According to tradition, the Mexica founded their twin altepeme of Tenochtitlan and Tlatelolco in 1325 on a small rocky island in the middle of the lake.[4] In the very

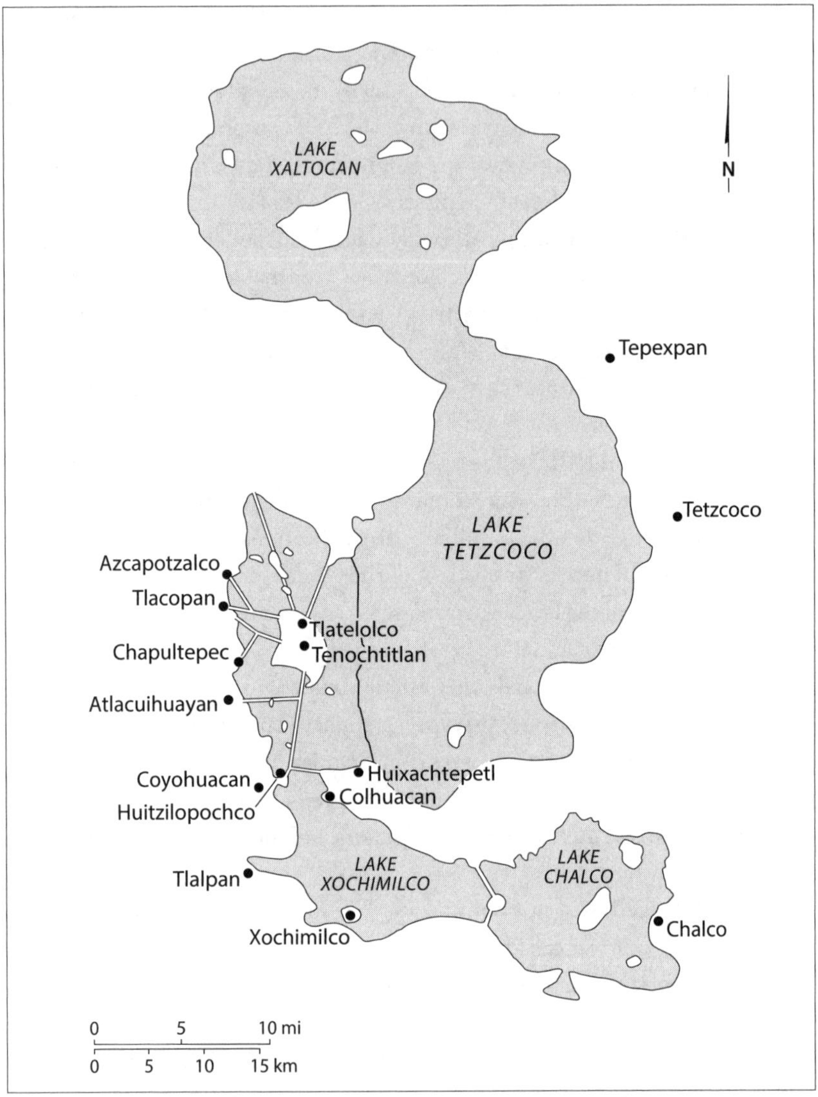

Map 1. Central Basin of Mexico. Map by Bill Nelson.

center of the island, a temple was erected to both Huitzilopochtli and Tlaloc, the rain god. Around this temple, a sacred precinct developed over the course of two hundred years. The small temple became the Templo Mayor, the most important religious building of the Mexica. Smaller structures surrounded it. Toward the west, in the direction of the setting sun, were two nearly equally important buildings. One was the *tzompantli*, the ritual skull rack. On this structure, skulls of sacrificial victims were threaded on horizontal poles in several ranks as a type of memento mori of the importance of death through sacrifice for the maintenance of the cosmic order. Just beyond it to the west was the *teotlachco* (divine ball court). *Tlachtli*, the Nahua ballgame, was an essential part of many rituals. While other ball courts no doubt existed throughout the city, this ball court was sanctified and associated with rituals and celebrations of the divine order. Recent excavations in downtown Mexico City have completely changed our understanding of the physical geography associated with the placement of these structures.[5]

Tenochtitlan and Tlatelolco were connected to the cities across the lake by a series of causeways in all the cardinal directions except to the east, where the lake is broadest (see map 1). The lakeshore was dotted with other altepeme. When the Mexica arrived in the thirteenth century, the basin had already been fairly well populated. To the northwest were Azcapotzalco and Tlacopan. The rocky prominence of Chapultepec, where the Mexica first settled upon entering the basin, was located due west. South of that were Atlacuihuayan (modern-day Tacubaya) and Coyohuacan (modern-day Coyoacan),[6] both of which were major altepeme of the southwest part of the basin. In the southeast were the altepeme of Chalco and Xochimilco, which controlled some of the richest agricultural land of the basin. Directly to the east, across the breadth of the lake, was Tetzcoco, considered by its residents to be the oldest and most sophisticated altepetl of the region.

The Mexica Calendar

The Mexica used two different calendars at the same time to place all their actions within a temporal context. One of these, the *tonalpohualli*, consists of thirteen numbers and twenty signs, which rotate throughout a 260-day cycle. Imagine two cogged wheels. On one are the numbers 1–13, on the other a set of names such as Alligator, Wind, House, Lizard, Snake, Death, and Deer. The two wheels rotate so that 1 Alligator is followed by 2 Wind, 3 House, etc. At the end of the numbers, 13 Reed, the next item on the name wheel (Jaguar) aligns with the number 1 (1 Jaguar). Turning on a few more spaces, what was the first sign at the start (Alligator) now aligns with 7 on the second rotation (e.g., 7 Alligator, followed by 8 Wind, 9 House, etc.). It takes 13 cycles of the names, which is 20 cycles of the numbers, to return to the starting point. Each set of the thirteen numbers was called a *trecena* by the Spanish.

This book is an analysis of the month of Panquetzaliztli, one of eighteen months in the *xihuitl* or *xiuhpohualli* calendar of the Mexica. This calendar is based on the perceived movement of the sun and thus is described as a "vague" solar year.[7] It consists of 365 days organized into eighteen months of twenty days each, with five unnamed days leftover that are collectively called the *nemontemi*. Because the xihuitl is a vague year and does not seem to have accommodated a leap day, over time the seasons slowly moved through the various months.[8] In the solar calendar, each of the eighteen months was marked by a series of ceremonies and rituals associated with a particular deity of the Mexica pantheon who was the patron of that month. These months are frequently referred to in Spanish as the *veintenas*, or counts of twenty, since each month has twenty days. Spanish sources differ regarding the names of each month, although by and large the order of the months remains the same. Following the organization supplied by Fr. Bernardino de Sahagún, the months are as follows.[9] Sahagún's name for the month comes first, followed by a rough translation, and any major variant name appears in the third column.[10]

MONTHS OF THE XIHUITL

Name	Translation	Variant
Atl cahualo	They Leave the Water	Quauhuitlehua
Tlacaxipehualiztli	Flaying of Men	
Tozoztontli	Short Watch	
Hueytozoztli	Long Watch	
Toxcatl	Dry Thing	
Etzalcualiztli	Meal of Maize and Beans	
Tecuilhuitontli	Small Feast of the Lords	
Hueytecuilhuitl	Large Feast of the Lords	
Tlaxochimaco	Flowers Are Given	Miccailhuitontli
Xocotlhuetzi	Xocotl Fruit Falls	Hueymiccailhuitl
Ochpaniztli	Sweeping the Way	
Teotl eco	Arrival of the Gods	Pachtontli
Tepeilhuitl	Feast of the Mountains	Hueypachtli
Quecholli	flamingo	
Panquetzaliztli	Raising of Banners	
Atemoztli	Falling Water	
Tititl	Wrinkled	
Izcalli	Resurrection	

The fifteenth month, Panquetzaliztli,[11] clearly had important ritual significance to the Mexica, because they chose it to be one of the four months during which subject peoples were required to pay their tribute to the Triple Alliance.[12] It also fell near an important celestial event, the winter solstice, and marked the beginning of the season of warfare for preconquest societies in central Mexico. Since the winter in the central highlands tends to be cool and dry and the harvest was completed by then, it was conducive to warfare. Moreover, the month also focused on the celebration of the Mexica national god, Huitzilopochtli. In the early sixteenth century, the month ran from late November into December of the European calendar.[13] Many of the months' names are evocative of the activity that occurred during them, for instance, during Panquetzaliztli, banners were raised. But as will be explored in greater depth, the banner was symbolic of sacrificial victims.[14] Consequently, the name of the month implies that it featured human sacrifices.

The tonalpohualli and xiuhpohualli calendars ran concurrently. Thus, any given day would have one date from each calendar. The two calendars would return to the same day/date combination every fifty-two years. The closing of this cycle was called the *xiuhmolpilli* (the binding of the years). It was celebrated with a complex ritual called the New Fire ceremony, which will be discussed further in chapter 5. While the Mexica were able to locate any event with a date from the two calendars, that date would only place the event within a fifty-two-year period. By analogy with the Western calendar, it would be similar to say that there was a war in the year '38 but not be able to specify which century. The Maya resolved that difficulty by also creating a zero day, a starting point from which all days were counted in succession, but the Mexica, and the Nahua in general, did not do this. Consequently, time could be slightly more flexible for the Mexica. If the calendars needed adjusting, this could be achieved by adding the same number of days to each calendar.[15]

In spite of Panquetzaliztli's importance to the Mexica, focusing as it did on their national god, thus far there have been no in-depth studies of the month. In fact, only one of the months of the xihuitl has received a monographic treatment, and that is the eleventh month, Ochpaniztli (Sweeping the Way), studied by art historian Catherine DiCesare. This study, however, does not analyze the rituals and ceremonies so much as chronicle the representation of the month's ceremonies over the early-colonial period.[16] Several modern works, however, have tackled the study of the xihuitl as a whole, with individual chapters focusing on particular months. Michael Graulich, a prolific author and keen scholar of the preconquest world, wrote the best of these studies.[17] At the same time, a host of scholars from the sixteenth century to the present have attempted to understand exactly how the calendar governed the everyday lives of the Mexica. As will be seen in chapters 1–4, many of the early-colonial observers provided modern scholars with the building blocks that allow us to better understand the intricacies of the calendar and the rituals and ceremonies that it governed. This study will both describe and analyze the activities of the month. Later, the focus will shift to consider how the month came to be celebrated in the exact manner in which it was.

The terms "ritual" and "ceremony" will appear on nearly every page of this book. There do not seem to be any hard and fast rules in Religious Studies about the exact meaning of these two terms. Nonetheless, after a very informal survey of the literature and of various scholars' opinions regarding distinctions between the two words, I have opted to use the words in this manner: the term "ritual" will mean any discrete series of actions dictated within a larger religious celebration, and "ceremony" will refer to a series of rituals that, taken together, constitute a whole. Using an example from Christianity, for instance, Catholics, Episcopalians, some Lutherans, and others celebrate the Eucharist (Communion, the Lord's Supper, etc.) on Sunday. The larger ceremony consists of several smaller rituals. The first part is frequently called the Liturgy of the Word while the second half is the Liturgy of the Eucharist, or Liturgy of the Table. Each of these liturgies can be considered a ritual, although there are also smaller rituals within each of them. For example, the Liturgy of the Eucharist contains the Eucharistic Prayer itself as well as various set prayers such as the Lord's Prayer, the Distribution of the Elements, and the prayers after Communion, each of which can be considered a ritual.

Each of the months of the xihuitl had a signature ceremony that usually occurred on the last day of the month. For example, in 1520 the Spanish conquerors of Mexico living in Tenochtitlan witnessed the celebrations of the month of Toxcatl. Over the course of the month, a young man was chosen to impersonate the god Tezcatlipoca and live the life of the deity, taking wives and banqueting. Then the young man slowly ascended the steps of the Tlacochcalco temple, discarding the accouterments of the god as he went, in order to meet his demise at the hand of a sacrificial priest at the top of the pyramid.[18] In the month of Ochpaniztli, the signature ceremony also included two running ceremonies involving warriors and god imitators. One person imitated the goddess Toci (Our Grandmother), then in the middle of the month, the goddess was sacrificed and then flayed. A warrior then donned a piece of her thigh skin and wore it for the rest of the month.[19]

Over the course of the twenty days of Panquetzaliztli, the celebration built as additional rituals were conducted, all culminating in a distinctive ceremony called "the Swiftness of Huitzilopochtli." The rituals of the last day focused the energy and attention of the entire city on the sacrifice of scores of prisoners and slaves. The signature ritual of the Swiftness of Huitzilopochtli consisted of a priest who ran on a long circuit (more than twenty miles) in the Central Basin while carrying a dough image of the god Huitzilopochtli.

In order to better understand the celebration of Panquetzaliztli, we fortunately have access to descriptions of it in the works of various Spanish missionaries who collected information on the preconquest lives of the natives. Several of the early- and middle-colonial chroniclers included information about the festivities in their writing. Fr. Bernardino de Sahagún and his informants were by far the most prolific, dealing with the celebration in several sections of his works. Another missionary friar, Diego Durán, who was raised in Mexico by Spanish parents, provides another detailed description of the month and its ceremonies. The Franciscan friar Toribio de Benavente, who was known as Motolinia, also includes in his writing some critical details about the month and its festivities. These and similar works provide a picture of the ceremonies that occurred on many of the days of the month and form the basis for much of this book. The use of these sources is not without its peril. There is little doubt that the picture of native society provided by the missionaries was distorted by the friars' own Christian beliefs and desires to convert the natives. Indeed, the suppression of native beliefs was one of the motives for their collection of data about native cultures. Because the material collected by these missionaries plays such a central role in our understanding of Panquetzaliztli, a bit more should be known about each missionary and the methods he used to collect, organize, and present his information.

Fr. Bernardino de Sahagún

Bernardino de Sahagún is well known for amassing a vast amount of information on the preconquest Nahua. Sahagún envisioned creating a collection of materials that would assist missionaries in their work among Nahuatl-speaking peoples. The purpose that he envisioned for this collection of books was to assist in the suppression of the last vestiges of native culture. Sahagún felt that if the missionaries were well versed in the culture, they would be able to better understand what bits had persisted and how to root them out. Those materials included not just descriptions of the native culture at the time of the conquest but also sermons, a confessional guide, translations of Bible readings for Sunday mass, and other Christian doctrinal works.[20] But it is the cultural—what some call ethnographic—material that provides the best look into rituals from the preconquest era.[21] Sahagún composed several versions of the work. Due to the vagaries of history, two works stand as testimonies to his efforts: the *Florentine Codex*, a bilingual (Nahuatl and Spanish) encyclopedia of cultural information about the Nahua, and the *Historia general de las cosas de la Nueva España*, the Spanish-only version of the same material. Sahagún collected much of the material reported in the *Florentine Codex* and the *Historia general* with the assistance of at least four Nahua natives.

Sahagún was living in the Franciscan convent of Santiago Tlatelolco (in the northern district of Mexico City) and served as an instructor in the Colegio de Santa Cruz Tlatelolco, where the friars trained the sons of the Nahua elite in Spanish Christian culture. He collected and composed his works in the 1560s until about 1575.[22] Because Sahagún used informants who lived in the neighborhoods near the convent, the material in these two works tends to reflect a bias toward Tlatelolco and Tenochtitlan, the twin cities that were the Mexica capital. The urban area came to be known collectively as Tenochtitlan after the conquest, and eventually just Mexico.

Sahagún's methodology has been debated among scholars in recent years. The degree to which his native assistants participated in the whole enterprise is also subject to debate. Initially, scholars considered the various works to be Sahagún's own. More recently, the role of the native assistants has emerged as significant to the degree that some might consider them joint authors, especially of the text written in Nahuatl.

As noted above, Sahagún was a committed missionary. His ultimate goal was the spread of Christianity and the elimination of other religions. Because he used questionnaires, native informants, and other trappings of modern ethnography, some scholars tend to downplay the ultimate goal of his work as he envisioned it. Others have noted that Sahagún worked during a period when medieval notions of culture and knowledge were fading but a modern conception had not yet taken hold. The degree to which Sahagún manipulated his data has only begun to interest scholars as more bits and pieces of his work papers are made more widely accessible and as more scholars have the linguistic skills, particularly in Nahuatl, to handle them. Sahagún's work seems seamless and not internally contradictory, but the important question is the degree to which it is a faithful reflection of Mexica culture or rather merely an artifact of Sahagún and his team. Because his information on the Mexica is some of the richest and is relatively approachable, it forms and will continue to form the core of studies such as this one. At the same time, we need to scrutinize Sahagún's work and evaluate it both in terms of its time and in how it supports or contradicts the information from other sources.[23] As a result, although this current book relies heavily on Sahagún, his observations are not accepted blindly.[24] The works of several other missionaries and the testimony of pictorial manuscripts also enlighten this study.

Within both the *Florentine Codex* and *Historia general*, Sahagún discusses the rituals associated with the month of Panquetzaliztli on at least three different occasions: twice in the book on the rituals and then in five chapters of the book on the merchants. Other references to specific aspects of the celebration also appear in numerous other parts of the work. Yet the *Florentine Codex* and *Historia general* were the last stages in Sahagún's process of learning and writing about preconquest culture. He initiated his studies in the late 1550s in Tepepulco, to the northeast of Mexico-Tenochtitlan, where he used young native men from the Colegio of Santa Cruz Tlatelolco. This work has been published as the *Primeros memoriales.* The information was not put into final form, however, until the friar's return to the Franciscan convent of Tlatelolco and to his duties in the Colegio at least a decade later.[25] Among other things, the *Primeros memoriales* focuses on the Nahuas' festivals, calendars, and gods and contains a concise description of the festival of Panquetzaliztli, again based on information collected by Sahagún in Tepepulco. Sahagún presents a different description of Panquetzaliztli's ceremonies in the *Primeros memoriales* than he reports in the *Florentine Codex.* While certain elements are consistent with what was reported for Mexico-Tenochtitlan, the Tepepulco celebration differs in several significant ways. Arthur J. O. Anderson points out that the two locales (Tepepulco and Mexico-Tenochtitlan) were very different types of places. Tepepulco was a minor district's capital that was subject to a larger altepetl, namely Tetzcoco, while Tenochtitlan was the most important altepetl and the capital of a large and vibrant collective of states. As a result, one would expect that ceremonies would differ significantly from one place to the other.[26]

After his return to Tlatelolco from Tepepulco, Sahagún continued his collection of firsthand knowledge about preconquest times. Some of the preliminary work that Sahagún compiled early in his research has also been preserved in two Spanish repositories located in Madrid: in the Royal Library, located in the Royal Palace (or Palacio de Oriente), and in the Library of the Real Academia de la Historia. These materials were collectively called the *Codices matritenses,* or "Madrid codices." These are materials that scholars now consider to have been rough drafts for the *Florentine Codex* and are called by some scholars the *Manuscrito de Tlatelolco*, since Sahagún was resident in that neighborhood during its production. Most of this information ultimately appeared in the final version of the *Florentine Codex*.[27] Moreover, unlike the case of the *Primeros memoriales*, very little of the information in the Tlatelolco manuscript deals with the celebrations of the months of the solar year, and what does appear is essentially repeated in the *Florentine Codex*.

Fr. Diego Durán

Durán was born in Spain, but according to his own words, he moved to New Spain before he was about six. He learned Nahuatl as a small child living first in Tetzcoco and later in Mexico City. He joined the Dominican Order and began a career as a missionary in various towns and villages such as Hueyapan and Oaxtepec, south of the Central Basin, in the shadow of the great volcano Popocatepetl. He also learned a great deal about the conquest and life before the conquest because of his friendship with Fr. Francisco de Aguilar, who had participated in Hernán Cortés's expedition. Like Sahagún, Durán felt compelled to learn as much as he could about preconquest culture in order to better evangelize to the natives. While he admired many aspects of preconquest Mexica culture, he believed that the natives had practiced and continued to follow a diabolical religion. He was not convinced of the earnestness of their conversion and saw idolatrous practices just below the surface of their devotions. At the same time, Durán also saw great parallels between the natives and the Hebrews, even proposing that the Mexica were descendants of one of the lost tribes of Israel.[28] Clearly, Durán's preconceived notions about the Mexica would color much of his writing. He was more open and obvious about his biases than Sahagún was, and his observations must be evaluated carefully. At the same time, Durán's work is also an essential source for beginning to understand the Mexica because of its rich content.

Durán's research method was slightly different from Sahagún's. Rather than rely principally on native informants, Durán had access to a significant number of preconquest native pictorial manuscripts. Yet these are difficult to interpret without training, so he solicited the support of natives who were trained to decipher the texts in the old ways. Beyond gaining information about the texts, Durán relied on native elders whose recollections took them back to the time before the conquest. Unlike Sahagún, Durán queried Spanish conquerors to tell him what things were like at the time of contact. These witnesses were notoriously untrustworthy in their memories of the native culture, but Durán found a few whom he felt comfortable interviewing, such as Fr. Francisco de Aguilar.[29]

Durán organized his information into three works. One was a history of the natives up through the conquest, commonly called the *History of the Indies of New Spain*. Another text with information on the preconquest culture, including descriptions of ceremonies and rituals, has reached the present day under the name the *Book of the Gods and Rites*, while his exposition of the Mexica calendar system is called the *Ancient Calendar*. Durán composed these works at roughly the same time that Sahagún was composing the *Florentine Codex*, approximately 1574–81.[30]

Fr. Toribio de Benavente ("Motolinia") and Fr. Andres de Olmos

Motolinia was one of the original twelve Franciscan missionaries to New Spain. A native of the village of Benavente in the Kingdom of Leon, little is known of his life before his arrival on the shores of New Spain as an ordained member of the Franciscan Order. He was a close friend of the leader of the expedition of twelve friars, Fr. Martín de Valencia. He took the name Motolinia from a comment made by the natives as the friars walked on their way from the coast up to Mexico. Seeing how poorly the friars were dressed, the natives exclaimed, "Motolinia!" meaning, "He is poor!" Motolinia was an indefatigable missionary, baptizing hundreds if not thousands of natives during his career. He also was one of the first friars to attempt to write down the cultural history of the natives among whom he worked. Unlike the cases of Durán and Sahagún, where scholars have been able to piece together snippets of insight regarding their sources and research methodologies, there are fewer clues about Motolinia, perhaps because he was working so early. While he authored several works, Motolinia is best known for two: the *Memoriales* and the *Historia de los indios de la Nueva España*. These works suffer from many of the same drawbacks as the accounts of Durán and Sahagún in that, while in some ways sympathetic with the natives, Motolinia was a missionary who sought the evangelization of the natives.[31]

Fr. Andrés de Olmos drew on Motolinia's experience. Olmos arrived in Mexico a bit later as a member of the entourage of the first bishop of Mexico, Fr. Juan de Zumárraga. Olmos was the first friar to formally study Nahuatl, writing a preliminary grammar and dictionary of the language and copying down many of the aphorisms that were a distinctive feature of Nahuatl.[32]

Fr. Juan de Torquemada

Juan de Torquemada, like Durán, arrived in New Spain along with his parents while still a child. In about 1579 he entered the Franciscan Order. He served in Mexico, New Galicia, and Guatemala as a missionary and came to know a variety of important figures, including Bernal Díaz del Castillo, the soldier-chronicler of the conquest, and important missionaries and Nahuatl scholars like Sahagún, Fr. Juan Bautista de Viseu, and one of Sahagún's research assistants and informants, Antonio Valeriano. Between 1605 and 1612 he served as the chronicler of the Franciscans in New Spain, collecting and organizing the papers of the various chroniclers and other friars who preceded him. In this way, Torquemada became familiar with the earlier works of Andres de Olmos, Motolinia, and Gerónimo de Mendieta. The result of Torquemada's efforts was his monumental work known as the *Monarquía Indiana* (Indian monarchy) published in Seville in 1615. The book's full title is *The Twenty One Ritual Books and Indian Monarchy, with the Origin and Wars of the Western Indians, of the Cities, Discovery, Conquest, Conversion, and Other Marvelous Things of the Same Land.* As the title indicates, it is divided into twenty-one sections and covers all aspects of native history and culture, from their origins up through the conquest and evangelization. Book 8 considers each of the months of the xihuitl, describing the rituals and ceremonies of each in some detail. While Torquemada learned Nahuatl and much about Nahua culture firsthand, his book is a retelling and reordering of material collected by other friars who were chronologically closer to the conquest. The work of Torquemada came to be reviled in the nineteenth century when scholars noted that some of his information was taken verbatim from the works of others without giving them credit, especially from other Franciscans such as Gerónimo de Mendieta and Bernardino de Sahagún. In more recent times his work has been reevaluated. While he does incorporate information from the works of others, the practice was very common when he wrote, and attribution was not yet a universally accepted norm. More important, Torquemada clearly had access to a rich collection of information, some of which has not reached modern times. Thus, his work is the only way in which scholars can access some lost texts. Like Sahagún and others, Torquemada also consulted native elders and others who might have had valuable information regarding the topics he covered.[33] Thus, Torquemada had a rich corpus of material upon which to draw when he set about writing his chronicle and history.

Several important pictorial manuscripts also date from the early-colonial period. Many of them contain material that describes the Panquetzaliztli festival.

In addition to the pictorial manuscripts from the native tradition, of which a few remain, works such as the *Primeros memoriales* and the *Florentine Codex* should also be considered because of their illustrations.

Birth of Huitzilopochtli and the Mexica Migration

The Templo Mayor, the principal temple in Tenochtitlan dedicated to Huitzilopochtli, was the focal point for the celebrations of Panquetzaliztli in the city. But the Templo Mayor was envisioned as more than just the largest religious building in the sacred precinct of Tenochtitlan. It also figured as a symbolic representation of the mythical mountain Coatepec (Snake Mountain). That locale played a central role both in the mythic birth of the god Huitzilopochtli and in the Mexica migration story.[34]

One of the myths concerning Huitzilopochtli's birth was intimately linked to the origin myth of the Mexica people themselves, creating a deep tie of reciprocity between the deity and the people.[35] One of the important stories describing the birth of Huitzilopochtli reinforces his role as a solar god. Coatlicue (Snake Her Skirt) was the mother of Coyolxauqui (Bells [on] Her Cheeks) and her brothers, the Centzon Huitznahua (Four Hundred Southerners). One day, while Coatlicue was sweeping the temple on Snake Hill (Coatepec), a ball of eagle down floated from the sky. Coatlicue placed the fluff in the bosom of her blouse and continued her chores. Later, when she tried to remove the ball of down, she could not find it. Instead, she discovered that she was pregnant. This infuriated the Centzon Huitznahua, who considered their mother's pregnancy to be intolerable and, assuming it to be the result of sexual intercourse outside of marriage, evidence of her sexual depravity. Without a known father, the parentage of the child was clearly suspect. The Centzon Huitznahua conspired with their sister, Coyolxauqui, to kill their mother and, at the same time, their as yet unborn brother. Huitzilopochtli, still in his mother's womb, discovered his siblings' plot and, at the appointed hour, emerged fully armed, wielding his signature weapon, the xiuhcoatl, the Fire Serpent. His brothers were clothed in paper armor that he ignited with his weapon. He beheaded and dismembered his sister, Coyolxauhqui, and threw her body parts off Snake Hill.[36] Because Huitzilopochtli had no known father, one of his epithets in Nahuatl was Tetzahuitl (Something Scandalous or Frightful). Sahagún expanded on this, adding, "For no one appeared as his father."[37]

In the famous sculpture of the dismembered Coyolxauhqui at the base of the Templo Mayor, the wounds of her death are clearly apparent (see fig. 1). Lying

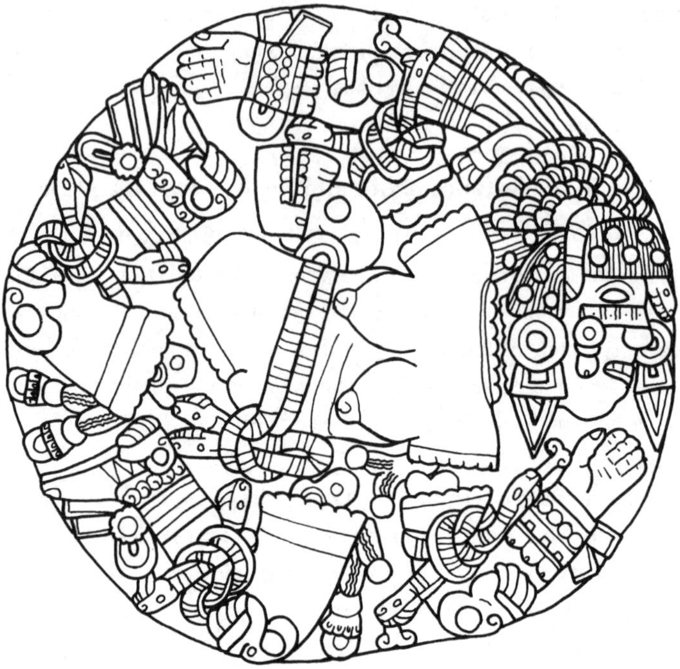

Fig. 1. Coyolxauqui Stone, Templo Mayor, Mexico. Drawing by Emily Umberger.

naked, she is beheaded and dismembered. She also carries symbols of her name in the bells that adorn her cheeks. On her forehead are the balls of down that were also representative of Huitzilopochtli, since that was the mechanism whereby his mother was impregnated (the down balls also appear on his shield, which was called the *tehuehuelli*).[38] Coyolxauhqui also has snake "garters" tied around each of her limbs just below the point of dismemberment, probably in recognition of her mother, Coatlicue.

Analyzing this birth myth, scholars have noted that if Huitzilopochtli were considered the solar deity, then Coyolxauhqui would be the representation of the moon while the Huitznahua were the stars. The coming of the sun inevitably drives away and defeats the moon and stars.[39] The xiuhcoatl has been interpreted as the burning rays of the sun, possibly a thunderbolt or a meteor.[40] Lastly, the Templo Mayor was considered to be Coatepec, the place where Coatlicue was impregnated and where Huitzilopochtli was born.[41] Everyone understood that it was a symbolic relationship—they knew that the pyramid was not the actual hill or mountain. The origin myths place the location of the original Coatepec somewhere to the northwest, possibly in the region of Tula.

The Mexica origin myth inserts a bit of circularity into the birth story of Huitzilopochtli. According to the legends of their origin, the Mexica came from an island home called Aztlan. In one account, the Mexica discovered the god Huitzilopochtli in a cave as they set out on their migration (see fig. 2). He was carried by one of their leaders, who became a *teomama* (god carrier), and he led them on their path (see fig. 3). Eventually, the migration reached Coatepec, where Huitzilopochtli was born of Coatlicue.[42] This version of the myth is necessarily circular, since the god existed before Coatepec. This seeming impossibility was explained in a sixteenth-century collection of myths that narrated the migration of the Mexica from Aztlan to Coatepec (spelled Cuauhtepec in that version): because Huitzilopochtli both accompanied the migrants and was born at the location, that variant explained, "She became pregnant without assistance of a male, and Huitzilopochtli was born of her, in addition to the other times when he was born, since he was a god, he could do and accomplish what he wanted."[43] This account had Coatlicue as a virgin, suggesting that Huitzilopochtli was her first child. In that version, Tezcatlipoca (Smoking Mirror), who died before the start of the current epoch and then came to life again, created the four hundred opponents who sought to kill Huitzilopochtli. Lastly, the author notes that the birth of Huitzilopochtli and the death of the four hundred opponents were celebrated annually, which is a reference to the feast of Panquetzaliztli.

Fig. 2. Departure from Aztlan. *Tira de Peregrinación/Boturini Codex*, plate 1. Drawing by Emily Umberger.

Fig. 3. Teomama (god carrier). *Tira de Peregrinación/Boturini Codex,* plate 2. Drawing by Emily Umberger.

Some of the legends and modern scholars hold that Huitzilopochtli was a man who was deified: an elder called Huitzilin (Hummingbird), who led his people on their migration. His name was significant because, according to belief, warriors who died in battle became hummingbirds who accompanied the sun on its daily course.[44] As a leader, he was infused with the power of the deity Tetzauhteotl (Frightful or Scandalous God), an avatar of Tezcatlipoca and a god of fishers who had presented himself as a wizard and manifestation of the moon.[45] Thus, the deity who directed the migration spoke through the medium of a leader named Huitzilipoch, or Huitzilin.[46] During the migration, Huitzilin died and underwent an apotheosis, according to the legend, born as Huitzilopochtli at Coatepec, where the Mexica had stopped on their migration.[47]

Running among the Mexica

Running figured as an essential element in the celebrations of Panquetzaliztli. In Mexica culture in particular as well as in Nahua culture, running was an important activity with both practical and spiritual purposes. In order to understand the larger context within which the running ceremony of Panquetzaliztli occurred, it is necessary to look at the various functions of running within the Mexica and Nahua cultures.

In addition to the information provided by writers such as Durán and Sahagún, some data regarding running and runners among the Mexica comes from Spanish accounts of the conquest. Cortés, in his letters to the Spanish crown, explains that the *huey tlahtoani* (great speaker, the Mexica ruler), Moteuczoma, maintained a corps of fast runners to carry messages from one part of the empire to another. Thus, when the Spanish finally landed on the Gulf Coast at a site they would call La Villa Rica de la Vera Cruz (the Noble Town of the True Cross), they were greeted within hours by emissaries dispatched by Moteuczoma. Cortés claimed that the runners had carried information 260 miles in less than a day.[48]

Mexica couriers were used for a variety of purposes. Clearly, one was to communicate quickly and efficiently with far-flung parts of the empire. These runners also brought rare and exotic goods from great distances in order to delight the ruler. Items mentioned include ice and snow from nearby volcanoes as well as seafood and other coastal delights. Some colonial writers explain that Moteuczoma regularly enjoyed fresh seafood brought up from the coast by the messengers. Using a relay system, the couriers could cover 200 to 350 miles per day with runners stationed at approximately two-league distances (5.2 miles).[49] Some of the sources report that a team of runners could cover four to five leagues (10.4 to 17.5 miles) in an hour (3.4 to 5.8 minutes per mile).[50] Marathon runners in modern times run on average at about six miles per hour for a 26.2-mile run (9.5 to 10 minutes per mile).

One of the Nahuatl words for these runners was *titlantli*, generally glossed as "messenger"; the other was *paina*, "swiftness."[51] While there was a special group of fleet runners called titlantli who served as messengers, this word was also applied generally to messengers and ambassadors. From the literature, it seems that the courier runners consisted of two different types. One was the messenger who sent regular communications from one part of the empire to the other and possibly carried small items as quickly as possible. This category may have included those who were called simply titlantli or paina and who carried messages or goods along a fixed route. The other was the *tequipan titlantli* (victory messenger). These were young men of marriageable age who traveled with the Mexica troops to military engagements. When the Mexica began to take prisoners and it seemed that victory was in their grasp, the messengers would be dispatched to notify the huey tlahtoani.[52] These couriers wore colored ribbons in their hair, which indicated the progress of the war. A white ribbon signified that victory was either at hand or had been achieved. They wore the traditional cloak, tied at one shoulder, but in order to run faster, it was belted around the waist. They also carried messages written in pictographs on paper to provide the same information. If the messenger was reporting a victory, he carried a *chimalli* (a round shield) in his left hand and a *macuahuitl* (a war club edged with obsidian). When the courier had to report a defeat, he left his hair untied and disheveled.[53]

Runners also participated in certain important ceremonies such as the New Fire ceremony. In this ceremony, to be discussed more fully in chapter 5, a fire was kindled in the chest cavity of a sacrificial victim. Priests who gathered around lit their torches from that new flame. Then they passed the fire to special runners who would carry this "new" fire to all locations in the valley. The most important of these runners sped directly to the Templo Mayor, where he first illuminated the image of Huitzilopochtli and put fire to the incense offered to the god. The fire was then passed to the priests of the sacred precinct and then to the rest of the city. In describing the runners, Sahagún wrote that these messengers were chosen from among the warriors who were valiant but also fast. They were called *in painani* or *in tlaczani* (the fleet or the swift), terms that used two of the common words for running, *paina* and *tlacza*.[54]

While little else is known of the messengers, it is possible that the office was either hereditary or at least limited to a small number of well-trained individuals. Future couriers were chosen when still quite young. They trained under the supervision of the priests of the sacred precinct. In order to strengthen their legs and build endurance, the boys were required to run to the top of the Templo Mayor repeatedly. Each trip was a total of 113 steps. To encourage them and provide incentive, prizes were given to the winners of these sprints.[55]

Bearers and Porters

The couriers were associated with bearers and porters because of the similarity of their social and economic functions in aiding communication and trade. Bearers also played an important role in the origin myth of the Mexica and in the conception of time. The couriers and porters used the same roads and stopping places and were frequently considered one group. The principal difference among them was speed. Indeed, one of the services of the messenger was to carry small items quickly over long distances. Others who carried larger loads over long distances were also essential in the trade system of the Mexica. In the absence of beasts of burden, all long-distance trade had to occur through the agency of human bearers and porters. These people were known generically as *tlamama* (he/she/it carries something).[56] Some evidence indicates that the porters and the couriers

Fig. 4. Tlamama (bearers). *Codex Mendoza*, folio 62r, Arch. Selden. A. 1, Bodleian Library, University of Oxford.

might have used the same way stations, since porters were also expected to carry burdens four to five leagues before being relieved, the same distance that lay between messenger stations.[57] While runners covered this distance in about an hour, porters required a day for the same distance.

The tlamama used a *mecapalli* (tumpline) and frame to carry their burdens on their backs.[58] A tumpline is a rope that attaches to a carrying frame and then passes over the back and shoulders, across the forehead, and down to the other side of the frame. The Mexica normally carried goods in either wooden boxes or baskets, depending on what was being carried, which were attached to the carrying frame.[59] Consequently, the carrying frame and tumpline became symbolic of bearers (see fig. 4).

According to comments from the conquest period and practices during the early-colonial period, the tlamama served in the towns or regions where they lived and were subject to the jurisdiction of the local tlahtoani. It is not clear whether third parties could contract the porters directly without the intervention of the local lord. As with couriers, porters might have been part of a clan or hereditary group within each polity. The *Codex Mendoza*, a pictorial history of the Mexica from the early-colonial period, shows young children being trained to become porters, using the tumpline, suggesting that porters were prepared from a young age.[60]

Long-distance trade was an essential feature of life in the empire and an area in which the tlamama played a central role. The *pochteca* and *oztomeca* (commercial traders and merchants) based in Tenochtitlan used hundreds of bearers on their journeys, taking articles from the core of the city to the periphery and vice versa.[61] This would seem to contradict the control of all tlamama by local lords unless they also oversaw all trade in their districts. Yet the evidence seems to indicate that the pochteca maintained ties to sources well outside the Aztec sphere of influence, well beyond areas controlled by local Mexica or Nahua lords. Nonetheless, for some of the long-distance trade, the pochteca employed a corps of specialized porters based in Tenochtitlan and its twin city, Tlatelolco. Yet this was an expensive proposition. Bringing porters with them to distant lands, the traders incurred costs that might not necessarily be recouped by sales along the way. Bearers were paid only when on the road and would not be paid during markets and trading opportunities. Because the merchants might be expected to transport more goods on the return trip than they had on the outward leg, the number of porters used on the return trip would tend to outnumber those on the outbound. It would thus be reasonable that merchants contracted additional porters to return with them to Tenochtitlan, dealing with local lords as needs dictated.[62] The long-distance merchants became important participants in the Panquetzaliztli celebrations.

Bearers also played an important ritual and symbolic role. In the legends of the Mexica migration, a teomama (god carrier) had carried the national god, Huitzilopochtli (see fig. 3). Just as the tlamama carried his burden on his back with a tumpline and carrying frame, the teomama had borne the god in a bundle on his back, using a cloak as a tumpline. In the *Tira de Peregrinación,* another Mexica codex that depicts the migration of the Mexica people from their mythical home to the Central Basin, four nobles are shown leading the people, with the god bearer in front. Indeed, in the Panquetzaliztli running festival, the priest who carried the image of the god was called a teomama. Three of the leaders were men, but one was most clearly a woman, who was called Chimalma and could be identified by her typical hairdo and garb.[63]

The role of these four migration leaders is not clear. While the Mexica people were traditionally divided into seven groups, called *calpolli* (neighborhoods, or sometimes kinship groups), the four-part leadership seems to have been broadly adopted among groups in Central Mexico.[64] In Tlaxcala, for example, four leaders governed the altepetl. Tenochtitlan itself was frequently depicted as encompassing four main districts. In the *Codex Mendoza* (see plate 1), the altepetl of Tenochtitlan had four main regions, each surrounded by symbols of water, signifying both Lake Tetzcoco and the canals that crisscrossed the city.

Not only was Huitzilopochtli pictured as being carried during the Mexica migration, different gods were also envisioned as carrying their responsibilities on their backs. The gods had the duty to see that the calendar continued to move in a regular order. Because of the organization of the various calendars, the gods were thought of as moving time along. Sahagún discusses the god One Rabbit bearing time along: "One Rabbit. It is said [that this was] the year sign and year counter of the south. For thirteen years it carried, set on its path, took with it, bore the burden [of the year]."[65]

Organization of the Study

The chapters of this book will analyze various aspects of the Panquetzaliztli celebration and the running of the Swiftness that takes place within it. The Mexica migration to the Central Basin of Mexico will serve as a point of departure. The Mexica established their twin cities in 1325. During the next one hundred years, they were subject to other altepeme, but after about 1427, they launched a political and military alliance with their neighbors called the Triple Alliance. In the century prior to Spanish arrival, that alliance came to dominate much of what is now central Mexico. Clearly, areas on the fringe of this region would be under less Mexica influence. Even some of the parts of the Central Basin only came under Mexica domination toward the end of the preconquest period. In order to discover some of the earliest forms of the Panquetzaliztli celebrations, the first chapter looks at narrative and pictorial manuscript sources from the outer reaches of the alliance along with some of the first information collected by the Spanish. These documents might reflect native traditions that were less subject to Spanish influence in the wake of the colonization. The chapter develops a picture of the rituals and celebrations of Panquetzaliztli, drawing on both narrative and pictorial sources. Using pictorial manuscripts, the chapter also explores essential iconographic elements to help identify the principal deity of the celebrations: Huitzilopochtli and his avatar Painal.

While both Durán and Sahagún collected reams of information about the native cultures, the content needs to be continually interrogated given the complex environment in which the missionaries worked and the shifting intellectual landscape of the times. Nonetheless, those two missionaries, along with others such as Torquemada, provide modern scholars with a wealth of detail about the celebrations during the month of Panquetzaliztli. The second chapter attempts to integrate these disparate authors' observations of the month's festivities into a single narrative, outlining the daily activities up to the point of the running of the Swiftness. Chapter 3, in turn, focuses in some detail on the rituals, including the Swiftness, that led up to and followed the sacrifices on the Templo Mayor. Both of these chapters are replete with details as the individual rituals practiced on each day of the month are described and analyzed. By looking at them in such detail, we can begin to appreciate the complexity of the symbolic realm within which the few signature ceremonies occurred. If we were to focus only on the impressive ceremonies toward the end of the month, the entire arc of the celebration would be lost. Indeed, the rituals were choreographed toward a particular emotional experience that culminated in the running of the Swiftness and the sacrifice of the victims on the final day. In chapter 3, comparisons are made with the tentative finds from chapter 2 in order to create a unified notion of the month's flow and the function of rituals within it.

In the fourth chapter, additional pictorial elements are added to the increasingly complex picture of the month's celebrations. Since the Panquetzaliztli ceremonies and rituals have cognates in the festivities of other months, this chapter also considers those elements of similarity, which are found in the various texts describing other celebrations. While many of these elements' symbolism is opaque to modern viewers, thanks to colonial chroniclers and our ability to interpret Mexica symbolic acts within a larger cultural context, we are able to see that many of the rituals and ceremonies have transcendent importance. The chapter demonstrates that the Mexica used elements of the month's celebration to impose their particular worldview and used human sacrifice on a massive scale in order to cow potential opponents and keep others within their sphere of influence. The many elements of the celebrations tend to reinforce several very simple and important messages about Mexica and Aztec power. The chapter concludes with a hypothesis considering what the Panquetzaliztli festival might have been like prior to the rise of the Mexica and the creation of the Triple Alliance.

The fifth chapter looks more deeply into Mexica myths, stories, deities, and belief systems in order to more completely interpret the nuances of the rituals and ceremonies. In particular, the migration legends and the stories of Huitzilopochtli's birth are analyzed in greater detail to see their relevance to the Panquetzaliztli celebrations.

Chapter 6 offers observations about the nature and history of the Mexica state and the Triple Alliance as seen in the ceremonies of Panquetzaliztli. The Panquetzaliztli celebrations of Tenochtitlan differed in three important ways from the proposed Nahua celebrations of the month. Each of these is considered in the chapter. These Mexica innovations include the centrality of Mexica national god Huitzilopochtli, the prominence of merchants in the Tenochtitlan celebration, and the alignment of the important New Fire ceremony with the month of Panquetzaliztli. Similarly, the Mexica introduced a new vision for the cycles of existence that is complementary to the other changes seen in Panquetzaliztli. The chapter attempts to determine when and why each of these innovations was included among the month's ceremonies.

This book offers a unique insight into the rituals and ceremonies of what is possibly the most important month of the Mexica solar year. The early-colonial chroniclers tended to present a static, asynchronous image of the monthlong ceremonies. Using a wide variety of perspectives and methodologies, we can begin to excise elements and determine their origin and potential utility within the monthlong celebration and even posit the historical and political bases for these changes. Thus, while the picture is of the celebrations as they transpired on the eve of the conquest, we can take a more historical look, analyzing the specific elements and how they worked together to create the final product. In this manner, it becomes clear that the celebrations as described by the chroniclers were not static but subject to changes from many sources. This, in turn, allows us to better piece together how ceremony and ritual both changed over time and played an important role in Mexica statecraft.

CHAPTER 1

PANQUETZALIZTLI OUTSIDE TENOCHTITLAN

The month of Panquetzaliztli had an important role in the life of the Mexica in Tenochtitlan. But before looking at the ceremonies and rituals associated with the month in the capital, this chapter will consider how it was marked outside Tenochtitlan. Similarly, it will attempt to determine how the month might have been celebrated prior to the rise of the Mexica. Both these perspectives can, then, better explain how the Mexica might have innovated the month's activities and what the implications of these changes might have represented.

The two major sources for knowledge of Mexica life and culture, written by friars Diego Durán and Bernardino de Sahagún, essentially draw from the experiences of Tenochtitlan. But in order to better consider the Mexica ceremony in its larger context, we need to look beyond Tenochtitlan and to the rest of the Nahua world. This chapter will consider how the month was celebrated in the Nahua world generally and in the Central Basin of Mexico outside Tenochtitlan more specifically. It draws on several sources. The richest, by far, is the information collected by Sahagún early in his career in Tepepulco, which lies within the Central Basin of Mexico but well outside the immediate influence of Tenochtitlan. Other missionaries also gathered bits of information about the preconquest celebrations that can help to re-create the broad strokes of the festival outside the city. Lastly, some of the pictorial evidence draws on experiences outside the Central Basin of Mexico or simply from outside Tenochtitlan. Some of the sources included in this chapter, such as the narrative of Motolinia, come from Tenochtitlan and other places in the Central Basin. Yet, because Motolinia was one of the very first missionaries, the information he collected potentially also came from the earliest times after the conquest.

As noted, the ceremonies described for Tenochtitlan at the time of European contact may or may not have been representative of how the festival was celebrated in other Nahua communities. Likewise, the descriptions may not even reflect how the festival was commemorated in Tenochtitlan historically. It is quite likely that ceremonies changed after the Mexica took leadership of the Triple Alliance. Fortunately, we have surviving descriptions, although fragmentary, of Panquetzaliztli celebrations, some of which are from other regions of central Mexico, along with glimpses of Tenochtitlan earlier in its history.

Looking at the "compact *veintena* icons," that is, the specific images associated with each of the twenty-day months found in pictorial manuscripts, H. B. Nicholson saw a movement toward greater consistency among the depictions of the months, especially in the iconography. There were significant differences in local practices, but at the same time, there was "widespread sharing of basic ideological concepts and ceremonial performances throughout the region" due to many communities' incorporation into the Triple Alliance.[1] Thus, looking across many different pictorial sources, Nicholson perceived a fairly high degree of homogenization, at least in the small images used to represent the months, which in the case of Panquetzaliztli was simply a banner.

Pictorial manuscripts, those from both before and after the conquest, can provide a great deal of information about the celebrations associated with Panquetzaliztli. The illustrations from Sahagún's *Primeros memoriales* of the Panquetzaliztli celebration and the descriptions of the gods' raiment can be particularly useful in providing a hint of Nahua religious practice outside the imperial capital city. A score or so of other pictorial manuscripts document practices from the xiuhpohualli (the solar calendar). Of these, only one comes from outside the Central Basin. One clearly comes from Tetzcoco, across the lake from Tenochtitlan, while the others originate in either the imperial capital or the Central Basin more generally. Nonetheless, these works can help to round out our knowledge of religious performances and practices.

Central to understanding the rituals of Panquetzaliztli, and all feasts, is the Mexica notion of *ixiptla* (plural, *ixiptlahuan*). Taken at its basic level, an ixiptla was a symbolic representation of something. This could be an object that represented some cosmic force or deity, or it could be a person who dressed up like a deity. Generally, the crucial examples considered here were objects or people who represented deities. In Nahuatl, things cannot exist in the abstract but must be possessed, owned, or part of someone or something. "Someone's ixiptla," that is, an ixiptla not possessed by a specific person, would be *teixiptla*, "someone's impersonator or symbolic representation." Molly Bassett has called the teixiptla "the localized embodiment."[2] While an ixiptla of a person is easily distinguishable from that person, the ixiptla of a deity might both look like the deity and embody the deity. These concepts will become crucial as we explore the details of Panquetzaliztli celebrations here and in later chapters.

Fray Toribio de Benavente, known as Motolinia, collected a great deal of information about preconquest life during the early days of the evangelization. He was active between his arrival in 1524 and his death in 1568, thus making him one of the first observers of preconquest culture. His missionary efforts focused largely on central Mexico, including Tenochtitlan and the Tlaxcala region. But his observations do not seem to be as tightly focused on Tenochtitlan as other commentators'. He describes the ceremonies and rituals of Panquetzaliztli twice, once briefly and once with a bit more detail. The brief description is evocative as much for what it says as for what it implies.

> Panquezalistle—This feast was the birth of Uchilobus [Huitzilopochtli] from the virgin. And they made a Uchilobus from seeds, and all those whom they had had [captured] in war they killed them and they all ate them. And one of them they dressed in blue, and painted his face blue with each two stripes of yellow. They killed him on Mutizuma's [Moteuczoma's] stone. They offered some seed buns. They did not eat from the rising of the sun until it was set, and it lasted one day.[3]

The outline of the feast is simple in this description. It celebrated the birth of Huitzilopochtli from a virgin. Immediately we can begin to question Motolinia's motive since this could be a clear reference to Christ's virgin birth, especially since both Christmas and Panquetzaliztli were celebrated roughly around the winter solstice. A figure of Huitzilopochtli was made of grain. Although the friar did not mention it, that figure of the deity was an ixiptla, a local embodiment of the god. Motolinia describes a festival having to do with the sacrifice of warriors captured in battle. The sacrifice also included ritual cannibalism. The general populace fasted during the daylight hours. One of the warriors/victims was dressed in blue and then sacrificed on the sacrificial stone dedicated by Moteuczoma I.[4] That victim, dressed in imitation of Huitzilopochtli, was also an ixiptla, although again

Motolinia did not recognize it as such. Thus, within Motolinia's brief description, he presented two of the forms that the ixiptlahuan can take: a figurine or statue and a person dressed in imitation of a deity.

In his longer description of Panquetzaliztli, Motolinia begins after having discussed the stars and the calendar. In addition to the information given in his brief description, he explains that the preparations for Panquetzaliztli were not simple. Each year, more than sixty or eighty men fasted for up to a year in preparation. The early missionary friars saw fasting as one of the desirable religious behaviors of the past that they could encourage. In the preconquest ritual, many women also fasted and prepared foods for the penitents. In addition, Motolinia suggests that the entire corps of priests and others involved in the rituals fasted for some eighty days (four native months). They performed self-sacrifices of blood, prayed, and offered incense to the principal gods. On the day of the feast, before dawn, the priests gathered at the Templo Mayor along with the lords and the general populace. Throughout this longer passage, Motolinia describes the Mexica priests as if they were part of the Catholic Church. He refers to the chief priest and his lieutenants as the "Supreme Pontiff with his Cardinals." Later he comments that the chief priest was dressed in "pontifical robes." The groups of priests revealed an image of Huitzilopochtli that had been finely dressed and decorated. This was, then, an ixiptla, a local embodiment of the god Huitzilopochtli. The chief priest took up the image of the god and carried it in a procession following those who carried incense before him. The procession went to Tlatelolco, then to a place called Acolman, to Azcapotzalco, then Tlacopan, passed in front of Chapultepec, then went to Huitzilopochco (modern Churubusco), and finally back to the Templo Mayor by midday. Along the way, four persons, war captives called *mamaltin*, were sacrificed at a temple in Acolman and another four were sacrificed outside Huitzilopochco. The route was some five leagues (about 21.5 miles) long. A similar set of fasts, sacrifices, and processions occurred in Tetzcoco.[5]

After that introduction, in the next section Motolinia expands on the subject of Panquetzaliztli by noting that it was a month during which there were many sacrifices and homicides through heart removal and that there was ritual cannibalism. He clarifies that the month was dedicated to both Huitzilopochtli and Tezcatlipoca. The latter deity represented many aspects of Nahua life. He was associated with warfare, the hunt, and youth. Motolinia explained that they were brothers, gods of war, and powerful forces of destruction. While

Tezcatlipoca was the older brother, the two were the principal gods revered throughout the region.

The feast of Panquetzaliztli was one of the principal celebrations of the native year. Motolinia explained that people would offer blood sacrifices by drawing their own blood from their tongues, ears, arms, or chests. It would be wiped on paper or sprinkled on the images of the gods in a manner, according to Motolinia, not unlike Christian priests' sprinkling of holy water. Again, this type of interjection raises many questions about veracity and intent. The place where blood was drawn differed from province to province, and one could determine a person's province of origin by how he or she drew blood.

The friar then goes on to detail the human sacrifice practiced during the month. He describes a large narrow stone (one palm's breadth thick by one and a half wide) that was placed upright on the floor in front of an image of a native deity, which Motolinia calls an idol. He writes that on this stone, the victim would be placed with the shoulders on the top point so that his breast was elevated. Priests, called the *tlamacazque*, would hold the hands and feet of the victim. The priests were very quick and dexterous. One took up a knife made of flint, like a flint for fire making, which he notes was not particularly sharp, contrasting it to an obsidian blade that would have an edge as sharp as a barber's razor. Although the knife was not sharp, the position of the victim, with the chest and abdomen flexed, meant that with a powerful stroke, the priest could cut open the chest and remove the heart. The officiating priest offered the heart in the sanctuary of the temple and then all around, leaving a trail of blood, until he finally dropped it to the ground. He picked it up and placed it in an offering bowl. Motolinia wrote that from time to time, the priests and their assistants would eat or sample the hearts. He used the word *alfaquí* for the assistants. It is a borrowed word from Arabic that describes a person trained in Islamic law, thus again raising concerns in a modern reader.

Motolinia continues, relating that after the sacrifice, the body was rolled off the top of the temple onto the steps below. If the victim had been captured in battle, the warrior who had taken him took charge of the body. Along with family and friends, the warrior would carry the body to his home, where the flesh of the victim would be prepared and served in dishes. If the warrior was wealthy, he would offer a lavish feast in testimony to his bravery, giving gifts of blankets to his guests. If the victim had been a slave, he would not be rolled off the temple but carried down. The person who had purchased him would also offer a feast, but not as lavish as the warrior's. Motolinia then briefly notes that in different feasts, slightly different procedures were followed. Nonetheless, at a feast such as Panquetzaliztli, the number of victims differed according to the size and importance of the city: from as few as twenty to as many as one hundred. In the major cities and in Tenochtitlan, more than one hundred victims were sacrificed.[6] Somewhat later in his narrative, Motolinia also suggests that the fasting of the priests and other participants was practiced similarly in Tlaxcala, Huejotzinco, and Chollolan. The fast meant that people could eat only small rations of tortillas, salt, and water.[7]

In discussing the widespread tradition of fasting, Motolinia comments that it was an integral part of the celebration of Panquetzaliztli. Throughout the solar year, the priests would conduct fasts of between ten and forty days, consuming only tortillas, water, and salt. Yet, in preparation for Panquetzaliztli, the priests would fast for a full eighty days, which made some of them sick. The general public, including children, generally only fasted like this for between five and ten days. The friar goes on to note that there were few general fasts but that each province would have its own schedule. The fasts and feasts would be dedicated to the most important gods for that place.[8]

Looking at the description offered by Motolinia, we can see certain essential elements comprising the festival of Panquetzaliztli. In all likelihood, Motolinia's information is some of the earliest chronologically, probably collected before Sahagún's and Durán's accounts. It manifests a focus on Tenochtitlan, detailing activities in specific places in and around that city. At the same time, Motolinia indicates that the festival was celebrated in a similar manner elsewhere, such as in Tetzcoco and even Tlaxcala. His experiences in central Mexico allowed him to make such comparisons. The preparations began several months out with fasting and other spiritual disciplines. The highlight of the feast was a ritual procession wherein a priest carried an image of the god over a route within the Central Basin of Mexico. We can imagine that upon returning to the Templo Mayor, sacrifices such as those detailed by Motolinia occurred. There was also feasting and gift giving, principally involving warriors who had captured enemies in battle. Others also participated by providing slaves for the sacrifices, but Motolinia was silent as to their identities.

Primeros memoriales—Tepepulco

Sahagún collected the material contained in the work that has come to be known as the *Primeros memoriales* in the altepetl of Tepepulco during the 1550s while he was a missionary friar living there. Tepepulco is located some one hundred kilometers northeast of Tenochtitlan. Historically it had closer ties to the city of Tetzcoco than to Tenochtitlan. Tetzcoco was associated with the Nahua ethnic group known as the Acolhua, who traced their lineage back to the historical city of Tula.

The rites associated with the month of Panquetzaliztli in Tepepulco continued over an eighty-day period (i.e., four Nahua months), although Sahagún does not explain exactly when they began or when they ended. The fast included not just reduced intake of food and drink but also abstinence from bathing and sexual relations. Elsewhere in the *Primeros memoriales,* Sahagún writes that the abstinence from bathing and sexual relations lasted only seven days, not the full eighty.[9] Specifically, on the fifth day of the month of Panquetzaliztli, everyone fasted, including children. While Sahagún does not detail the nature of the sacrifices that were performed during Panquetzaliztli, he merely notes that there were deaths similar to those associated with the month of Tlacaxipehualiztli. He also refers to a festival for Painal, but Sahagún fails elaborate on that comment anyplace else in the work.

The celebration of Panquetzaliztli in Tepepulco included much singing and dancing in addition to fasting and abstinence. Young people were allowed to hold hands and to dance, probably making the festival something that they eagerly anticipated. During the celebration, residents of the surrounding villages would come into the city, in this case presumably Tepepulco, to sing in the sacred precinct. Along with these ceremonies, they made offerings of tortillas to Huitzilopochtli. Sahagún describes them as being long and large. He implies that the teixiptla featured in this ritual was of some edible material, because at this point in the ritual performance it was broken, presumably to be eaten. While Sahagún does not explicitly say that the pieces were consumed, he does link the breaking of the figure with the consumption of one of two kinds of pulque (*matlalloctli,* "blue pulque," and *macuiloctli,* "fivefold pulque") that were drunk on the top of the temple.[10] The brewing of this pulque was the responsibility of the priest who had the title of Ometochtli Pahtecatl (Two Rabbit, Lord of the Medicine).[11] During the ritual drinking of pulque, an ixiptla of Huitzilopochtli named Chonchayotl would descend and seek out passersby to cut their ears. This also involved a ritual skirmish or battle, although the details of the battle are not included in the *Primeros memoriales.* Elsewhere, Sahagún suggests that the priest called Cuatlapanqui Ometochtli (Head Breaker, Two Rabbit) was responsible for dressing the god impersonator during this ceremony.[12]

In summary, during the celebrations in Tepepulco, a figure of the god Huitzilopochtli was fashioned for the celebration of Panquetzaliztli, but Sahagún does not indicate the nature of this image. The celebration included a series of sacrifices involving the god Painal, although Sahagún provided no details. Lastly, in Tepepulco, there was a ritual battle. In this ritual, an ixiptla of Huitzilopochtli named Chonchayotl came down from the top of the temple. Assistants would grab people who happened to be passing by in the roads and streets and bring them to Chonchayotl/Huitzilopochtli. The unfortunate ones would be grabbed by the hair and suffer cuts to the earlobes. This ritual was called the *Chunchayocacalioaya* (Battle of Chonchayotl).[13]

Sahagún's comparison of Panquetzaliztli with Tlacaxipehualiztli is curious. He writes only that there were deaths. The latter festival included the flaying of sacrificial victims, after which priests would wear their skins. Sahagún's comparison might have to do with the number of sacrificial victims slain during each month. Nevertheless, in the text of the *Primeros memoriales,* Sahagún only obliquely suggests that there were any deaths at all in Panquetzaliztli. The reader has no idea who these victims might be or the manner of their death. The reference to Painal is curious because the friar does not further elaborate the nature of the sacrifices to that god in the *Primeros memoriales,* nor does he state in which month they might have occurred. He provides no indication that Painal was the focus of some Panquetzaliztli rituals, nor is there any indication that he was included in rituals for Tlacaxipehualiztli, which were dedicated to the god of regeneration, Xipe Totec, (Flayed One, Our Lord). The other similarity between the feasts of Tlacaxipehualiztli and Panquetzaliztli is that both included much singing and dancing, but again, these were elements common to many months. In yet a different section of the *Primeros memoriales,* Sahagún notes that individuals sang and danced at the two feasts, as they did in the months of "Huey Tozoztli, Toxcatl, [Huey]Tecuilhuitl, and Xoco Huetzi [Hueymiccailhuitl]." This could imply a similarity of repertoire, possibly confirming what he had written.[14]

In the *Primeros memoriales,* Sahagún also provides the reader with some descriptions of the gods' raiment. The first two deities listed are Huitzilopochtli and Painal, reinforcing the relationship between the two deities suggested in the earlier description of Panquetzaliztli rituals. The descriptions of their costumes are filled with words not found in other contexts, thus making it more difficult to determine exactly what Sahagún intended with the descriptions. Fortunately, both descriptions are accompanied by illustrations that help to clarify the text and fill in gaps of understanding (see plate 2).

The Array of Huitzilopochtli

On his head is a headdress of yellow parrot feathers with a quetzal feather crest.
His blood bird is on his forehead.
There are stripes on his face, on his countenance.
Ear plugs of lovely cotinga feathers.
On his back he bears his fire serpent disguise (*xiuhcoanahual*), his *anecuyotl.*
On his arm is an armlet with a spray of quetzal feathers.
The knotted turquoise cloth is bound around his loins.
His legs are painted with blue stripes.
On his legs are small bells, pear-shaped bells.
His lordly sandals.
His shield is the *tehuehuelli.*
Across the shield lie stripped [arrows].
His serpent staff is in his other hand.[15]

There are several unique features to the costume of Huitzilopochtli. The "blood bird" probably refers to the hummingbird insignia frequently found on his forehead. The xiuhcoatl (fire serpent or turquoise serpent) was his special weapon. In this description, it appears as a disguise that he wears on the back of the ixiptla. Consequently, the fire serpent might have served purposes other than as simply a weapon but also as an insignia and costume. From the text, it is not clear whether the xiuhcoatl is different from the other item included in the phrase "the *anecuyotl* (*aneucyotl*)," though they clearly are different. One description has it being a headdress covered with white feathers,[16] although it literally means "water honey/nectar." Angel María Garibay believed it to be some sort of belt, while other descriptions imply that it was more of a basketlike headdress of paper and feathers.[17] The bells worn on the legs are similar to the apparel of Tezcatlipoca.[18] The staff that the Huitzilopochtli ixiptla carries is probably a symbol of his fire-snake sword, being a *coatopil* (serpent staff), perhaps an insignia of his lordship.[19] Many scholars have studied the nature of the god's shield, the tehuehuelli. The word only appears in limited places in the *Florentine Codex,* where it metaphorically refers to the shield that pregnant women carried into their labor, possibly representing the unborn child.[20] The word, while not translated by Charles Dibble and Arthur J. O. Anderson, means something like "very powerful stone." The dots that appear in the decoration on the shield probably depict tufts of down that are unique features of Huitzilopochtli, probably referring to his birth legend.[21] The combination of the shield and the arrows is also a visual metaphor for the Nahuatl diphrase (two words that together signify a third concept) *in mitl in chimalli* (the arrows, the shield), which signifies war.[22] This symbol of the arrows and the down-tufted shield appear as part of the representation of the city of Tenochtitlan in the *Codex Mendoza,* located just below the iconic eagle standing on a cactus. The Tenochtitlan design, which includes the four down tufts around a central feather signifying cosmic order, is called the *ihuiteteyo.*

A song about Huitzilopochtli found in the *Primeros memoriales* provides a bit more of the metaphorical impact of his birth. The song is entitled "Chimalpanecatl icuic" (the One on the Shield, His Song), and is about the mother Tlaltecahua (One Who Possesses Earth). The song tells of the birth of a child from a virgin onto a shield at Coatepec. The shield was called the tehuehuelli. The gloss of the poem clarifies that this was a tale of the miraculous birth of Huitzilopochtli, who emerged fully armed with his distinctive shield and with his face painted for war. It also associated his mother, Coatlicue, along with the earth god Tlaltecatl (Earth Lord).[23]

The description of the god called Painal is equally detailed and it immediately follows that of Huitzilopochtli (see plate 3). Sahagún mentions Painal but does not explain his role. While there are some differences between the two costumes, the overall impression is of similarity, as one would expect from an avatar or alter ego of the principal god.

The Array of Painal

> On his head is a headdress of yellow parrot feathers.
> A cagelike design is painted across his face.
> His face is painted with the star design called darkness.
> In his nose is his turquoise nose arrow adornment.
> His blood bird he places [on his forehead].
> [His hummingbird disguise is on his back]
> On his chest is his gold ring [his breast mirror].
> His turquoise shield, the shield covered with a mosaic of turquoise,
> is in his hand.
> He wears the turquoise knotted cape.
> The fire sticks [and] the golden banner are in his hands.[24]

Clearly, the central color theme of Painal's raiment is turquoise with accents of gold and yellow. Yet, like Huitzilopochtli, the ixiptla also has the "blood bird" insignia, which ties him to the principal god. The gold mirror on his chest, however, could suggest some influence of Tezcatlipoca. Most indicative of the celebrations of Panquetzaliztli, Painal's ixiptla holds the signature banner in his hand: *teocuitlapanitl,* (a golden banner).[25] The fire sticks of the narrative do not appear in the illustration. They probably relate Painal to fire making festivities, the most important of which was the New Fire ceremony.

The major and important difference between the illustration of Huitzilopochtli and that of his companion Painal is that the major god is depicted standing upright while Painal is shown seated. All the other deities in the *Primeros memoriales* save one are shown standing. Only the very last, Omacatl (Two Reed), a deity named for a date from the tonalpohualli calendar, which served as one of the names of the god Tezcatlipoca, is also seated. A reed mat was one of the unique characteristics of Omacatl, and thus he was depicted seated upon it. He was also celebrated in Toxcatl along with the creation of amaranth-dough images.[26]

Although the *Florentine Codex* was written and produced later than the *Primeros memoriales,* a comparison of just the deity images of Huitzilopochtli and Painal can provide some additional information about the nature of these two gods and their depictions. Also, the *Florentine Codex* certainly is based on Tenochtitlan and Tlatelolco, not Tepepulco. Just as in the *Primeros memoriales,* Sahagún describes the array of the gods in the *Florentine Codex.* Again, the first god was Huitzilopochtli. Among other features of the god, Sahagún notes: "And when a feast was celebrated [for him], captives were slain; ceremonially bathed slaves were offered up. The merchants bathed them."[27] The written description of his array is quite brief compared to the one found in the *Primeros memoriales*: "And he was thus arrayed: he had an ear-pendant of blue *cotinga* feathers; he had the fire serpent disguise, the blue netted cloth, the arm band. He wore rattles and shells."[28]

The accompanying picture in the *Florentine Codex* (see plate 4) shows an ixiptla standing and looking to his right. This is clearly the picture of a man wearing the god's array. On his head, he has a headdress with three horizontal stripes, yellow, white, and red, from the bottom to the top. In these bands, one sees green feathers standing straight up, giving the effect of a very colorful toque or chef's hat. He wears an ear decoration of red feathers. On his face are two yellow bands of face paint, one along the lower jaw, the other at the height of the eyes. In his right hand, he has a serpent staff, the coatopil. On his back is a very large feathered device, possibly the xiuhcoatl, with a similar headdress, but it has only a red band encircling the green feathers. The device's mouth is open, seemingly attached to the deity impersonator only at the lower jaw by means of a red sash around the waist. The upper jaw shows a row of squared-off teeth. On his left arm, the deity has a paper device tied with a red ribbon, and he holds a shield with three arrows in his left hand. The shield is white with five clusters on it, no doubt depicting the down balls associated with Huitzilopochtli's shield. He wears what looks like pinstriped pants, tied at the knee and ankle. His sandals are like most of the other figures.[29]

The description of Painal immediately follows that of Huitzilopochtli (see plate 5). In the text, Sahagún notes that Painal was the deputy, delegate, or substitute for Huitzilopochtli. Interestingly, here Sahagún uses the word *moteixiptlatianj* to describe Painal. The *teixiptla* was the localized embodiment of the god,[31] and this is a verb form of the word, meaning "to assist in the place of another or to represent someone in a play."[31] This means that he represented the god in processions; he urged people forward. Sahagún then notes: "And the people followed [the impersonator], jostling, howling, roaring. They made the dust rise; they caused the ground to smoke. Like people possessed, they stamped upon the earth. And one man carried [the image] in his arms." The array of Painal follows, and is equally brief compared to the *Primeros memoriales*: "And he was adorned thus: he was garbed in the costly cape of precious feathers, with the quetzal-feather head-ornament in the manner of coastal people. Bars were painted on his face; and a star design. He had a turquoise nose-plug. His was the hummingbird disguise. He had the breast mirror; he had a shield set with mosaic of turquoise."[32]

The drawing that accompanies this description is slightly different from that found in the *Primeros memoriales*. Like the other drawing, the god is shown sitting down. Again, in the *Florentine Codex*, the only other god shown sitting is Omacatl. Painal has a headdress similar to Huitzilopochtli's. There is a yellow cap surmounted by a red band, from which the green feathers rise. But at the forehead of Painal, there is a device that looks like three small balls at the end of sticks. He has gray paint around his eyes, with small white circles around them, and some sort of nose plug, which is also painted white. The gray items should have been blue, but possibly the paint has faded over the years. Following the narrative description, the nose plug is turquoise while the circles around the eyes are symbols of the stars. Like Huitzilopochtli, he has two yellow stripes of face paint: one at the forehead, the other at the level of the mouth. He wears a smoking-mirror earplug and has a red knot at his shoulder, probably tying up the ends of his headdress's band. The cloak is fishnet, edged in red with white disks, a typical star-eyes design common to many deities. There is a white circle at the breast held by a red knot, a shell pectoral. He also seems to wear a short white garment over his shoulders. In his right hand is a white shield composed of what should be a turquoise mosaic with four yellow pendants. In his left hand, he holds a yellow-striped banner topped with a flint.[33]

Several items, such as Painal's shield, his cloak, and his nose plug, the narrative description notes, should be turquoise. The cape was of costly feathers (*teuquemetiuja* [*teoquemetihuia*]), which one can assume was blue in color, since that was the color associated with royalty and power. The rulers are normally depicted wearing blue capes, *xiuhtlapalli tilmahtli*.[34] In the *Florentine Codex*'s illustrations of the gods, what should be blue appears gray. Taking the written description and the illustration together, one gets a fairly complete idea of what the god (or god imitator) was supposed to look like, but neither is complete by itself. Just as in the depiction of Huitzilopochtli, Sahagún and the artist who worked for him took pains to make it clear that this was a man in the disguise of the god.

The painted image may have had as much to do with Nahua thought as with Sahagún's concerns about the continuation of certain features of Mexica religion. Some minor variations in the details of the images might have been the result of a conscious effort to deprive the image of its power as a teixiptla. Diana Magaloni Kerpel argues that the painted image could take on the power of the deity if it were, in fact, completely adorned in the proper manner. The omissions of details would deprive the image of its power. After chemical analysis of the colors used in the manuscript, Magaloni Kerpel concludes that the colors appear as intended, rather than having changed in appearance as a result of chemical changes over time. Thus, she proposes that the use of gray rather than a brilliant blue might just be one way of depriving the image of its power.[35]

When taken together, these descriptions and illustrations of Huitzilopochtli and Painal from the *Florentine Codex* help to explain some things that are not made clear elsewhere in the narrative. Dibble and Anderson, the translators of the *Florentine Codex*, indicate that both a god impersonator and the amaranth image of the god appeared in the running ceremony of the month of Panquetzaliztli. They do this through inserting the phrase "the impersonator" in their translation: "'*Auh in maceoalti, quitocaia*' (And the people followed [the impersonator])."[36] But Sahagún's Nahuatl actually reads, "And the people followed it." It is notable that the Nahuatl states "it" rather than "them."[37] The earlier description of Painal states that he was the "substitute" for Huitzilopochtli, where Sahagún used the word *moteixiptlatianj* (*moteixiptlatiani*). Clearly Sahagún, in the Nahuatl, referred to either the teixiptla who carried the image or to the image itself, or to the two as one, but not to them individually. The procession manifested multiple layers of impersonation: the dough image, the priest who carried it, and possibly yet more members of the entourage.

The illustrations in the *Florentine Codex* and the *Primeros memoriales* dealing with Panquetzaliztli and the gods Huitzilopochtli and Painal differ rather significantly from one another. The pictures of the *Primeros memoriales* are somewhat closer to the old native tradition than those of the *Florentine Codex.* While in both instances the figures are presented strictly in profile, the depictions of the *Florentine Codex* show more rounding and are clearly portraits of humans wearing the attire of the gods. The colors of the *Florentine Codex* are not as strong as Sahagún's earlier work, but this might have to do with having used different paints and with the aging of the different pigments over time. But the celebrations of Panquetzaliztli are barely illustrated in the *Florentine Codex,* whereas the *Primeros memoriales* contains a complex and detailed image. Magaloni Kerpel, however, argues that the less intense colors of the illustrations focusing on the gods and the less complex depiction of the celebrations also had to do with Sahagún's own concerns about the preservation of certain aspects of Mexica culture. Those topics that were closer to core of the ancient religion received fewer visual depictions.[38] At the same time, the narrative descriptions of the ceremonies, rituals, and performances of the *Florentine Codex* are much richer than in the *Primeros memoriales.*

On the basis of the illustrations for the *Primeros memoriales,* H. B. Nicholson proposes a set of indicative elements of Huitzilopochtli's array and insignia. The nineteen elements he proposes can be collapsed into thirteen by providing either/or distinctions. As a result, these are the essential elements of the iconography of Huitzilopochtli:[39]

Headdress of blue/green or white feathers
Hummingbird helmet, costume, or back device
Xiuhcoatl or feather back device
Facial striping, usually blue and yellow
Black eye mask with star design
Quetzal feather armlet in a spray design
Circular white shell pectoral with ties
Serpent staff or serpent spear thrower (atlatl)
Plain white shield or one with five down balls
Spear-thrower darts without points or spear with point
Sacrificial banner tipped with stone point
Smoking mirror at temple or elsewhere
Striping of arms and/or legs

Not all these elements need to be present, but the presence of a set of these elements would imply an identification as Huitzilopochtli or a strong relationship to him. All representations of the god manifest a significant number of these elements. Among all the characteristics, the hummingbird device is probably unique and nearly definitive.

The *Primeros memoriales* includes a painting of the ceremonies conducted during Panquetzaliztli. This illustration is extremely important because it offers a few glimpses beyond the brief narrative provided by Sahagún (see plate 6).[40] The picture has four loosely organized horizontal registers. On the very bottom level are three figures wearing traditional cloaks. These men seem to be dancing in a line. Their legs are painted black. They might represent the warriors who were known to dance during the Panquetzaliztli rituals. Of course, the narrative description of the Panquetzaliztli ceremonies also notes that the feast is one celebrated with singing and dancing.[41]

On the third level from the top are four figures. Two of these are priests, distinguished by their black color. One is the chief priest. His hair is tied near his neck and flows down his back. In his left hand, he holds a stylized bag adorned with three starlike symbols. The bag, *copalxiquipilli* (copal bag), is used to hold copal, the pine resin incense used in native rituals.[42] Around his shoulders, he wears a gourd slung over the back and tied with a red cord and tassels. He confronts another priest, dressed as a secondary priest, wearing paper ornaments on either side of his head. The secondary priest holds a firebrand in his hand and stands on a small mat, *petlatl.* To the right of these figures are two others carrying white shields. These two men wear black paint on the upper parts of their faces. With white hair, white bodies, and black face stripes and carrying banners, they represent victims prepared for sacrifice and are indicative of the theme of raising banners.

Just above this, five priests perform a sacrifice. On the far left, there is a temple or palace seen sideways, with the main priest standing in front of it. He has just performed the sacrifice taking out the heart of the victim. All the tlamacazque (priests) are painted black. The chief priest wears his hair flowing down his back, tied at the neck. In his right hand, he raises the flint knife used in the sacrifice. The four other priests wear pleated paper ornaments on the sides of their heads, which are associated with Mictlanteuctli (the deity of the underworld) and other deities of death. They hold the sacrificial victim by his hands and feet. The sacrifice has already occurred because the victim bleeds profusely from a wound in his chest. The victim is arrayed like Huitzilopochtli, with a blue-and-yellow-striped face and blue arms and legs. He wears the same blue headdress as the other god imitators. Immediately to the right of this group is another teixiptla, also dressed in the array of Huitzilopochtli. Just like the figure immediately above him, he also carries a white shield. He has both the banner and flint in his headdress, which are possibly associated with the aneucyotl and the quetzal-feather array on his back. At least in Tepepulco, according to the *Primeros memoriales*, the victim was indeed a teixiptla.[43]

In the very top register, reading from left to right, we encounter the raised banner symbolic of the month's name. In the center of the drawing, the god Huitzilopochtli sits with his famous weapon, the xiuhcoatl, or coatopil. He is seated inside a sanctuary that is perched atop a larger temple, although the illustration makes it look like it is floating in the air above the larger temple since the depiction has the sanctuary facing left while the larger temple has the sanctuary facing forward. In this instance, his xiuhcoatl is colored blue-green since the word *xiuhtic*, from which the term derives, means blue-green.[44] His face is striped. Although he should wear a cloak of turquoise, the artist preferred to color it green.[45] He carries a round shield that is white. While Painal was best known for a turquoise shield, Huitzilopochtli's was generally white and tufted.

In the far-right corner of the top register is a standing figure wearing the array of Huitzilopochtli, holding the flag associated with the feast in his right hand. This figure most likely represents the teixiptla, the local embodiment of the deity that was featured in the Panquetzaliztli celebrations. His face, too, is striped like Huitzilopochtli, and he wears the quetzal-feather headdress and has a banner topped by a flint knife. The banner relates to the name of the festival and refers to the sacrificial victims. He carries the same round white shield as the other image of the god seated in the sanctuary. On his back, he has the quetzal ornament that is unique to Huitzilopochtli. It is quite possible that the two figures to the far right in the upper and middle register, both dressed in raiment evocative of Huitzilopochtli, are, in fact, sacrificial victims attired as teixiptlahuan. Clearly they are attired in a manner exactly like that of the victim depicted in the illustration.

The ceremonies described by Sahagún in the text of the *Primeros memoriales* differ significantly from what one sees in the illustration. While he wrote about the capture of passersby and bleeding them from their earlobes in the Battle of Chonchayotl, nothing like that appears in the illustrations. Similarly, the cultic consumption of pulque is not depicted. However, the dancing that is mentioned in the narrative description is reflected in the attitudes of the three figures at the bottom of the page. They seem to be dancing, all facing the same direction and possibly holding hands. Thus, the main points of similarity converge on a festival to honor Huitzilopochtli in which there is singing and dancing and the raising of banners. The centrality of Huitzilopochtli is confirmed by the illustration. The presence of what must be interpreted as god impersonators adds additional information that is absent in the narrative. The fact that the sacrificial victim appears to be a god impersonator is extremely important since this was not implied in Sahagún's narrative in the *Primeros memoriales.* Yet he equates the festival to that of Tlacaxipehualiztli, which implies human sacrifice, although he does not detail how the sacrifice was performed. As a result, the presence and type of sacrifice are only clarified in the illustration.

Early Pictorial Manuscripts from beyond Tenochtitlan

Three important pictorial manuscripts come from places beyond Tenochtitlan, and one possibly dates from either before or approximately during the period of the conquest. These works offer the best likelihood of describing the way that Panquetzaliztli was celebrated outside the area of immediate Mexica control and possibly outside the influence of Tenochtitlan. Just as looking at the celebrations in Tepepulco allow us to better understand the underlying traditions of the month, these illustrations assist us in focusing on the salient features of the celebrations that are less influenced by the Mexica.

Codex Borgia

The *Codex Borgia* is one of a handful of preconquest divinatory and calendrical manuscripts that has survived the depredations of time. Scholars agree that the manuscript comes from the region of Puebla–Tlaxcala, a region just south of the major influence of the Mexica. Richly illustrated, it forms the basis for much of what modern scholars know about the interlocking calendar systems in use among the Nahua. It comes from an area of Nahuatl speakers, but they were not immediately under Mexica domination. Thus, scholars believe that it reflects many of the traditions that the Nahua inherited. The manuscript is pictorial and was not glossed in any language subsequent to its creation. Consequently, the images that it presents need to be interpreted in the light of other sources. Because of Sahagún's stature as an observer of preconquest culture, his descriptions serve as the point of departure for many interpretations of the *Codex Borgia.*[46] At the same time, because the *Borgia* dates from a period approximately twenty years before Spanish arrival, it is a better representation of the native culture for not having passed through the lens of European culture.

An important portion of the *Codex Borgia* deals with the eighteen months of the solar year called the veintenas.[47] Susan Milbrath has identified one particular image in the cycle, leaf 46 (see plate 7), as a representation of the rituals of Panquetzaliztli. In particular, this illustration suggests the burning of sheets of paper that were placed in a *cuauhxicalli* (sacrificial basin) at the foot of the Templo Mayor.[48] For Milbrath, the theme of this page of the *Codex Borgia* is the beginning of the dry season, symbolized by the fire rituals and fire serpents that predominate in the illustration. The page corresponds to the period between approximately November 26 and December 15, 1496 (of the Julian calendar), which would have included the winter solstice. She sees the sacrificial stone represented on the far-left side of the page and the two bowls with fire coming out of them decorated with eagle heads and wings. In the lower-middle section, Quetzalcoatl, representing the planet Venus, uses a fire stick to make a fire on the back of a large fire serpent "encasing Xiuhtecuhtli [*sic*], the fire god," who wears a blue bird on his headband, which she identifies as a deity she calls Lady Cotinga. In the temples on the upper left and right of the page, the same god, Xiuhteuctli, holds a small Tezcatlipoca. Tezcatlipoca appears again just below on the left-hand throne, now as a full-size warrior, holding a banner in his hand, which is symbolic of the name of the month, Panquetzaliztli, "the raising of the banners." In the lower-right throne, we find yet another manifestation of Xiuhteuctli the fire god, while four forms of Chantico, goddess of the hearth, stand on either side of the central figure. The central figure consists of an image of Quetzalcoatl undergoing a transformation by fire and heat as he is boiled in a vessel surrounded by fire serpents. Milbrath notes that while, in Tenochtitlan, the month was dedicated to Huitzilopochtli, in the *Codex Borgia* his place is taken by Tezcatlipoca since the manuscript comes from outside the Mexica sphere of influence.[49]

This interpretation by Milbrath is not without its critics. Most note that the plate supposedly illustrating Panquetzaliztli does not fall where is should in the order of months. The organization of the rituals also has little to do with any known celebrations of the month. Lastly, the banner, the one unique, ubiquitous, and important iconographical marker for the month, which is present in practically every other illustration, plays a very small and almost unobtrusive role here, held in the right hand along with a small shield. Its presence, however confirms the association with Panquetzaliztli. In addition, the interplay of Tezcatlipoca and Quetzalcoatl in the illustration is evocative of other manuscripts where the two characters are sometimes allies, sometimes adversaries, as will be seen later.

The suggestion promoted by Milbrath, that the month of Panquetzaliztli was dedicated to Tezcatlipoca in a Nahua region outside of immediate Mexica control, has some confirmation in descriptions of other celebrations in Tenochtitlan. Several scholars have noted that as the Mexica gained power and influence, they inserted their national god into various rituals and celebrations that had previously been dedicated to Tezcatlipoca and other deities.[50]

Other scholars have held that what is depicted in the leaf of the *Codex Borgia* as the feast of Panquetzaliztli is not that at all but rather a symbolic representation of the New Fire ceremony, the celebration that occurs every fifty-two years when the calendrical cycles renew and start again.[51] This relationship will be studied in chapter 4. According to that analysis, what is depicted in the *Codex Borgia* is not the immolation of the paper offerings in the final rituals of Panquetzaliztli but the celebration of the New Fire ceremony and the beginning of another fifty-two-year cycle. The central figure acting in the depiction is indeed Quetzalcoatl, who, along with Tezcatlipoca (depicted twice on the left-hand side), appears as the protagonist in most of the stories portrayed in the codex. In that reading, the leaf in question represents the origin of the New Fire ceremony, with Quetzalcoatl performing the actual ceremony on the body of Xiuhteuctli, the fire god. Unfortunately, other scholars, including Milbrath, note that there is little evidence for elaborate New Fire ceremonies in the Puebla-Tlaxcala region, where the manuscript originated.[52]

Boban Calendar Wheel

In approximately 1545, don Antonio Pimentel Tlahuitoltzin, one of the descendants of the famed ruler of Tetzcoco, Nezahualcoyotl, ordered the creation of various documents in order to assert his claims to the Texcocan throne. The author of the work included a depiction of the preconquest calendar as part of its documentation. This includes the image that is now known as the Boban Calendar Wheel.[53] The document gained this sobriquet from its first European owner, Eugène Boban, a French antiquarian and archeologist. The document was painted on native paper, *amate*, and among other images, depicts the month of Panquetzaliztli.

The outside rings of the wheel depict the veintenas, and like many other images symbolizing Panquetzaliztli, the Boban Wheel image consists of the iconic flag (see figure 5). It is located on the left-hand side of the wheel, just above the midpoint. The flag itself is decorated with black stripes while a cluster of what appear to

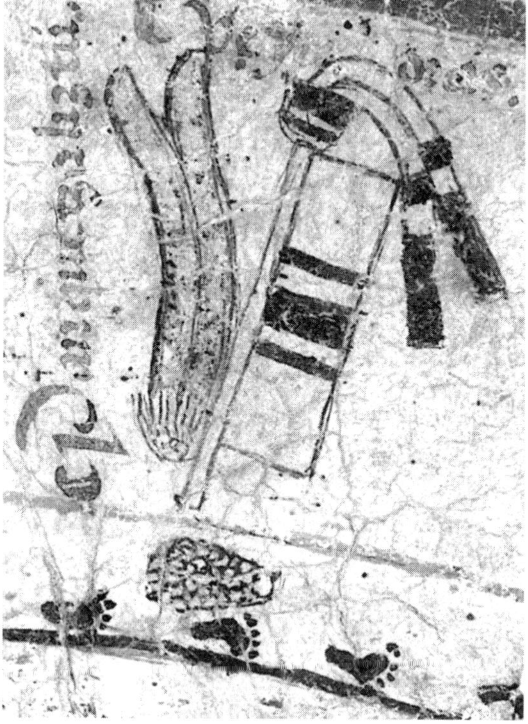

Fig. 5. Panquetzaliztli. Boban Calendar Wheel, John Carter Brown Library.

be quetzal feathers springs from the staff on which the banner is attached.[54] The symbol is labeled "Panquetzaliztli," and just on the top of the image are written the words "*veinte dias*," signifying the length of the Nahua month.

Tovar Calendar

Jesuit missionary Juan de Tovar collected detailed information about the preconquest calendar during the 1570s and 1580s. He included this information, along with illustrations, in the manuscript known as the Tovar Calendar, which probably dates to 1586–87. Tovar was born to Spanish parents in Tetzcoco, where he spent his childhood. Most sources indicate that he was related to the Dominican Diego Durán.[55] In his illustration for the month of Panquetzaliztli, Tovar features the banner that was raised quite prominently. Yet, unlike any of the other illustrations

Fig. 6. Panquetzaliztli. Tovar Calendar, John Carter Brown Library.

of the month, the very large banner is held not by a god but by what seems to be a wizened old man (see figure 6). The man, who is wrinkled, balding, and somewhat emaciated, wears a hip cloth with a traditional fringe, as is seen in many other illustrations from a variety of sources.[56] He also wears a necklace with two strands of turquoise beads that is further adorned with little jingle bells. Turquoise beads and golden bells were both seen as precious items and were often associated with supernatural beings.

The text that accompanies the illustration explains that "Pāquetzliztli" was the fourteenth month.[57] The banner illustrated on the page signifies the name of the month "the raising of the banners." The explanation continues that the banner was erected in the center of a patio and that military leaders performed ceremonies around it. Having put aside any differences, the military leaders celebrated and sang songs of their prowess and accomplishments. This might harken back to a time before Tenochtitlan's dominance or to practices outside the area of Mexica supremacy. Tovar also adds that the month corresponded roughly to December and included the Christian festivals of Saint Catherine of Alexandria the Virgin (November 25) and of Saint Andrew the Apostle (November 30).[58] Clearly, Tovar considered the month to be dedicated to military leaders and warriors who would raise the banners and celebrate their victories. He did not indicate that the feast was associated with any particular deity. Tovar also wrote a small work about the history of the natives of Mexico, with short sections that discussed the principal gods. Yet, upon scrutiny, one can see that the material was taken intact from Durán's works on the natives. The small portions of Tovar's work that are not copied from Durán probably represent information that he collected in Tetzcoco.[59]

Conclusions

Several works, both narrative and pictorial, describe the traditions of the Panquetzaliztli festival as it occurred outside Tenochtitlan. None of these are extensive. They do not offer day-by-day accounts of activities. Some of the pictorial documents are very equivocal and are subject to a great deal of speculation by modern scholars. Nonetheless, taken as a whole, the picture that emerges is of a festival that was most likely dedicated to Huitzilopochtli or possibly also to Tezcatlipoca. The oldest narrative account, that of Motolinia, supports the dual-advocation hypothesis. The older pictorial manuscript of the *Codex Borgia* supports a celebration of Tezcatlipoca, perhaps with Quetzalcoatl. With regard to the *Borgia*, in spite of Milbrath's interpretation, some scholarship holds that the leaf in question depicts the New Fire ceremony and not the veintena. This will be the subject of a longer analysis in chapter 5.

Considering, then, the areas of similarity among all these sources, a few things are clear. First, the month of Panquetzaliztli did not have any other name. Though a few months had several different names, that was not the case with Panquetzaliztli. The depiction of the month in the pictorial manuscripts always includes the symbol of a flag, which represents the name of the month.

Additionally, the celebrations of Panquetzaliztli included several aspects that were generic to nearly all veintena celebrations. There were fasting and penance to prepare for the month. Individuals also participated in small, personal blood sacrifices as part of the penance. There were food offerings and probably the consumption of pulque or some other beverage.

Some of the month's activities centered around an ixiptla of Huitzilopochtli. Three different variants have been described: Motolinia describes a seed-paste image; another was a statue or similar construction; and in Tepepulco, a person called Chonchayotl served as an ixiptla.

Lastly, one of the activities of the month was human sacrifice. While Sahagún only obliquely suggests that such sacrifices occurred in his narrative in the *Primeros memoriales*, he depicts it rather graphically in the illustrations. Motolinia describes the sacrifices in some detail. In Motolinia's description of the paste ixiptla and the procession of priests who carried it, he also mentions the sacrifices that were made along the way and the final sacrifices of warriors. He also claims that there was ritual cannibalism. Although he does not mention it explicitly, the procession that he describes has many of the same features of the running ceremony that appear in greater detail in the *Florentine Codex*. In the *Primeros memoriales*, although Sahagún mentions and illustrates dancing and goes on about the mock battle of Chonchayotl, the text includes nothing that is similar to the procession that Motolinia describes. Even though Motolinia's narrative is slightly older than Sahagún's, it focuses, in whole or in part, on Tenochtitlan. All the sites mentioned are in the Central Basin of Mexico. Consequently, it is quite clear that Motolinia has, at least in part, taken the Tenochtitlan celebration of Panquetzaliztli as the example for his book. By contrast, in the *Primeros memoriales*, Sahagún suggests that he focuses only on the practices of Tepepulco.

The next two chapters will consider the two longest and most detailed descriptions of the ceremonies and rituals of Panquetzaliztli. They are contained in Sahagún's massive work, the *Florentine Codex*, and in Diego Durán's work on the religion of the natives of Mexico. These two narrative accounts concentrate on the practices of Tenochtitlan and provide a wealth of details that are absent from all other accounts. Much of what they describe is consistent between the two accounts, but lamentably, more details are unique to one or the other than are shared by both.

CHAPTER 2

PANQUETZALIZTLI CELEBRATIONS IN MEXICO-TENOCHTITLAN

Looking at the older texts and pictorial manuscripts detailing the ceremonies of the veintenas, we can begin to understand some of the major elements of the feast. Motolinia outlines a procession that traversed some of the route. According to Sahagún in the *Primeros memoriales,* the mock battle of Chonchayotl was important in Tepepulco as the ixiptla chased his victims. Most sources agree that the month celebrated warriors and warfare. The pictorial evidence demonstrates that a celebration of Huitzilopochtli was central to the month, although some sources indicate the prominence of Tezcatlipoca or even Quetzalcoatl. Sacrifice played an important role, but authors disagree about its centrality. Consequently, we must look in greater depth at the two key sources for a more complete and detailed description of the practices in Tenochtitlan on the eve of the conquest: the *Florentine Codex,* a project directed by Sahagún, and the *Book of the Gods and Rites* by Diego Durán.

According to these sources, the culminating ceremony of Panquetzaliztli focused on a runner who traveled through the city of Tenochtitlan and surrounding areas.[1] This ceremony and others associated with it during the month were the focus of great attention among colonial observers who collected information about preconquest culture and rituals. Durán, Sahagún, and Juan de Torquemada have all described the running ceremony in great detail, although there are some significant differences among them and inconsistencies in their descriptions. This chapter will focus on integrating into a single thread the narratives of the Panquetzaliztli ceremonies leading up to the running event. Unfortunately, the authors chose to focus on different aspects of the celebrations. Some of the authors provide detailed descriptions, such as Sahagún. Others, like Motolinia and Durán, dedicate a chapter to the month but only describe a few bits of the larger celebration. Nearly all the observers sprinkle information throughout several chapters, with some appearing in descriptions of the veintenas, other details in chapters dedicated to Huitzilopochtli, and still other bits in sections about sacrifice and other topics. By and large, the descriptions are complementary in that they all agree on the general trajectory of the ceremonies. But as we focus on the details, there are discrepancies.

Because of the discrepancies among the various sources, there has been no single description of all the events of the month from start to finish. Consequently, it has been difficult to see how all the disparate rituals worked together to create a monthlong series of religious events. As commentators focus on one or another ritual or ceremony, the greater arc of the celebration is lost. The ceremonies and rituals did not occur in a vacuum; they were not isolated one from the other. As we will see, the rites of the month proceeded in an orderly and integrated manner, each day building on the previous, until the final flurry and hecatomb of sacrifice on the last day. Admittedly, it is difficult to describe all the detailed rituals and ceremonies in a narrative manner. Nonetheless, without the step-by-step narration of each day's events, the major themes seem to be more pronounced than they probably were to the participants of the day.

The celebrations of the month were so important to Sahagún that he includes several different descriptions of them in three different portions of his massive *Florentine Codex* and makes numerous other references to them throughout the work. The longest narrative that describes the ceremonies of Panquetzaliztli is found in book 2, chapter 34, which details the month's celebrations.[2] In book 2, Sahagún describes the feasts and celebrations of all the veintenas. Each chapter describes one of the eighteen months and how it was celebrated.

One of the other books where Sahagún provides valuable information about the rituals of Panquetzaliztli is book 9, which focuses on the merchants, who traditionally were based in Tlatelolco. The merchants played an important role in the celebration, providing many of the sacrificial victims for the final rituals of the month and participating in daily rituals along the way. It should come as no surprise, then, that Sahagún also dedicates a large section of book 9 to the festivities of Panquetzaliztli. In that book, he spends some five chapters discussing all the elements of the celebration. Many of his descriptions are essentially repetitions from book 2, but he also provides unique material regarding the merchants in the book. The greatest amount of new material has to do with the feasts, banquets, gifts, and private ceremonies involving the merchants.

In the principal description of the ceremonies of the monthlong festival in book 2, Sahagún does not at first make it clear that the merchants were centrally involved. He relates the specific rituals, describing the participants simply as "they."[3] In some instances, he clearly means that priests engaged in some activities. In other instances, he describes the action of "the bathed ones" and "the bathers." It is only in book 9, where Sahagún discusses the merchants, that one learns that the principal actors in these ceremonies were merchants.[4] There, he makes it clear that the "bathers" are the merchants who participate in the ceremony while the "bathed ones" are their sacrificial victims. In introducing all the monthly ceremonies, Sahagún notes that, in addition to the celebrations, there was debt paying. He does not elaborate on this observation, but its implications become clear as we explore the details of each month.

This chapter and the next will, then, integrate bits of information from the various sections of the *Florentine Codex* along with details from a handful of other observers. Sometimes the descriptions are complementary, essentially describing the same event; other times there are great discrepancies. These chapters will work to put all these together into a single, integrated narrative of the events of those twenty days along with some interpretation. The symbolism and meaning of the rituals and ceremonies will be dealt with in a later chapter, after the detailed description of all the month's events.

An Overview of Panquetzaliztli

Durán, Sahagún, and Torquemada place Panquetzaliztli as the fifteenth month of the year. While there is much speculation, most observers agree that, at least during the years immediately prior to the conquest, the month began as early as late November and lasted through mid-December.[5] These sources also agree that the ceremonies and rituals of this month were dedicated to Huitzilopochtli.

The participants in the activities of the month of Panquetzaliztli included four main groups within Mexica society. First, the priests of Huitzilopochtli and a few other ritual specialists oversaw many of the rites. Second were lay participants, mainly warriors who had captured enemies on the battlefield and merchants who had risen to distinction. Included with the warriors and merchants were their wives and members of their households; in this context, prostitutes were also explicitly included. The third group consisted of war captives and slaves who had been purchased to be sacrificial victims and were the focus of many of the rituals. Lastly, the entire population of Tenochtitlan and Tlatelolco, especially particular residents of certain neighborhoods, both witnessed and took part in events.

In order to better understand the dynamics of the celebrations of the month of Panquetzaliztli, a general synopsis of events will help to provide an overview. Although the month began in late November, preparations began months earlier. Once the month had officially begun, participants went through a series of additional rituals involving singing and dancing. The merchants purchased slaves for sacrifice, then hosted a series of banquets and gave gifts to important individuals. The merchants who were part of the ceremonies were elite members of the merchant class. Warriors already had captives from battle and also participated in banqueting. In one of the key rituals, the merchants, and possibly the warriors, supervised the ritual bathing of the victims in preparation for the final sacrifice. For this reason, a merchant or warrior became known as *tealtiani*, "one who bathes people." The victim was then known as the *tlaaltilli*, "bathed one." The merchants then departed for the trading post of Tochtepec, located far to the southeast on the edge of what is now the state of Oaxaca bordering Veracruz. At Tochtepec, the merchant-bathers performed a series of rituals to receive the blessings of their fellow long-distance merchants. Once those rituals were accomplished, the merchants would return to Tenochtitlan. During the second half of the month, the merchants and warriors performed another series of preparatory rites in anticipation of the final ceremonies. On the last day of the month, three threads all came together. The central feature was the running ritual, wherein a priest carried a dough image of Huitzilopochtli along a twenty-two-mile counterclockwise course (see map 2) that began at the Templo Mayor, went north to Tlatelolco, west to Tlacopan, south to Chapultepec, along the lakeshore to Coyohuacan, and then straight north to return to the Templo Mayor. As this run was ending, the sacrificial victims battled men from the Huitznahua neighborhood of the city. The runner carrying Huitzilopochtli returned to the temple, followed by the sacrificial victims for the culminating immolation. Some minor rituals followed, lasting some four days into the next month.

A detailed description of the events of Panquetzaliztli follows. The differences among the main sources are considered as an attempt is made to create

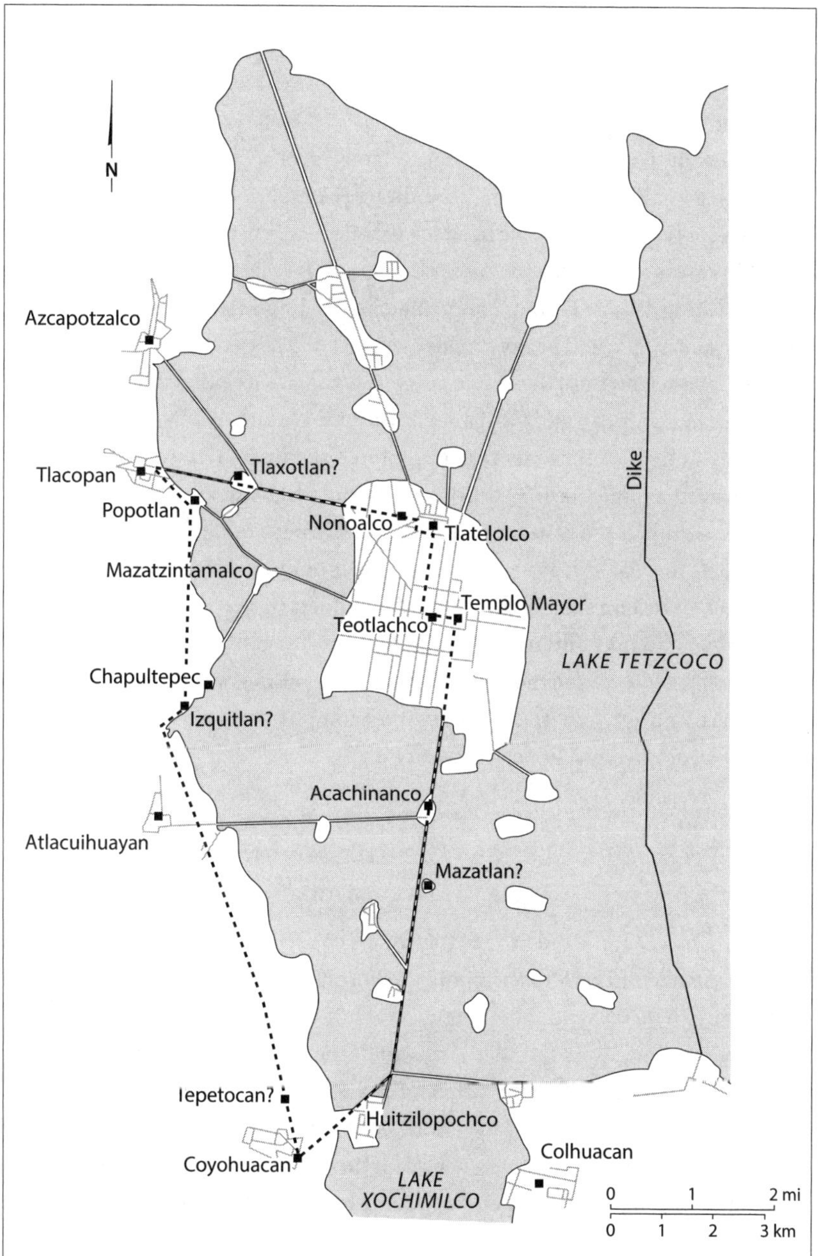

Map 2. The Swiftness of Huitzilopochtli. Map by Bill Nelson.

a consensus scenario for the celebrations. As the previous synopsis indicates, at various points several activities occurred at the same time. This adds to the difficulty of the narration and the complexity of the symbolism inherent in the celebrations.

The descriptions that follow are taken largely from Sahagún because he provides such a wealth of detail in his accounts of the month's celebrations. At every step in the process, however, we need to evaluate his descriptions in terms of what other observers report and any biases that the friar might have allowed to enter into his writing. Where Durán, Torquemada, and Motolinia differ with each other and with Sahagún, it will be noted. Furthermore, as we saw with Motolinia in the previous chapter, many of these authors continually insert either direct or oblique references to European and Christian traditions. Unfortunately, it is impossible to know exactly how these sentiments colored the overall narrative, but where possible, overt comments or insertions will be noted. Lastly, all these authors were trained in a different manner of thinking than we have today. We can attempt to compensate for that, but as with extracting bias or cultural intrusion, it is nearly impossible to be completely thorough. As Walden Brown points out, Sahagún (and we can add his contemporaries) stood on the medieval side of the divide between the medieval and modern. The medieval outlook was disintegrating, but the modern had not yet arrived. This further complicates the effort to determine anything approaching a historical reality.[6]

Preparations Leading Up to the Month and Singing the "Tlaxotecayotl"

According to Sahagún and others, the rituals of preparation for Panquetzaliztli began eighty days (four Mexica months) before the month itself.[7] On the first day of Ochpaniztli (early September), right at midnight, the priests of Huitzilopochtli spread out fir boughs on circular altars and other holy places on mountaintops at quite a distance from Tenochtitlan.[8] These same priests would take charge of the sacrificial offerings much later, at the end of Panquetzaliztli. While working with the tree branches, completely naked, the priests had processions in these remote places during which they carried the boughs, green reeds, and thorns. It seems that any type of greenery was used. The raising of the boughs was one of the unique acts associated with the month and is always used as an explanation of the month's name. Thus, in these rituals, the boughs represented the banners that gave the month its name. Whistles and shell trumpets provided a musical accompaniment to the processions. The displaying of boughs accompanied by music continued throughout the eighty days that followed. The priests also engaged in fasting during this preparatory period. When Panquetzaliztli finally arrived, the priests had several other rituals to complete.

Beyond the fasting, the specific rituals associated with the celebration of Panquetzaliztli commenced right at the beginning of the month. The highlight of the opening moments was the singing of the hymn dedicated to Huitzilopochtli, called the "Tlaxotecayotl," although Sahagún is not explicit about who participated. There are suggestions that the whole populace joined in song and dance. Certainly, one assumes that warriors and merchants and their wives and concubines engaged in ritual dance and sang the hymn on the very last night and closing moments of the previous month, Quecholli. During each night of the month of Panquetzaliztli, these participants would repeat the song along with designated dances, always between dusk and midnight.

The hymn, which is one of a series of songs dedicated to various deities, praised Huitzilopochtli.[9] These songs were used throughout the year as part of the monthly commemorations and may have been tailored for use by the Aztecs in their impressive imperial ceremonies.[10] Sahagún provides two somewhat different versions of the hymn. The one that appears in the *Florentine Codex* is rather spare and is placed in the appendix to book 2 without a translation of the Nahuatl. The other version, from the *Primeros memoriales*, is more expansive, is translated into Spanish, and has long glosses that interpret the meaning of the obscure words and phrases. The *Primeros memoriales* version is probably the older of the two.

In the following, the text in the left-hand column is from the *Primeros memoriales* while on the right is the text from the appendix to book 2 of the *Florentine Codex*. Following each stanza, the explanation provided by Sahagún, taken from the *Primeros memoriales* and originally in Spanish, helps to clarify the text. Charles Dibble and Arthur J. O. Anderson provide a quite literal translation of the poem from the appendix of the *Florentine Codex* while Thelma Sullivan is more lyrical in her translation of the *Primeros memoriales*. This is seen in the reference to Tlaxotlan and Tlaxotecatl (the genitive form). Rather than translate these as "a place called Tlaxotlan" and "a person from Tlaxotlan," Dibble and Anderson, following the lead of Angel María Garibay, translate it quite literally to be "the hot region" and "a hot region dweller." The explanations provided earlier by Sahagún, however, do not support that translation.

"TLAXOTECAYOTL"

Primeros memoriales	*Florentine Codex*
Huitzilopochtli, the wayfaring warrior. None is my equal. Not for nothing did I take the yellow parrot feather garb. Because of me the sun has shone. *This means . . .* *I am Huitzilopochtli; no one is my equal, no one is like what I am like. . . .* *Not in vain did I take the quetzal feathers, the green stones; all are my possessions [as well as] the yellow parrot feather vestment . . .* *because of me the sun has shone, the day has dawned.*	Uitizilopochtli Leader in war. Whose work is on high. Who goes on his way Not in vain I take the yellow feathered cape Which through me is the sunshine.
He is terror! Now the Mixtec, the Pichahuaztec have one foot. There he's gone! *This means:* *Tetzahuiztli: i.e. he went terrifying the Mixteca when they warred with him.* *He removed the feet of the Pichahuazteca and of the Mixteca.*	Evil of omen Dweller in cloudland You have but one foot Dweller in chill land of wings You open your hand.
Oh, the walls of Tlaxotlan! Feathers have been given out. Churning up the earth he goes. He gives the call to war. He is my god. One known as Tepanquizqui [he who makes war]. *[This] means, he stirs up fire on the walls of those on whom war is made . . .* *there he places the chalk, the feathers . . .* *thus he goes into battle churning up the earth and it means he offers the people war; he makes them meritorious . . .* *it is he who makes war.*	Feathers are given the hot region's ramparts Broadcast they fly Proclaimers of war My god is entitled "defender of men."

In all the versions, the Nahuatl is obscure. The text is largely the same in the two versions, given slight differences in orthography. Complicating translation and interpretation, Nahua singers would insert nonsense syllables to fill out a line, perhaps to keep a stable rhythm, not unlike "hey-nonny-nonny" or "fa-la-la" in old English songs. Extracting the nonsense syllables from the real text is a daunting task. The following is the first stanza in Nahuatl, with the nonsense syllables in italics.

Primeros memoriales	*Florentine Codex*
The Tlaxotec[11] is fearful. The dust, the dust is whirling. The Tlaxotec [is fearful]. The dust, the dust is whirling. *[This] means, first he became frightened before the battle was fought . . .* *war has stirred; it has commenced. No one was fearful any longer when the dust rose, when the dust [day] became night.*	Already he rises all covered with paper A hot region dweller He circles in dust A hot region dweller He circles in dust.
The Amanteca are our foes. Join yourself to me! The foe is battled in his house. Join yourself to me! *[This] means, his enemies are those who are gathered in their houses, where there is fighting; their houses will burn.*	The Amanteca are our foes About me place yourselves In battle form there's going to war About me place yourselves.[12]
The Pipitecas are our foes. Join yourself to me! The foe is battled in his house. Join yourself to me! *[This] means, the Pipiteca became his enemies; in the town there is fighting in the houses.*[13]	[there is no corresponding stanza in the *Florentine Codex*]

Vitzilobuch
iaquetl *aia,*
yiaco n ai,
in ohujhujhujia
ane njcujc tociquemitla, *yia, ayia, yia, yio, vjia,*
que *ia* noca, oia, tonaquj *yiaia, yia, yio.*[14]

Huitzilopochtli defeats his opponents and then cripples them by removing one of their feet. This last action is important because both Huitzilopochtli and Tezcatlipoca were frequently depicted as having one foot, the other being supplanted by a bird foot or some other device. In the *Primeros memoriales* translation, Huitzilopochtli is identified as the person from Tlaxotlan. This is of great importance because one of the stops on the running ceremony was in a place called Tlaxotlan. Both versions describe the defeat of the Amanteca, while only the *Primeros memoriales* includes the Pipiteca. In many ways, this song must have become the theme song for the celebrations of Panquetzaliztli since it was sung every evening of the month.

The hymn summarizes many of the important aspects of Huitzilopochtli. He is characterized as a warrior and a leader. Of all the deities, he is the first. He instills terror in his foes. The basis for this terror is his power and might, although other terrifying aspects of his personality will become more evident. Garibay suggests that the phrase "He is terror," from the word "Tetzaviztli" (*tetzahuiztli*), is, in fact, an epithet for Cihuacoatl (Female Snake), one of the female deities; others associate it with Tezcatlipoca. Garibay further notes that the epithet and Huitzilopochtli's name became interchangeable. In several sources, the god is known as "In Tetzahuitl, in Huitzilopochtli" (the Scandal/Terror, Huitzilopochtli).[15] Garibay defines the word closer to "horrendous" or "frightful," with a further meaning of a fatal or mortal announcement or premonition. Alonso de Molina, glosses the word as "something scandalous or frightful, or an augury."[16] Because one definition is "scandal," one of the suggestions is that Huitzilopochtli received the epithet not because of his fearful countenance or ability to instill terror but because he was born illegitimately. In his discussion of the miraculous birth of the god, Sahagún recounts, "And Uitzilopochtli was also called an omen of evil, because only from a feather which fell, his mother Coatl Icue [Snake Her Skirt] conceived [him]. For no one appeared as his father."[17] In all likelihood, this notion of scandal or fright had to do with notions of family structure and legitimacy. Although the Nahua allowed for a man to have several wives, and other female partners were also recognized within elite households, a child without a known father threatened the social order. The *Codex Mendoza* also gives an additional glimpse into the repercussions of violating the social order. In it, the punishment for adultery, another violation of societal norms, was death by stoning.[18] At the same time, the word *tetzahuitl* was also used to describe omens and premonitions. Thus, in the descriptions of Spanish arrival, native accounts recall the various omens and portents of the conquest using that word.[19] Tetzahuitl, then, provided a wide range of possible meanings that were exploited in Nahuatl rhetoric. Huitzilopochtli, with his epithet, could represent the notion of premonition, the vengeance of an illegitimate child, or even the terror and horror of battle and sacrifice. These were all within the breadth of the meanings of the word.

The first part of the song associates Huitzilopochtli with the power and strength behind the movement of the sun; the second glorifies war. Throughout, the imagery clearly associates him with the sun. The fact that he is a wayfarer, moving back and forth, suggests the motion of the sun that wanders across the sky as the seasons change. The yellow feather cape, as explained by Sahagún, means that the sun shines because of him; it is symbolic of the sun.

In the second section, the god becomes associated with the warrior from Tlaxotlan. This is fully consonant with the general understanding that Huitzilopochtli was a warrior deity. One should note that the name of the song, "Tlaxotecayotl," refers to the essence of being a Tlaxotec, that is, one from Tlaxotlan. One of the neighborhoods of Tlatelolco carried the name of this place and thus was probably associated with warriors and things martial. The description of war is filled with fire and dust. It then goes on to list the victories of the Tlaxotec warriors, who are here associated with Huitzilopochtli.[20] When the song says that the Mixteca and Pichahuazteca have one foot, it could possibly be a reference to Tezcatlipoca. Another aspect of Tezcatlipoca was that he became the sun of the darkness, that is, the sun as it made its course from the west back to the east.[21] In general, throughout the celebrations of Panquetzaliztli, individual rituals recall the birth of Huitzilopochtli, as in the reference to Cihuacoatl, a variant and avatar for Huitzilopochtli's mother, Coatlicue. There is ample confusion about the role of Tezcatlipoca in the festivities of Panquetzaliztli and about his rivalry with Huitzilopochtli, as was seen in the earlier description provided by Motolinia and the illustrations of the *Codex Borgia*. Interestingly, the song makes it clear that fear is an essential element of battle, but it is something that the warrior overcomes, just as he overcomes his foes. The warrior of the song is called Tepanquizqui. Garibay interprets this to mean "he who emerges among the people." In Molina's translation, the word refers to an actor in a farce.[22] Thus, it might have a metaphorical meaning of a representative: that the god was playing a role in the cosmic struggle. Indeed, one might remember that Painal was also described as a representative or one playing a part, a *moteixiptlatiani*. The annotations provided by Sahagún in the *Primeros memoriales*, however, describe the deity as one who makes war. Garibay interprets this section, and most of the song, as metaphorically elaborating the cosmic struggle of the sun in its daily journey.[23] However, more concrete readings are also possible. If this deity is associated with war, then he would be a manifestation of Tezcatlipoca, one of whose names was Yaotl (War). Thus, throughout the song, because of several references, there is a subtle confusion or melding of aspects of Tezcatlipoca and Huitzilopochtli. In short, the song characterizes Huitzilopochtli as an aspect of the sun and as a patron and exemplar of warriors, and these are two features that he shares with Tezcatlipoca.

The singing of the "Tlaxotecayotl" hymn was part of a dancing procession through the city.[24] Musicians sounded on conch shells around midnight, which was the signal to end the singing and dancing. Although some of the participants in this ceremony were clearly priests, and other sources inform us that merchants took part, here Sahagún explicitly notes that some of the participants were women, including prostitutes (*ahuianime*), who also sang and danced among the men.

One of the first divergences of the Spanish text in the *Historia general* from the Nahuatl text in the *Florentine Codex* has to do with the singing of the "Tlaxotecayotl." The Nahuatl text indicates that women and pleasure girls (*in cioa in avienjme* [*in cihua in ahuianime*]) sang the hymn and that it continued daily for twenty days.[25] In the Spanish text, however, Sahagún states that with this song men and women sang and danced, mixing with one another, with no reference to whether it continued or was a one-time ceremony and also not mentioning that some of the women were prostitutes.[26] Later, the Spanish text further notes that the men and women danced together, while the Nahuatl states that the owners danced with the female slaves who would become sacrificial victims.[27]

Purchase of Slaves for Sacrifice

In book 9 of the *Florentine Codex,* Sahagún begins his description of the ceremonies of Panquetzaliztli by elaborating on how the slaves who would become sacrificial victims were chosen.[28] The merchants purchased the slaves in Azcapotzalco, the former capital of the Tepaneca Empire, which was located on the western shore of the lake. The Azcapotzalco slave market was the largest in the region if not the largest in all of ancient Mexico. Among the Mexica and many other Nahua groups, each warrior would seek to capture enemies in warfare. He would offer these captives later in sacrifices.[29] If he happened to capture several enemy combatants, or if some were captured who could not be assigned to any particular warrior, these captives would be assigned to the emperor and eventually sold in the slave market. Some of the slaves who were offered for sale to the public for the purpose of sacrifice came from this category.[30] In the marketplace, the slave dealers provided ritual garments for their slaves. They gave the men *tilmahtli* (capes), *maxtlatl* (breechclouts), and *cactli* (sandals). The dealers adorned the slaves with labrets made from amber and leather earrings that hung down from their ears. The male slaves' hair was cut short in the style of warriors. They wore flower garlands on their heads and carried flower shields. The slaves also had tobacco in smoking tubes and small bouquets of flowers to smell.

Merchants also purchased female slaves to become sacrificial victims. While not necessarily captured on the field of battle like their male counterparts, they were nonetheless taken as prisoners of war, sometimes with the sacking of enemy cities by Mexica armies. Some estimates calculate that as many as one-third of sacrificial victims were female.[31] The female slaves received slightly different garments and accouterments. They received a flowered *huipilli* (over-blouse), which might also have downy yellow parrot feathers woven into the fabric. The *cueitl* (skirt) had an irregular design or a design based on square cornerstones. The women's hair was cut in a pageboy style, just under their ears, quite unlike most Mexica women, who wore their hair long and pinned in a unique manner to the top of the head. The only other adornments for the female slaves were necklaces. Like the men, they were given flower garlands and shields, smoking tubes, and bouquets. Sahagún wrote that the slaves, both male and female, were made to dance, smoke, and smell the flowers in order to attract buyers.

Continuing in book 9, Sahagún notes that the process of purchasing slaves for sacrificial victims had its own rituals. The slave dealer hired men to sing and to drum on the *teponaztli* (two-toned log drum). They sang songs so that the slaves would dance, encouraging sales. Rather than have all the slaves displayed together in one central place, each slave merchant kept his slaves separate in his own enclosure or area.

The merchants who were participating in the Panquetzaliztli ceremonies exercised caution in buying the slaves. Sahagún lists the various criteria taken into consideration in the purchase. The slaves were to be intelligent and good singers and dancers. They needed to be good looking, well built, healthy, slender, and free from scars, bruises, and blemishes; in short, they needed to look like "a round, stone column."[32] They needed to walk well, not shuffle along. They should not have sunken foreheads, cysts, or any blemishes on their heads. The merchant would negotiate with the slave dealer over price. For mediocre dancers, the price would be thirty large capes; for particularly handsome, good dancers, it might go as high as forty.

Durán explains that the sacrificial victims all came from foreign city-states, such as Tepeaca, Calpan, Tecali, Cuauhtinchan, and Huaquechula. In each of the cities they represented, there were Mexica war captives who were also being sacrificed in the same manner on the same day. Durán then begins a short exposition on what was known as the Flower War, the war fought with neighboring city-states expressly for the purpose of gaining sacrificial victims. Scholarship has downplayed the importance of ritualized warfare for the purpose of gaining captives, instead emphasizing warfare as a part of statecraft and imperial politics.[33]

After purchase, the slave would be stripped naked, and all the clothing and adornments were returned to the dealer. Only a very few slaves continued to wear the clothing and jewelry provided by the dealer after the sale. The merchants who were buying slaves for sacrifice were aware of the custom and brought clothing with them for the slaves they planned to purchase. The clothing they brought was practical, not fancy: simple breechclouts, capes, skirts, shifts, and sandals.

Once the merchant returned home with his newly acquired slaves, he locked them in small flat-roofed wooden jails or cages that had been built, called *quauhcalco (cuauhcalco)*, literally "a wooden house."[34] They were flat roofed so that the slaves would be able to dance on them. During the daytime, the merchant allowed the slaves to be outside of their confinement. While the women might be asked to spin cotton into thread, the men were not asked to perform chores. At night, the slaves were confined to their cages but allowed to use a traditional sleeping mat, a petlatl.

At this point, the vocabulary that Sahagún uses to describe the merchants involved in these ceremonies changes. Rather than call them merchants, he begins to refer to them as "the bather," tealtiani (singular) or tealtianime (plural), while the slaves who would be sacrificial victims were called "the bathed ones," tlaaltilli (singular) or tlaaltilhuan (plural).[35] He also makes a specific distinction between general sacrificial victims, tlaaltilhuan, and the war captives who would be sacrificed along the procession, whom he calls mamaltin (captives).

Banquets and Gift Giving

Sahagún reinforces the notion that the merchants who sponsored the slaves and participated in the bathing ritual and other Panquetzaliztli performances were known for their wealth and lacked for nothing. The middle part of the month of Panquetzaliztli was filled with a series of banquets that the merchants offered to other leading merchants, to warriors and military commanders, and to members of the royal household. The banquets and associated ritual gift giving had several functions. As some of the wealthiest members of society, the merchants were careful to not be overly ostentatious in their own dress and behavior. Giving valuable gifts to others was an acceptable activity, however. In addition, Mexica society greatly valued military prowess, and the inclusion of leading merchants into the central rituals of the month of Panquetzaliztli tacitly included them into the ranks of the warriors. The banquets and gift giving that would occupy much of the month thus allowed the merchants to rub shoulders with the military and political leaders of society.[36]

The preparations for the banquets and gift giving began well before the month of Panquetzaliztli, but must have especially occupied the merchants in the days immediately preceding the month. In order to demonstrate wealth publicly, the merchants commissioned the creation of a very large number of capes and breechclouts to be given away as gifts. The Nahuatl text reports that this meant four hundred breechclouts and between eight hundred and twelve hundred capes. In Nahuatl, four hundred signified a very large number, so these figures represent huge quantities of these items. Sahagún describes the designs on the capes in some detail: "These were capes with plaited flower ornaments and with carmine-colored flowers, made with eight blotches of blood, and with orange flowers; and netted capes; and capes with whorl designs; capes with spiral designs; and long, narrow ones, two fathoms long."[37] There were several styles of breechclouts listed, including some with long ends, some with coyote fur or netting, and tawny-colored or white ones.

The merchant-bathers gave these articles of clothing to high-ranking military officers. In the text, Sahagún lists fifteen different ranks of warriors including the commanding general and princes of the royal house. Beyond these gifts, the merchants gave more presents to other merchants, including others who were also providing slaves for sacrifice as well as the two groups of merchants who traveled into foreign lands: the disguised merchants and the spying merchants.[38] The sacrificing merchants also gave clothing gifts to the slave dealers and to merchants from outlying cities who had been invited to the ceremonial performances during the month.

With these preparations complete, the merchant-bathers then began to organize food for the banquets that would punctuate the celebrations of the month. They put aside stores of corn, beans, two kinds of chia, squash seeds (to put on top of a special *atolli* [a drink made with masa flour]), chilies, and salt (forty to sixty jars). Other foodstuffs were more perishable and had to be purchased when they were needed, such as tomatoes, eighty to one hundred turkeys, twenty to forty dogs (for cooking), and twenty sacks of cacao beans. The recipe for dog meat called for it to be placed in the bottom of the dish, then sauce was added, and it was topped with the turkey meat. Other preparations included grinding the cacao into powder and then beating it into the frothy chocolate drink that was prized by the Mexica. Sahagún suggests that they needed an astounding two to four thousand chocolate beaters, small wooden implements that were whirled between the hands to mix and froth the chocolate. Beyond that, the merchant needed to provide plates and cups for his guests along with wood and charcoal for heating and cooking. Lastly, he assured that there was a sufficient supply of water to drink, as many as four boats full. The merchant-bathers paid for all these items using two types of currency: cacao beans and small capes. Sahagún notes that the capes ranged in value from sixty-five to one hundred cacao beans, depending on the size and quality of the cape.[39]

Trip to Tochtepec

Sahagún is the only source of information about many of the activities of merchants who participated in the Panquetzaliztli rituals. As a result, although he collected a wealth of information, there may be gaps that remain problematic. Moreover, there simply is no corroboration for this particular series of events.

There were two ceremonies in which the merchant announced his intention to participate in the Panquetzaliztli ceremonies to the leadership of the merchant guild. One of these occurred in Tenochtitlan-Tlatelolco. Before that, there was a similar ceremony in a place located some distance away. Sahagún implies that after all the gifts had been organized and the food purchased and arranged, the merchant-bathers left for Tochtepec, a residential and staging area for all types of merchants from the Central Basin of Mexico.[40] Looking at the logistics of the trip, this hardly seems likely. Even using modern roads, the town is some 418 kilometers from Tenochtitlan. The walk today would take nearly ninety hours using modern highways. In Mexica times, a trip to Tochtepec and back would easily take the entire twenty-day month, if not more. As a result, one has to conclude that once the merchant had made his full commitment to participate in the rituals and begun to amass the goods and supplies necessary, he would make the trip to Tochtepec, well before the onset of Panquetzaliztli. In Tochtepec, the merchant-bather went to the guild house of the Tlatelolco merchants.[41] Merchants based outside the major cities of the Central Basin of Mexico could not enter into the basin but had to depend on trading partners from the capital district. Representatives of many trading cities had bases in Tochtepec so that they could negotiate deals with one another.

The merchants who were participating in the Panquetzaliztli sacrifice had long-distance porters carry all the gifts they intended to distribute in Tochtepec, including the chocolate beaters. First, the merchant went to the temple of the god of the vanguard merchants, Yacateuctli (Lord Nose).[42] He swept the area in front of the god and then spread out a petlatl (reed mat), and he placed new vestments for the god on it as an offering. He took out as many traveling canes or walking staves as he had slaves to sacrifice. The walking staves were symbolic of both the god and the guild of long-distance merchants. He wrapped up the canes in a proper array and tied it all up. He placed the bundles on paper on the mat in front of the god. On top of these bundles, the merchant added the appropriate items of clothing for the sacrificial victims: capes for the men, skirts and overblouses for the women. The clothing had the design and ornamentation mentioned above: coyote-fur capes with a red-eye border, long breechclouts, skirts with either a corner-square or irregular design, and shifts with a radiating flower design or yellow parrot feathers. This allowed the merchant to display the items so that people would notice them later during the ceremonies. The display of goods served to publicize his participation in the ritual performance and to indicate his wealth in a very concrete manner.

After the initial ritual, the merchant-bather reentered the guild house of the Tlatelolco merchants to supervise the preparation of food, including turkeys and chocolate, for a banquet that he would host for the other merchants. From the assembled leadership, he invited a number of people to be his guests at the performance of the Panquetzaliztli ceremonies back in Tenochtitlan. His invitees included other vanguard merchants, the people who assisted him in bathing the slaves, and the slave dealers. His guests came from throughout the twelve cities of the trading network of the Central Basin of Mexico. The banquet for his guests began at midnight with hand washing. They then feasted on all the food and afterward washed hands and faces again. The merchant-bather offered his guests chocolate to drink and tobacco to smoke. At the end of the banquet, he distributed gifts to the guests.

After taking care of his guests, the merchant withdrew for more rituals. Based on how many slaves he would bathe and offer for sacrifice, he sacrificed the same number of quail, which he had brought with him for this occasion. This ritual consisted of beheading the quail and then tossing them into the fire.[43] He burned copal incense, raising it four times toward the east for the rising of the sun and then to each of the other cardinal directions. Then the merchant-bather returned to his guests and addressed them in a formal speech. The Mexica were exceedingly fond of formal oratory, and this speech is just a very small example of it. After greeting the guests with all formality, he compared them to warriors, extolling their courage in traveling to difficult places—mountains, peaks, gorges, and deserts—and expressed the desire that their property never be lost or destroyed. He then formally pledged to offer a slave to be beheaded for the great god Huitzilopochtli.[44] In return, the guests praised their host and thanked him for offering up the secrets of the god and for his kindness. He, too, was compared to a powerful warrior. Then the host, the merchant-bather, took up his feathered staff and departed for Tenochtitlan.[45]

Rituals in Tenochtitlan

Sahagún implies that the trip to Tochtepec occurred within the first few days of the month of Panquetzaliztli, but that is unlikely. Therefore, the banquets and feasts began not upon the merchant-bather's return but on about the fifth day of the month, after the purchase of the slaves and the organization of food and gifts. Sahagún notes that the timing of the feasts and banquets was important. They should fall on ritually significant days. This probably explains why Sahagún is somewhat vague about the timing of certain banquets and other ceremonies; they were timed to fall on propitious days from the tonalpohualli.

The merchant-bather assembled everything that he would need for the series of banquets.[46] He sent out special invitations to the leading merchants and disguised merchants. Continuing in the section on the merchants, Sahagún lists three officers within the merchant guild who would receive special attention in the ceremony: the Quappoyaualtzin (a merchant military commander), the Uetzcatocatzin (Huetzcatocatzin), and the Zanatzin.[47] During the feast, the merchant offered them food and drink along with tobacco and gifts, much like in the earlier banquet in Tochtepec. This group of merchants received special gifts of capes with plaited paper ornaments and the special and unique long breechclouts. The merchant-bather then addressed them in a highly ornamented speech in which he thanked them for their presence and invited them to witness the sacrifices to Huitzilopochtli. Interestingly, the merchant-bather confided to his colleagues that he would benefit from his participation in the ceremonial sacrifice and even profit from it. This reinforces the multiple levels on which merchant participation in these events operated. On one level, they fulfilled a religious obligation. But at the same time, they demonstrated their wealth while recycling some of it back into the community through banquets and feasting. But it was also a strategic act in which the merchants tried to curry favor with the warriors and political leaders of the society.

In response, the merchant leaders called the merchant-bather a youth and charged him to dissimulate regarding his wealth since merchants generally avoided pride and ostentation. In equally flowery speech, the other merchants observed that the merchant-bather had already been preparing himself for this moment for as many as two years, filling himself with weeping and sorrow as befitted such a solemn act. They called upon him to prepare well for the coming events, admonishing him not to live foolishly, execute the rituals poorly, or commit some other outrage lest he bring shame on all the ranks of merchants including the slavers, the vanguard and outpost merchants, and other merchant-bathers. Lastly, they chided him for not preparing well for the banquet, claiming that he had hidden provisions away, holding back from his guests. In reply, the merchant-bather described all his preparations up to that point in order to demonstrate his readiness. Part of his report was to list the gifts and food that he would give away.

The elder merchants outlined the rituals that the merchant-bather was to follow, urging him to acquit himself well. He was to hold four special banquets in conjunction with specific rituals. These included the rituals called the *teyolmelaua*, the *tlaixnextia*, the *teteualtia*, and the *tlamictia*.[48] During the last ceremony, in particular, the merchant-bather was urged to avoid coveting other people's property. Translating the names of ceremonies can be extremely complex. *Teyolmelaua*, on the surface, would mean something like "straighten a person's heart." The Mexica used the expression of "heart straighten" (*neyolmelahualiztli*) to describe a preconquest confessional rite. Louise Burkhart suggests that in that instance, the purification rites the slaves underwent provided spiritual benefits for the merchant and his family.[49] *Tlaixnextia* means "to reveal something" or "to acquire something, to gain goods." In this context, it suggests that the ceremony imparted esoteric knowledge to the sacrificial victim or the merchant-bather or that this was a mechanism to acquire more possessions.[50] *Teteualtia* (*tetehualtia*) refers to the washing ceremony that was one of the distinctive features of the preparation of slaves as sacrificial victims.[51] *Tlamictia* could mean "to cause something to be killed," although the indefinite object pronoun, *tla-*, could also refer to "someone" not just "something."[52]

The merchant-bather addressed the other merchants and thanked them for their advice. He used very elegant and distinctive speech to recognize the assistance they provided to him and his happiness at receiving their counsel. They replied that all that was left was to decide on a day that was ritually beneficial on which to begin the process of bathing the slaves and then performing the other rituals called upon in the ceremony. To accomplish this, they sent forth for a soothsayer, a calendar priest, to determine the best date to begin, such as 1 House, 2 Flower, or 2 Monkey from the tonalpohualli. This observation is important because it is one of the few instances in the description of the rituals and ceremonies of Panquetzaliztli that mention how it might interact with the 260-day ritual calendar. It demonstrates that the rituals were not confined to specific days of the month of Panquetzaliztli but could be shifted to maximize the interconnections between the two calendars.

With all this concluded, the leading merchants offered a benediction to the merchant-bather. They called upon him to be humble and embrace charity. In that way, he would live a long life with good health. Specifically, they admonished him to offer charity to the poor and to old people because they are the representatives of the god called Totecuio (Our Lord), which one assumes, in this context, to be Yacateuctli or Huitzilopochtli.[53] Failure to embrace this charity might result in becoming blind, crippled, or in some other way afflicted. The parting counsel was to avoid coveting another's wife or daughter.[54]

Book 9 of the *Florentine Codex* provides some details about the activities occurring between the eleventh and the nineteenth days of the month.[55] Again, Sahagún does not indicate that certain events occurred on specific days, undoubtedly because many had to be coordinated to fall on beneficial days from the tonalpohualli. At some point before the eleventh day of the month, but after having received the benediction of the other merchant leaders, the merchant-bather gave the slaves, both men and women, the special clothes he had already set aside. These included the capes, breechclouts, skirts, shifts, earplugs, labrets, and jewelry. In addition, he added crushed paper that was adorned with quetzal feathers with red cord ties to serve as ear decorations. These may be similar to the paper-flower ornaments worn by the priests in the illustration of the *Primeros memoriales*. The male slaves wore anklets made of ocelot skin on which rattles had been sewn. The hair over the slaves' temples seems to have been plaited with turquoise and gold, coral shells, and black obsidian in a design called *petzotzocolli* (shining hair strands).[56] The merchant then brought all the slaves together and commanded them to dance. As they danced, they held the flower shields, garlands, necklaces, and bouquets and tubes of tobacco, smelling the flowers and smoking through the tobacco tubes. In addition, the female slaves were dressed with good skirts, shifts, and sandals. Their hair was braided in a rope that had red, yellow, blue, and black threads added and then was finished with white feathers. The flowers would be replaced daily.[57]

Dressing the slaves was the first ceremony of the four, called teyolmelaua ("to straighten a person's heart"), and it took place at midnight. The merchant offered the victims food and drink while they sat on reed mats near the front entrance of the house so that anyone who might pass by could see them. The other guests of the merchant would come and go during the night, eating, drinking, and admiring his slaves. On another night, the merchant-bather would invite his guests to come back for the second ceremony, the tlaixnextia ("to reveal or to acquire something"), which was similar to the first. At this point, it is nearly impossible to determine on which night of the month this second ceremony occurred, especially since the exact timing was probably determined from the tonalpohualli.

The Bathing Rituals

Central to the relationship between the merchant and the sacrificial victims were bathing rituals that occurred on the eleventh and fifteenth days of the month in anticipation of the sacrifice on the final day. These two rituals seem to have been fixed on specific days of the xiuhpohualli and were not dependent on the vagaries of the tonalpohualli. Ritual bathing was an important part of the larger complex of human sacrifice, not just the ceremonies of Panquetzaliztli.[58] Bathing prepared the victim through ritual cleansing. According to several texts and scholars, the victims were cleansed to remove the stain of slavery.[59] In the case of the Panquetzaliztli ceremonies, it also created a special bond between the victim and the patron who sponsored the sacrifice, whether he was a warrior or a merchant. This is seen acutely in the way Sahagún and others refer to the sponsors and their victims, who came to be known as "bathers" and "bathed ones," respectively. Nonetheless, Sahagún does not explicitly report that the warriors bathed their captives in anticipation of sacrifice. If the bathing did serve to cleanse a person of the condition of slavery, it might not have been needed for the captured warriors, since they had not been bought or sold but captured on the field of battle.

In several places, Sahagún recounts that on the eleventh day of Panquetzaliztli,[60] the merchants ritually bathed the slaves whom they had chosen for sacrifice. The bathing ceremony to which he invited his guests was the teteualtia ("bathing offering papers"). This name is particularly evocative because it associates the slaves with pieces of paper offered in sacrifice. It is typical of the Mexica to depersonalize the victims, in this case, calling them pieces of paper. In a similar manner, warriors captured on the field of battle were compared to warm and tasty tortillas for Huitzilopochtli.[61] The first bathing ritual was performed at the foot of the Templo Mayor, the temple to Huitzilopochtli. Continuing the metaphor of sacrificial victims as food for the god, the area was frequently called Itlacuayan Huitzilopochtli (Huitzilopochtli's dining place).[62] The water for the bath was carried from a spring located near Huitzilopochco, the "Place of Huitzilopochtli" (modern Churubusco), by the elders and old men of the neighborhoods participating in the ceremonies. The spring was called Huitzilatl (Hummingbird water) and was located in a cave. As one can see from the name of the spring and the town, both these places were intimately related to the god Huitzilopochtli, whose name they shared. The elders of the neighborhoods collected the water in bottles that were stoppered with plugs made from cypress branches before carrying them back to the sacred precinct of Tenochtitlan. The use of the cypress stoppers also continues the symbolism of using branches as a theme of the month.[63]

Sahagún is vague in book 2 of the *Florentine Codex* about who sprinkled the slaves with the sacred water on the patio at the foot of the Templo Mayor, yet one could assume that it was the merchants and their wives.[64] Although Sahagún does not explicitly include the wives in this ritual in the *Florentine Codex,* he mentions that the merchants were assisted or accompanied by their wives as they departed.[65] Anderson posits that there were three types of bathing rituals among the Mexica. One was "washed in god's water," that is, twice bathed in the god's lake, the lake that surrounded Tenochtitlan and Tlatelolco. A second, the ceremony described here, consisted of elders from Huitzilopochco bringing water from the Huitzilatl Spring and bathing slaves at the base of the Templo Mayor. The last was when bathers continually bathed the victims in warm water in front of the Templo Mayor until the sacrifice.[66] A bit later in the Panquetzaliztli ceremonies, there is a fourth type, wherein the slaves are taken to the water's edge for a bathing ritual performed by elderly women.

After this ritual bath, the owners then dressed the slaves in the paper clothing that would be their attire for the rest of the month until their death. The slaves wore beautiful ornaments, earplugs, nose pendants that looked like arrows, and feather headdresses. The slave owners decorated the paper clothing of the slave victims with blue stripes on their legs and arms and blue-and-yellow stripes on their faces.[67] This decoration is very representative of the face paint and vestments of Huitzilopochtli. By having been dressed and arrayed in this manner, the sacrificial victims became teixiptlahuan, local embodiments of Huitzilopochtli.

The *Historia general* adds that the slaves remained clothed, both men and women, while the sacred water was splashed on their heads. Afterward, they were undressed and then dressed with the paper garments that they would wear to their sacrifice.[68] While the ornaments placed on the victims are described similarly in the two texts, in the *Historia,* Sahagún gives the added detail that the headdresses given to the females had yellow feathers tufted up in the middle, while the men's feathers were white.[69] The Nahuatl text describes the headdresses somewhat differently. Dibble and Anderson translate the passage as "reed headdresses surmounted by feathers." The original Nahuatl reads *yoan anecuiotl* (*ihuan aneucyotl*).[70] The aneucyotl thus complemented the rest of the clothing given to the slaves as teixiptlahuan of Huitzilopochtli.

Book 9 of the *Florentine Codex* provides even more detail about this bathing ceremony and especially the clothing provided to the slaves. In this section, Sahagún explicitly calls it the teteualtia, a detail that is absent in his other descriptions of the festival. This description focuses on the ritual headdress associated with Huitzilopochtli: the aneucyotl.[71] The merchant-bather would place them on the heads of the slaves so that they looked like headdresses of white feathers. He then dressed them in their special ritual array: multicolored wooden earplugs, an obsidian nosepiece, and a short jacket in imitation of the god Huitzilopochtli with a frayed edge decorated with feathers. The jacket was blue, black, and red with skulls and bones painted on it, tied at the waist with a red sash. Each slave had shoulder epaulets of a prairie falcon's wing tied on with paper strips. The paper was painted red and black with specks of iron pyrite (fool's gold) sprinkled on it. A single armband was placed on each slave along with wrist bracelets. Lastly, they received obsidian sandals. These must have been sandals decorated with pieces of obsidian, or perhaps they were shiny black in color, since as a volcanic glass, it would be impossible to actually have obsidian sandals. Again, this was imitative of Huitzilopochtli's full array, as discussed earlier.

Once the slave-victims were dressed, the merchant-bather summoned the priests who would officiate at the sacrifice. Some of the priests would now watch over the slaves until the sacrifice. The merchant-bather also called for the various washing assistants, face washers, ceremonial bathers, and the priests with matted hair. The gifts for them consisted of capes decorated with carmine-colored flowers, breechclouts with long ends, and sandals. The women bathers received skirts and shifts. Everyone had their faces painted and adorned with colored feathers.[72] This description implies that at this first bathing ceremony, the merchants were assisted by a fairly large contingent of people. Again, the ceremony's description in book 9 offers far more details than the one given in book 2.

In book 2 of the *Florentine Codex*, Sahagún notes that after singing and dancing at the conclusion of the ritual bath, the slaves were taken home to the various neighborhoods of their owners. The owners took off the garments and adornments and stored them away in reed baskets until later in the month when they would be needed again. On their way home, the owners sang and danced in keeping with the continuing ceremony of the month. Again, Sahagún makes a point of noting that the wives (*incioaoan* [*incihuahuan*]) of the slave owners accompanied them in these rituals.[73]

According to book 2 of the *Florentine Codex,* the second bathing ceremony occurred on the fifteenth day of the month.[74] Those in charge of bathing the slaves went to a place called the Aiauhcalco or Ayauhcalco (Mist House) along with the elders of the neighborhoods. Sahagún does not enumerate who the bathers and elders were or how many people participated. Once the group arrived at the Mist House, they fasted, eating only at midday, and bathed themselves in the Mist House in the middle of the night. While there were at least four Mist Houses near Tenochtitlan and Tlatelolco, the one used during Panquetzaliztli was located in Huitzilopochco, using essentially the same source of water from in the first bathing ceremony.[75]

One woman in particular had the responsibility to bathe the sacrificial victims. First, she bathed herself at the edge of the lake, probably at or near Huitzilopochco. After her bath, she made a personal blood sacrifice using four thorns. She left one thorn on the lake's bank. Another was thrown into the water, and the remaining two were offered to Huitzilopochtli. The context implies that she bathed the sacrificial victims in the same place, although it is not completely clear. Using Anderson's typology, this bath at the edge of the lake near the Mist House would be a fourth type.[76] When this ritual was completed, the participants would return to their home neighborhoods singing and dancing. Here Sahagún specifically notes that everyone, bathers, merchants, wives, and victims danced the serpent dance. They would continue to fast until the final day of the month.

In book 9 of the *Florentine Codex,* Sahagún suggests that several women, not just one, assisted the merchants in the bathing of the slaves: "*mochintin cihoa, in tealtianime*" (several women [were] bathers), perhaps referring to the same women seen above in book 2.[77] The merchant-bathers gave these women special outfits that carried a variety of designs: heart and spiral designs on their skirts, downy feather pendants painted like stone vases, and overblouses with an eagle-head design and a border of twisted cords.

The Spanish text in the *Historia general* provides more details regarding the mundane description of the personal sacrifices made during this second bathing ceremony. The women who owned sacrificial slaves bathed daily in the Mist House at the water's edge. The passage reads, "las mugeres y señoras de aquellos esclavos bañabanse," which could refer to the wives of the sacrificial victims, but that does not make sense in this context, since these slaves were not assumed to have wives or female relatives nearby and certainly not ones who would be prepared to either make sacrifices or be sacrificed themselves. Thus, these are the wives of the merchant-bathers. Both texts indicate that the women carried maguey thorns with them for personal bloodletting. The Spanish notes that the women would cut their ears until blood flowed. They would get some blood on the thorn's tip and then toss it into the water; they then got blood on another thorn that was dipped into the water's edge. Women who bathed at home would perform the same ritual.

The use of the Mist House is quite symbolic. As a spring in a cave, it serves as a liminal space, a locus between the outside world, the entrails of the earth, dry land, and the wet world of water. Thus, the Mist House is a point at which many paired forces met: light and dark, inside and outside, dry and wet. The ritual bathing prepared the sacrificial victims and their patrons for the ceremonies that lay ahead. It stripped away that which had come before and focused them on that which was to come, again creating a point in which another set of paired forces, past and future, met ceremonially.

As noted, on the way to their homes after this second bathing ritual, all participants sang and danced the *coanecuiloa* (serpent dance).[78] In book 2 of the *Florentine Codex*, Sahagún offers a few more details about the dance. In performing the dance, the participants held hands while lining up. They held on to circular jar rests, bits of plaited reed that allowed a round-bottomed jar to sit on a flat surface. While others danced, it seems that the sacrificial victims ran around and through the line, becoming breathless and unable to sing at all. The old men of the neighborhood provided the drum beat and kept up the singing. At this point, Sahagún also notes that the participants still maintained their fast, especially the bathers. Part of that fast was abstinence from sexual intercourse.[79] In all likelihood, this is the dance that was represented in the illustration from the *Primeros memoriales*. That text notes that young men and women held hands while dancing, thus including participants of both sexes.[80]

This is the most extensive description of the serpent dance in the Panquetzaliztli section of the *Florentine Codex*. We can assume that this was the same dance that was performed every night of the month, since we learned earlier that on each night, the various participants sang the "Tlaxotecayotl" song and danced a dance. The serpent dance was not unique to Panquetzaliztli, but it might have been used particularly in honor of Huitzilopochtli, because most of the known instances where it was performed had to do with that god. It was considered a sexually suggestive dance that simulated copulation.[81] This might explain why Sahagún emphasized that the participants continued their fast, including abstinence.

Final Preparations for Sacrifice

Continuing in the general discussion of the feast in book 2 of the *Florentine Codex*, at dawn on the nineteenth day,[82] the sacrificial victims would take leave of their owners (the bathers) at their homes, placing a handprint of red, blue, or black on the doorpost or lintel where they exited. This and the other rituals that followed might well be parts of the ceremony of called the tlamictia (cause something to be killed), which Sahagún mentioned earlier as one of the four merchant-sponsored ceremonies subsequent to his return from Tochtepec. In book 9, Sahagún implies that this was the case without explicitly calling it the tlamictia. Instead, he states that for the fourth time the merchant-bather invited his guests to join him in the ritual performances.[83]

According to the narrative in book 2, as the victims left the house of the merchant, they sang in a strained voice as if they were hoarse.[84] On this occasion, the victims went to visit relatives, but then returned to their owners' homes for the final rituals.[85] Upon their return, the owners offered food, but it was seldom accepted.

The owners dressed the victims, providing capes and breechclouts for the men, skirts and overblouses for the women. While not clearly stated, this clothing seems to have been the same as the outfits given on previous days, although it is possible that it was special for this occasion. The merchants and their servants put out the reed baskets with the ritual clothing and ornaments from a few days earlier. The victims dressed, placed banners on their backs, and walked through the residences. The banners were particularly important since they reflected the name of the feast, "the raising of banners." Banners were symbols of sacrificial victims. Women put the slave victims' other belongings in wicker baskets and carried them away on their backs. There were others who were designated to carry the gifts and possessions for the victims. These porters went to the doors of the houses and arranged themselves. The victims walked through the houses, the women's rooms, the hearth room, and then left. The porters left first, followed by the victims. The first destination of this group was the government palace of the neighborhood.[86]

At the neighborhood palace, the sacrificial victims danced in the courtyard. They then placed their gifts in the palace and prepared to greet their owners and patrons. They arranged themselves in front of the palace and had a ceremonial greeting, with women arranged separately but alongside the men. The owners gave additional gifts to all their guests, both men and women. This final ritual was reserved to the merchants, the bathers, and the slave merchants.

Finally, when the victims were completely arrayed in their sacrificial garb, they were taken for the bathing ritual known as *xalaquia* (the entering of sand).[87]

According to Doris Heyden, this ceremony conveyed two concepts. Sand was seen as a cleansing agent, used in conjunction with the water in which the slaves were bathed. It also marked a place of transition from land to water, a permeable place, as water flows through sand.[88] It might have also referred to the passage the victims made from the secular world into the divine world. The Templo Mayor and the sacred precinct surrounding it consisted of several essential elements. The forecourt of the temple, part of the space in front of the temple, to the west near the base of the monumental stairway, was known as the Coaxalpan (Snake-sand place). In descriptions of various sacrifices, the victims underwent the xalaquia ceremony and then immediately went to be sacrificed. This would be possible if that particular cleansing occurred in the Coaxalpan in front of the Templo Mayor.[89] Recent excavations in the Templo Mayor have confirmed this, where the floor that represented the Coaxalpan was uncovered.

The day before their sacrifice, the victims were made to go through this sandy area, or a symbolic sandy area, in an act of presentation to the gods. The sand represented the edge of the watery storehouse of the sacred temple and the place where the riches of the temple were spread out, the place where their bodies would be offered as sustenance to the god. It adjoined the place known as Itlacualoyan Huitzilopochtli.[90]

In book 9 of the *Florentine Codex*, Sahagún adds that the slaves were also made to drink a potion called the *itzpahtlactli* (obsidian medicine) or *teuctli* [*teoctli*] (god pulque).[91] This was a very strong potion, and it had the effect of making the slaves act as if they were quite drunk, possibly to lessen their dread about their upcoming execution. It has been posited that this potion was a mixture of the water in which obsidian sacrificial blades were washed with the addition of cacao and intoxicants.[92]

After the xalaquia at the foot of the Templo Mayor, the victims climbed up one side of the dual staircase to the top of the temple, made a circuit around the sacrificial stone on top, came back down the other side of the dual staircase, and then slowly walked back to their neighborhoods. They were given their paper garments from the earlier ritual a few days before. That night, they sat on mats and kept vigil during which they were offered food and pulque.[93] In book 9, Sahagún notes that from this point, the sacrificial victims would never return to the homes of the merchant-bathers but were taken to the neighborhood temple of either the Pochtlan or Acxotlan districts, the principal merchant neighborhoods. There, they participated in singing and dancing while holding vigil all night. They were offered food and pulque.[94]

Both book 2 and book 9 describe the vigil held the night before the sacrifice. At midnight, a lock of hair was cut from the sacrificial victim. The hair was kept for posterity along with the victims' clothing and ornaments. Sahagún then notes that everyone throughout Tenochtitlan, not just the sacrificial victims, ate amaranth-seed tamales that were sliced with a maguey thread, not broken by hand. The traditional sleeping mats were stored away near the entrances to the slave cages. The victims and everyone in the city slept the remainder of the night on the floor or on old maguey fiber cloaks, awaiting the arrival of Huitzilopochtli in his disguise as the god Painal. The description offered in the *Florentine Codex*, book 2, abruptly stops at this point and shifts focus to concentrate on the ritual of the runner, which began at dawn of the twentieth day. Yet Sahagún provides essential details as to the nature of the vigil of the sacrificial victims and merchant-bathers in the book on the merchants.

In book 9, Sahagún repeats most of the details about the night before the sacrifice, but he adds a few items.[95] After the shell trumpets sounded at midnight, those who were fasting performed ritual self-sacrifice, drawing a little blood. The priests placed the victims on reed mats that had been rolled out, although in book 2 they remained on the floor or on old blankets. The merchant-bather then dressed in the costume for the ritual performance. It consisted of a short jacket like that worn by Huitzilopochtli and similar to what the victims wore. He also had pleated paper flowers, painted papers, and special foam sandals. He dressed as quickly as he could, then the fire in the household hearth was extinguished. Also in book 9, we learn that the amaranth tamales were sweetened with honey and that each victim symbolically received four pieces.

After feeding the victims, while everyone assembled in the courtyard of the neighborhood temple, the helpers of the merchants snipped some of the victims' hair, prompted to do so by a man blowing a whistle and shushing them along, making a sound like "Chich."[96] He carried a *cuauhcaxitl* (an eagle bowl, a sacrificial bowl), into which some of the hair was placed. This done, he hurried away. The helpers kept some of the hair and went around shouting, crying, and popping their lips with their hands. The merchant-bather returned with a censer and offered incense to the four cardinal directions, standing in the middle of the courtyard. The slave victims remained awake the rest of the night, not being able to sleep, one assumes, because of apprehension about what would happen the next day. At dawn, they were offered food, which they normally refused because of their anxiety at their forthcoming death.[97]

The description of the vigil differs slightly between the Spanish and Nahuatl texts. In the *Historia general*, Sahagún explains that only the merchants who purchased sacrificial slaves participated, but in the Nahuatl version, the ceremony included the merchants, the bathers, and the persons who brought the victims down after the sacrifice.[98] Then, in describing how the sacrificial victims slept in the hours before dawn, the Nahuatl text offers greater insight into the nature of their beds. In the *Historia general,* Sahagún implies that everyone in the city, not just the victims, slept on some worn old blankets.[99]

Conclusions

The narrative of Motolinia, the *Primeros memoriales,* and the early pictorial manuscripts are silent regarding much of the preparation and the complex organization of activity behind the early weeks of Panquetzaliztli. Sahagún (and Durán to a lesser degree) provides us with insights into the complexity of the celebration, the manifold little details that needed to be arranged. People moved from the Central Basin to Tochtepec. Ceremonies were conducted in front of the Templo Mayor, in the neighborhood temple areas, at the spring of Huitzilatl, and in the homes of the merchants and warriors.

The preparations and activities of the month of Panquetzaliztli that led up to the final running ceremony and human sacrifice manifest the complexity of the celebration. In anticipation of the event, some members of Mexica society began fasting and engaging in other activities many months in advance. The services of hundreds if not thousands of people were enlisted to acquire the goods, food, and clothing that were used in the month. Porters and merchants were active in the preparations. But, perhaps more important, many of the activities involved the whole community. While certainly the warriors, merchants, and their families undertook the daily singing and dancing, Sahagún implies that it spread into the community as well. On the night before the final sacrifice, the entire population dined on symbolic tamales and slept on old maguey capes or the hard floor. The month required the choreography of thousands of people, all acting in concert for the common end of the celebration of Huitzilopochtli that would occur on the final day. Yet, if one is taken aback at the complexity of the details of the preparation and first weeks of the celebration, the events of the final day overshadow them completely.

CHAPTER 3

THE FINAL DAY OF PANQUETZALIZTLI

All the activities outlined in the previous chapter had the purpose of preparing for the final day of the month of Panquetzaliztli. The day was complicated and dynamic. Throughout the day, at least two and sometimes three different ceremonies occurred simultaneously. They overlapped with one another and in many ways complemented each other. Describing them in an orderly and linear fashion defies the imagination since, at some points, two distinct ceremonies occurred simultaneously in two different parts of the Central Basin. Taken as a whole, one can see the parts moving like a well-oiled machine, all working to bring the attention of all the residents of Tenochtitlan to the Templo Mayor for the final paroxysm of sacrifice that was the hallmark of the month. But central to all the ceremonies and rituals of the final day was the teixiptla, and teixiptlahuan, of Huitzilopochtli.[1] Not only are the movements and choreography of people possibly befuddling to modern observers, the layers of symbolism and the local embodiments of deities were as complex as can be imagined.

At the high point of the Panquetzaliztli festivities, on the last day of the month, spectators witnessed a dizzying blur of ceremonies and rituals as the celebrations came to their inevitable end in human sacrifice atop the Templo Mayor. The denouement to the celebrations continued for several days into the subsequent month of Atemoztli. The logistics of the final day of Panquetzaliztli were exceedingly complex, but they all led up to the final sacrifice. The events of the day began with the emergence of a dough figure of Huitzilopochtli from his sanctuary on the Templo Mayor. That was followed by the ritual run through part of Tenochtitlan and the Central Basin of Mexico, called Ipaina Huitzilopochtli, "Huitzilopochtli's Swiftness."[2] At the same time, the bathers and sacrificial victims had a series of rituals to fulfill, with other, smaller rituals feeding into these. All these threads came together at the Templo Mayor for the hecatomb of human sacrifice.

Preparation of the Image of Huitzilopochtli/Painal

Central to the Swiftness of Huitzilopochtli was the figurine called variously Painal, Painaliton (Little Painal), or Painaltzin (Honored Painal).[3] It was a dough figurine that represented Huitzilopochtli and thus was an ixiptla, a localized embodiment of the god. This figure was the key element that linked all the day's ceremonies and performances. Painal was considered a distinct manifestation or avatar of Huitzilopochtli. There were three levels of symbolism at work in this ritual as Sahagún describes it in the *Florentine Codex*. The figurine called Painal was an ixiptla of Huitzilopochtli. Sahagún later contradicts himself and notes that the figurine representing Painal was made not of dough but of wood, but the composition does not affect the fact that it was an ixiptla.[4] In a different section, Sahagún also notes that Painal was not simply an ixiptla of Huitzilopochtli but was also his deputy or vicar. The priest who carried the Huitzilopochtli figurine had the title of Topiltzin Quetzalcoatl and was considered an ixiptla of the god Quetzalcoatl. Yet, in this ceremony, he also became an ixiptla of Huitzilopochtli.[5] Thus, the human localized embodiment of Quetzalcoatl carried a dough image of Huitzilopochtli that represented Painal, which was also a localized embodiment of the same deity.

As a result of this complexity, the sources become somewhat confused as to whether there were one or two physical images. Some contexts seem to indicate that there were two figurines, one of Huitzilopochtli made of amaranth dough and another of Painal made of wood.[6] Potentially there were three ixiptlahuan: the two figurines and the priest impersonator. Also adding to the confusion, during the celebrations of the month of Toxcatl, there were two dough figurines that are very much like the ones for Panquetzaliztli: one of Tezcatlipoca (in his manifestation as Titlacahuan) and one of Huitzilopochtli, which some observers may have conflated with the Panquetzaliztli ritual.[7]

According to Sahagún, the figurine image of the god that emerged on the last day of Panquetzaliztli was dressed in the raiment of Huitzilopochtli. It wore a feather device from its shoulder to its waist, carried an aneucyotl, and had a golden banner along with a green stone necklace. It wore a mirror device on its back along with other adornments of turquoise. Lastly, there seems to have been a herald who preceded the god, carrying the deity's unique weapon, the xiuhcoatl, or fire/blue snake. These were all specific markers of the god Huitzilopochtli.[8]

Diego Durán, in the section of his work focusing on the gods, provided his reader with a glimpse into how the amaranth dough image of the god was manufactured. Two days before the final ceremony, young women, aged twelve to thirteen, who were dedicated to the god, made his image. The young women, called Maidens of Penance lived in a cloister near the temple of Huitzilopochtli. When they entered the cloister, their hair was shorn, but thereafter they allowed it to grow. They only served the god for a year, after which they left to pursue a secular life and marry.[9]

The amaranth image of the god consisted of several ingredients.[10] The main item was ground *huauhtli* (amaranth seeds) mixed with toasted corn. Dark maguey syrup was then added to make the *tzoalli*, the paste used for the image. It has been suggested that the tzoalli was similar to what in modern Mexico is now called *alegría* wherein small edible seeds are made into candy. In reality, the two are somewhat different. Alegría is made from whole or toasted amaranth seeds, not unlike treats made from puffed rice and marshmallow. The tzoalli was made from a flour of ground amaranth seeds and thus might be more like a cookie but without any leavening.[11] To give the image a bit more realism, green, blue, and white beads were inserted to make the eyes while white corn kernels represented its teeth.

Unlike the detailed description of the manufacture of the dough image provided by Durán, Sahagún does not inform the reader that the image was even made of amaranth seed until the very end of his description of the ritual.[12] In book 3 of the *Florentine Codex*, Sahagún explains that the dough was *michioauhtzoalli* [*michihuauhtzoalli*] (dough of fish amaranth) also called *chicalotl*. Sahagún then details the complex process of making the final dough. Rather than being created by the hands of young women, Sahagún writes that the work fell to priests. First, they ground the amaranth seeds into flour. Then it was moistened, divided into pieces, and kneaded in bowls. In the process of kneading, they were careful to remove any bits of rubbish, chaff, or other foreign material. They were also looking for bits of a related type of amaranth, *petzicatl*, known as mirror-stone amaranth, which would have imparted a speckled look to the dough. Sahagún does note that once the dough was complete, it was quite firm, even hard, like pine resin or like the oil from an insect that was used as a binder for colors in painting (*coccus axin*).[13] The manufacturing process was extremely important because it was the means through which the ixiptla became animate: it became the local embodiment of the deity. Sahagún is very specific about where and when the image became animate.[14]

Durán suggests that the figure was somewhat large, as large as the actual figure of the god housed in the sacred cell atop the Templo Mayor. Once the amaranth dough image was complete, the maidens proceeded to dress and decorate it in the array of the god. The figure was placed on a blue bench or litter with handles to be carried by four people.[15] A few pages earlier, Durán gives a description of the image: "[The priest] descended from the summit of the temple carrying a dough image made of tzoalli dough, which is made of amaranth seeds and maize kneaded with honey. The priest brought down an idol made of this dough. Its eyes were small green beads, and its teeth were grains of corn."[16] Later Durán continues, "The dough was dressed in the form of the god. On it was placed the bird's beak of shining, burnished gold; the feather headdress on his head; his apron of plumes; his shield, staff, bracelets, and anklets, his splendid sandals; and his breechcloth, a magnificent piece of needlework and feathers."[17] It seems that Durán is describing two different but similarly attired images. One was loaded onto a large platform or bier and carried by four men; the other was small enough to be carried by a single person.

In Nahua thought, Painal was considered a captain for Huitzilopochtli. In some stories that tell of a time when both gods were men, Huitzilopochtli would send Painal in the vanguard. Because Painal was swift, he would lead the troops into battle. He thus represented the speed that was necessary in war. Sahagún notes that Painal represented Huitzilopochtli in processions and was his ixiptla.[18] Painal was also a messenger of the gods, and for Huitzilopochtli in particular. Thus, the Europeans associated him with the Greco-Roman god Mercury. He carried sticks used for making fire and a golden banner in his hands.[19] This description is very similar to the one provided by Sahagún in the *Primeros memoriales*.[20] He credits the name of the ceremony (Ipaina Huitzilopochtli, "the Swiftness of Huitzilopochtli") to the legend that the god was never taken captive, always defeated his enemies, and was so fast that his foes could never catch him; rather, he caught them.[21] The relationship between Painal and Huitzilopochtli in Mexica thought must have been so close that they became largely indistinguishable. When discussing the Panquetzaliztli ritual in the context of describing the god Huitzilopochtli in book 3 of the *Florentine Codex*, Sahagún ceases to call the dough figurine Painal, but rather always refers to it as Huitzilopochtli.[22] At the same time, even though it featured an ixiptla of Painal, the ritual was called Ipaina Huitzilopochtli, "the Swiftness of Huitzilopochtli."

Durán does not resolve the confusion about the size, number, or construction of the images. But he concurs that the principal image was made of tzoalli. In the chapter on the veneration of Huitzilopochtli, he implies that the figure was rather large, being carried to the Templo Mayor on a litter by four men and then lifted ceremoniously to the sanctuary on top with ropes.[23] But later, in his account of the ceremonies of Panquetzaliztli, he observes, "It was about as large as a man could carry in his arms while fleeing so swiftly that others could not catch up with him."[24]

In the appendix to book 2, Sahagún again discusses the images used in Panquetzaliztli, but the description matches what was already described earlier in book 2. In the appendix, he writes that there were two images: one of Huitzilopochtli and the other of Tlacauepan Cuexcotzin (or Tlacahuepan Cuexcotzin). The Huitzilopochtli image was the size of a man, made only of amaranth seed, but carried by a contingent of youths and priests. Tlacahuepan Cuexcotzin was an aspect of Tezcatlipoca. The figurine was smaller and also made of tzoalli. According to the legend, Tlacahuepan-Tezcatlipoca appeared in the market of the semimythical city of Tula with a little child dancing in his hand. The child was none other than Huitzilopochtli.[25] Olivier also suggests that Tlacahuepan was the patron god of the Tepanecs, who were members of the Aztec Triple Alliance.[26] The association of Huitzilopochtli with Tezcatlipoca in this instance is important because of what can be seen as a rivalry between the two gods that underlay the celebrations of Panquetzaliztli and Toxcatl. Indeed, although Sahagún indicates that these two figures appeared in Panquetzaliztli, they seem to be closer to images used in Toxcatl.

The Nahuatl text in the appendix to book 2 implies that the two images (Huitzilopochtli and Tlacahuepan) were made or became animated in different places. The verb used in Sahagún is *tlacatia*, meaning "to give birth," and *tlacatilia* means "to take on human form."[27] Sahagún indicates that the figure of Huitzilopochtli was made, or became animated, at the place called Itepeyoc (His Hill Heart Place). The corresponding ceremony for the Tlacahuepan Cuexcotzin occurred in the Huitznahuac neighborhood of Tenochtitlan. In these ceremonies, the teixiptla became animate during the course of the eighteenth night of the month.[28] The next morning, the images were revealed, and gifts were given to them, while in the afternoon, there was a procession that continued until sunset. At that point, the image (or images) was (were) taken to the Templo Mayor. A priest called Yiopoch (Yopoch) guarded the images all night.[29]

Continuing in the appendix to book 2, Sahagún describes the image of Painal, there called Painaltzin (Small or Honored Painal). This image was carried in the arms of the priest and made only of wood, unlike the other teixiptla that was of amaranth. This tends to contradict what he wrote earlier in the main portion of book 2. Elizabeth Hill Boone, in her study of Huitzilopochtli, notes that the amaranth images were built upon a wooden framework, and so possibly this image might have been finished in the same way.[30] In all respects, this image of Painal from the appendix to book 2 seems to be the same as the one described elsewhere in the *Florentine Codex*, except for the issue of its composition of wood or amaranth or a combination of the two. Consequently, Sahagún suggests in the appendix that there could be three images: two of tzoalli, the other of wood. The issue of Painal being made of wood seems to contradict what Sahagún reports elsewhere and what other authors such as Durán wrote. Although in the appendix to book 2, Sahagún explicitly notes that these figures were used in the celebration of Panquetzaliztli, they seem to correspond more closely to the feast of Toxcatl, when both Huitzilopochtli and Tezcatlipoca were represented with images.[31] Nonetheless, the remainder of the discussion in the appendix to book 2 deals with the Swiftness of Huitzilopochtli.

Once the image of Huitzilopochtli had been constructed, it was ritually bathed. The ritual specialist named Yiopoch, who was also an ixiptla of Huitzilopochtli, had undergone a year of fasting and penance in preparation for this moment. When he began his penance, he danced, putting on the array of the god that he would wear throughout the course of the year. Similarly, once the tzoalli image was completed, Yiopoch again adorned himself with the regalia of the god and danced. A procession began with one dancer leading Yiopoch: the master of the young men from the Huitznahua neighborhood. Next in the order of the procession came the leaders of the other youth groups, seasoned warriors, and some special ranks among the seasoned warriors: the eagle and ocelot warriors. Since this was the night before the final ceremonies of Panquetzaliztli, the way was illuminated by pine torches that the men carried. Adding solemnity to the procession, some participants provided incense, and others played flutes.[32]

The procession wound its way through the southern part of Tenochtitlan to the *Aiauhcalco* (*Ayauhcalco*, "House of Mist") in the Huitzilopochco neighborhood. The sanctuary was the place where ritual bathing had occurred and where the ashes of sacrificial victims were frequently deposited. In the sanctuary, the tzoalli image was set down, and the ixiptla took off the raiment of the god in preparation for the ritual. The high priest of Huitzilopochtli collected some water in a blue gourd, which he placed in front of the image. The priest then picked up four fresh, green reeds that he dipped in the gourd bowl of water and then bathed the face of the image four times. At the same time, he also ritually bathed Yiopoch, the god impersonator. This bath was a cognate ritual to the sacrificial victims' preparation for the final sacrifice.

At the conclusion of the bath, the impersonator dressed again in the raiment of the god and picked up the tzoalli image in his arms to the accompaniment of flute playing. From the House of Mist, the procession then went back to Itepeyoc. The tzoalli image was stored there until the following morning. Many of the men who had done penance returned home to await the final acts of the celebration.[33]

Durán wrote that before dawn on the day of the final ceremony, the young women who had originally worked on the dough image emerged from their cloister to escort the god to his temple. As his escorts, they were called the Ipilhuan Huitzilopochtli (Huitzilopochtli's Children).[34] The girls wore new white skirts and blouses, with garlands of *momochitl* (toasted or popped corn) around their heads, as necklaces, and over their left arms. They also wore red paint on their cheeks and red parrot feathers on their forearms. The chosen girls lifted the litter and carried the amaranth image to the temple. As they entered the courtyard, the boys from the *telpochcalli,* the religious school attached to the temple, took over carrying the litter. The boys, too, were adorned with garlands and necklaces of toasted corn. The boys carried the image to the foot of the Templo Mayor. There, the assembled multitude paid honor to the image of the god in the traditional manner by bowing down, touching the ground, and bringing dirt to their lips.[35]

Ipaina Huitzilopochtli—The Swiftness of Huitzilopochtli

According to Sahagún, right before the dawn of the last day of the month of Panquetzaliztli, when darkness still lingered, the person designated to carry the image, the priest called Topiltzin Quetzalcoatl, emerged from the sanctuary of Huitzilopochtli on the Templo Mayor.[36] In Nahuatl, he was the teomama, or "god carrier," the person who carried an image of a god. Although the dough image was of Huitzilopochtli, it was called Painal after the god's lieutenant. Sahagún does not describe the image being carried but rather narrates the event as if the image moved by itself: "Painal came down from the top of [the Temple of] Huitzilopochtli."[37] It seemed as though the image moved by itself: "Thereupon Painaltzin came forth."[38]

Throughout book 9 of the *Florentine Codex,* Sahagún uses the diminutive to describe the image of the god Painal, calling him Painalton/Paynalton (Little Painal), as does Torquemada from time to time.[39] In the Spanish text of the *Historia general,* when describing the powers and array of the god Painal, Sahagún mentions that the person carrying the god was himself sacrificed at the end of the ceremony after handing the figurine to one of the priests of the cult.[40] This grisly detail does not appear in the Nahuatl text describing the ceremony or in the section on the merchants. Thus, we must assume that the death was not of the teomama, the person who carried the divinity, but only of the amaranth dough image, which was ritually killed later in the ceremony. However, it is possible that Sahagún is simply contradicting himself, as occurs multiple times in the work. The sacrifice of the figurine does tend to confirm that the notion of ixiptla was so powerful that the local embodiments were completely assumed to be synonymous with the deity.

Torquemada supports the idea established by Sahagún that a second amaranth figurine of Tlacahuepan Cuexcotzin also departed from the sanctuary atop the temple and participated in the ceremony.[41] Torquemada, for his part, dissents from the others in asserting that the runner carrying the image of Huitzilopochtli was dressed in the raiment of Quetzalcoatl. While the priest held the title of Quetzalcoatl, there is no other mention that the priest was adorned with that god's raiment. Yet Torquemada adds that in addition to these two *teomamaque* (plural of teomama), "god bearers," a third person joined the procession, carrying a long waving and twisting snake.[42] This confirms one of Sahagún's observations that a herald carrying the xiuhcoatl preceded the procession. Torquemada calls the snake an *espanitl*, which was probably the Nahuatl word *panitl*, meaning "flag" or "banner."[43] The Spanish text of Sahagún's *Historia general* describes the first phases of the procession as though there were only one participant, using a singular verb. However, after an encounter with another deity about one-quarter of the way through, the verb becomes plural, as if both the figures led the procession.[44] Because of colonial orthography, it is frequently impossible to tell whether a Nahuatl verb is in the singular or plural.

Torquemada suggests that, at least at the outset, the sacrificial victims assembled to witness the running procession. They could not have accompanied it for long because there were other rituals in which they were involved during the remainder of the run. Torquemada also notes that there was singing as the spectators bade farewell to the image and that several persons used incense to reverence the image.[45]

Upon emerging from the sanctuary of Huitzilopochtli, the runner descended the stairs of the Templo Mayor and went first to the teotlachco, the divine ball court, an imposing ritual space within the sacred precinct (see map 2). Arriving there precisely at dawn, four persons (or two slaves) were sacrificed to two different gods: Amapan and Uapatzan (Huapatzan).[46] When discussing the first sacrifices, the Spanish text notes that statues of the gods, Amapan and Huapatzan, were located beside the ball court, while the Nahuatl text is silent regarding either images or their location. Very little is known of these two gods; their names resemble place-names rather than proper names. Later, in the appendix to book 2, Sahagún further notes that only impersonators of the god Amapan were sacrificed in the ball court and that the ritual occurred at dawn.[47] Following the sacrifice in the ball court, the bodies of the victims were dragged into the dirt so that it appeared that the ground had been painted with their blood. Although the ball court normally hosted ritual competitions of tlachtli (the preconquest ballgame), on this occasion, no ballgame was played. Rather, the locale was used specifically for this sacrifice. The smearing of the sacrificial victims' blood into the dirt of the court seems to have had an important ritual meaning. Durán does not include the sacrifice in the ball court nor any other event until the runner reached the western shore of the lake and stopped at Chapultepec. Motolinia similarly does not include the ball court sacrifices, but has the runner leave directly for Tlatelolco once this stop was concluded, as does Sahagún.

Torquemada has a longer description of the running ceremony than Durán, but neither of them provides as much detailed information as Sahagún. At the teotlachco, Torquemada indicates that quail were first sacrificed. Then two war captives were tied by their heels and sacrificed at the conclusion of a ceremony.[48] This description suggests that the two captives had possibly engaged in mock gladiatorial activity. In other celebrations, the Mexica tied a captive by the heel to a gladiatorial stone called a *temalacatl*, arming him with a feather war club and feather shield. A Mexica warrior carrying a macuahuitl or a macana (wood and obsidian battle-ax), would attack him. This ritual combat was one of the highlights of the month of Tlacaxipehualiztli. The gladiatorial combat, moreover, does agree with Motolinia's account.[49]

The runner carrying the image of Painal left the sacred precinct, which housed both the Templo Mayor and the Teotlachco among other temples, and proceeded to Tlatelolco, the twin city to Tenochtitlan. Tlatelolco had enjoyed autonomy as an independent altepetl after the two cities' founding, traditionally believed to be in 1325. As the Mexica of Tenochtitlan amassed power, their rulers no longer wished to share their home island with another independent city-state. In 1473, war broke out between the neighboring cities, with Tenochtitlan emerging victorious.[50]

It was not clear whether the runner stopped in the sacred precinct of Tlatelolco or just passed nearby. Torquemada states that the procession did stop in Tlatelolco and that an even more significant sacrifice was offered there than the one in the ball court, but he does not provide any details.[51] Sahagún indicates that rather than Tlatelolco, per se, the runner's destination was a place called Nonoalco. Tlatelolco is still a district of modern Mexico City, home to the Plaza of the Three Cultures, an area with preconquest and colonial buildings in juxtaposition with modern ones. The plaza corresponds to the ancient sacred precinct of the city-state of Tlatelolco. There is also a place within the larger Tlatelolco district still called Nonoalco.[52] In Mexica times, Nonoalco was listed as one of the original calpolli (neighborhoods) of the Mexica, located on a small island just to the northwest of Tlatelolco.[53] It eventually became part of the larger island. In the *Historia general,* Sahagún gives further indication of Nonoalco's location by noting that the church to Saint Michael could be found there.[54] Unfortunately, there is no church dedicated to Saint Michael in present-day Tlatelolco.

At the place called Nonoalco, the runner participated in yet another ceremony. At this point, the teomama greeted the image of Huitzilopochtli. A new figurine represented the god Cuahuitl Icac (Wood His Shoe),[55] who was known as Painal's helper or his elder brother. That god was decorated in a manner similar to Painal, but striped with chalk.[56] Cuahuitl Icac played an important role in the origin myth of the Mexica, as will be explored in greater depth later in this book. At the time of Huitzilopochtli's miraculous birth, Cuahuitl Icac became his ally and friend.[57]

From Nonoalco, the runner carrying the image of Painal circled around to arrive at Tlaxotlan. It is likely that the image of Cuahuitl Icac also joined the procession. In their translation of the *Florentine Codex,* Dibble and Anderson assume that, from this point, there were two runners carrying two images. Indeed, upon close examination, in the Nahuatl, one can see that at least one verb is clearly in the plural. Thus, Dibble and Anderson inserted the word "both" and made all the verbs plural to convey the notion that there were at least two runners, two ixiptlahuan. When one considers the Spanish text in the *Historia general,* things become clear. There Sahagún clearly notes that following Nonoalco, until shortly before the runners return to the Templo Mayor, there were, in fact, at least two runners, since the verbs describing them are in the plural.[58]

Unfortunately, there are no modern places in Mexico City that still bear the name Tlaxotlan. Nonetheless, we have already seen the place-name since it provides the name of the hymn sung to Huitzilopochtli throughout the celebrations of Panquetzaliztli, the "Tlaxotecayotl." We must conclude that it was located somewhere to the west of Nonoalco because the subsequent stop on the ceremonial path was Popotlan. As it turns out, there is a modern subway station called Popotla located more or less midway between Tlatelolco and Chapultepec, one of the subsequent stops on the ceremonial transit. There was a causeway that stretched over the lake from Nonoalco-Tlatelolco to Azcapotzalco.[59] In all likelihood, both Tlaxotlan and Popotlan were located along this causeway. Yet the route to Tlaxotlan must not have been a direct one, because Sahagún mentions that the runners "circled about." The Spanish text, again, gives more precise directions for the route, noting that Tlaxotlan was in the direction of Tlacopan, while the Nahuatl text merely notes that the pair of god imitators circled about to that place. Tlaxotlan must have been a critically important ritual stop because of its association with Huitzilopochtli, as evidenced by his hymn.

After Tlaxotlan, the runners proceeded to Popotlan. There, the two god carriers participated in the sacrifice of several victims, whom Sahagún states were executed very quickly. In the appendix to book 2, Sahagún further notes that people came out to greet the images; they offered incense, and many quail were beheaded in sacrifice.[60] The Spanish text of the *Historia general* notes that Popotlan was located near where the church of San Esteban stood.[61] There is no modern church in this part of Mexico City dedicated to San Esteban. To complicate matters even more, in the section of the *Florentine Codex* dedicated to the merchants, Sahagún lists a slightly different route for the runner. That route went from Nonoalco to Popotlan and then to Mazatzintamalco (the Honored Deer, the Place of the Tamalli), and from there to Chapultepec.[62] Mazatzintamalco is a reference to one of the dikes that protected the ancient city from flooding. To the west of Tenochtitlan, beyond what is now known as the Puente de Alvarado, was the dike called the Mazatzintamalco (also spelled Mazatzin-Tamalco). It was also the place where the Spanish regrouped as they fled from Tenochtitlan on the Noche Triste (Sad Night), when the Mexica drove them from the city early in the conquest. The Spanish launched one of their final assaults on Tlatelolco from there, using the causeway from Chapultepec to assist them as they pushed toward Nonoalco and Tlatelolco.[63]

Durán provides a rather different route for the ceremony. In his account, the runner left the Templo Mayor with Atlacuihuayan as his first destination, passing by Chapultepec. According to Durán, the runner did not visit the ball court, Tlatelolco, Nonoalco, Tlaxotlan, or Popotlan, as described by Sahagún. Durán notes that the runner, leaving the Templo Mayor, ran along the street later called Tacuba, because it was the direct route to Tlacopan, then to an orchard, which in Durán's time was called the Orchard of the Marqués (suggesting that it had been owned by Hernán Cortés), and then on to Atlacuihuayan. While Spanish names for these towns seem similar (e.g., Tacuba and Tacubaya), in Nahuatl one can see that they are quite distinct and suffered from transcription issues early in the colonial period. Tlacopan is located some five miles to the north of Atlacuihuayan on the western shore of the lake. Then, from Atlacuihuayan, Durán has the runner go to Coyohuacan.[64]

While Durán has the route go directly from the Templo Mayor to Chapultepec and Atlacuihuayan, eliminating any of the stops in the Tlatelolco region, Motolinia describes a route that is somewhat more similar to Sahagún's. According to Motolinia, the runner first proceeded to Tlatelolco, then Popotlan, then Azcapotzalco. Prior to reaching that city, in Motolinia's version, the procession stopped at a place called Acolman for sacrifices. Then it went to Tlacopan and to Chapultepec.

This route would have had the procession backtracking for some distance. It also would have the runner running much farther north than the Durán and Sahagún routes. After this northern circuit, Motolinia's route largely matches the others, sending the procession to Huitzilopochco, near Coyohuacan, where another four captives were sacrificed.[65]

According to Sahagún, after Popotlan, the runners proceeded along the western shore of the lake. They reached Chapultepec (Grasshopper Hill) and passed in front of it, probably near where the effigies of the Mexica *huey tlahtoque* (supreme rulers) were carved into the rock.[66] The procession went on to a riverbank, probably where the extension of the Avenida Chapultepec (or Gral. Pedro Antonio de los Santos) currently passes.[67] At a place presumably called Izquitlan, an additional sacrifice was performed.[68] The individual slain was called the Izquitecatl, or "the person from Izquitlan," thus giving a name to the place. In the *Primeros memoriales*, Sahagún indicates that the Izquitecatl was one of the principal deities dedicated to the traditional alcoholic beverage pulque (*octli* in Nahuatl). The place-name Izquitlan means something like "Place of Toasted Maize Kernels." The Izquitecatl, dressed in a sleeveless shirt, bells, and foam sandals, collected maguey sap that was then fermented in the making of pulque.[69] Izquitlan has a historical importance for the Mexica. One of the first groups of the Mexica migration, a calpolli, was called Izquitlan. The reference dates from about the time in the myth when Huitzilopochtli ordered the Mexica to camp and to establish communities at Coatepec, the mythic Serpent Mountain, somewhere to the northwest of Mexico. Later, when the Mexica first arrived in the Central Basin of Mexico, one of the first places they established a community was near the spring at Chapultepec, which they then called Izquitlan, after the group.[70]

From the sacrificial location beside the river near Chapultepec, Sahagún has the runners proceed to a place called Tepetocan on the outskirts of Coyohuacan.[71] Given the contours of the lake, in all likelihood, a runner going from Chapultepec toward the region of Coyohuacan would have proceeded through Atlacuihuayan anyway, as Durán suggests. Thus, for this part of the circuit, Durán and Sahagún describe the same route in two different manners.

From Tepetocan, near Coyohuacan, the runners went directly to Mazatlan and then doubled back and proceeded to Acachinanco.[72] Neither Mazatlan nor Acachinanco appears on modern maps. Mazatlan is very common as a place-name, meaning "the Place of the Deer." Acachinanco is more unique, and references to this place dating from the time of the conquest indicate that it was located on a small island just on the south side of Tenochtitlan. There was a causeway that ran from the south shore of the lake, beside Coyohuacan, and on directly into Tenochtitlan, traditionally believed to be more or less where the modern Calzada de Tlalpan passes. Mazatlan might have been off of this causeway, since Sahagún indicates that the runners could not proceed directly from Mazatlan to Acachinanco, perhaps because of paths onto and off of the causeway.

Mazatlan might have been an alternate name for a neighborhood known as Tetecpilco. Tetecpilco was located in about the right place, just a bit north of Coyohuacan but on the eastern side of the perpendicular causeway.[73] In identifying the place called Mazatlan in the *Historia general,* Sahagún notes that it was near the church of San Matias Iztacalco and that Acachinanco was located near homes owned by the Alvarado family.[74] There still is a church of San Matias Iztacalco, which is to the east of the old causeway and partway between Coyohuacan and what was the southern edge of Tenochtitlan.

To complicate matters more, in the section on the merchants, Sahagún lists the town of Xolloco as being a stop between Mazatlan and the Templo Mayor.[75] This was another place mentioned in the narratives of the city's conquest. In Sahagún's account of the conquest, he notes that the Spanish artillery knocked down a wall there located near the southern causeway into the city.[76] Modern studies place it very near the edge of the island of Tenochtitlan, perhaps closer to the sacred precinct than Acachinanco.[77]

Acachinanco could not have been too far from the Templo Mayor since Sahagún wrote that the arrival of the runners at this point triggered a separate ritual back in the sacred precinct. In his history of the conquest, Bernal Díaz indicates that it was at Acachinanco that Cortés met the great Mexica leader Moteuczoma II.[78] On some maps, it appears as a small island just south of the main island of Tenochtitlan, one-quarter of the distance to Coyohuacan, but on the causeway and surrounded on all sides by the lake. It also figured as the location of a skirmish in the conquest of Mexico, placing it near Xolloco. It was listed as one of the three places where Spanish troops massed in the final assault on Tenochtitlan.[79] At Acachinanco, Sahagún notes in the appendix to book 2, many people came out to greet the images. They offered incense and beheaded quail in sacrifice. After leaving Acachinanco, the runner proceeded directly to the sacred precinct that surrounded the Templo Mayor.[80]

While the runner carried the image of Huitzilopochtli/Painal, the sacrificial victims and others engaged in a series of several other rituals. As the runner arrived back at the Templo Mayor, in his narrative in book 2 Sahagún begins to bring two distinct sets of rituals together, for they not only occurred simultaneously, they eventually merged to became one large ceremony. When Painal was sighted, one assumes by a priest on the Templo Mayor, others finished rolling up paper that was to be used later in the ceremony. Sahagún does not provide any further details in this section of the *Florentine Codex* about the importance of paper or the significance of rolling it up, but in other sections, he describes this ritual in greater depth, as will be seen.

The Battle of the Huitznahua

While the runner carrying the image of Painal/Huitzilopochtli undertook his journey around the western and southwestern shore of the lake in the Central Basin, the bathed sacrificial victims (in tlatlaaltilti) were prepared for the events of the day. Having been awakened, they were then dressed in their ritual garments and assembled into a single group, possibly in the forecourt to the Templo Mayor. In book 9, Sahagún records that the victims were taken to the outskirts of the calpolli of Coatlan toward the end of the running ceremony.[81] There, they were herded into the temple courtyard to confront a cohort of warriors. This locale was also called the temple of Huitzcalco. This was the name given to the district temple for the Huitznahua region.[82] In book 2, Sahagún does not specify where this encounter took place.

Confronting the sacrificial victims was a group of warriors and others from Huitznahuac. Huitznahuac was one of the traditional calpolli of Tenochtitlan, closely associated with the cult of Huitzilopochtli. The name of the neighborhood means "south" in Nahuatl.[83] Added to the contingent from Huitznahuac were warriors from the imperial forces. This whole army was dressed in yellow quilted-cotton jackets and carried shields decorated with bears' eyes. Sahagún notes that Moteuczoma gave the uniforms to them. The Huitznahua also carried pine staves and spears as weapons.[84] The Spanish text includes important information about this ritual battle. Sahagún notes that the battle included "one group which was from Huitznahua, and, in another group, other slaves, and, in the Huitznahua faction, soldiers of the Huitznahua assisted."[85]

In book 2, Sahagún explains that the sacrificial victims remained in a single cohort and used flint-tipped short arrows called "bird arrows," probably as stabbing spears. In the section on the merchants, Sahagún adds that the slave victims also carried shields and macuahuitl (obsidian-bladed clubs). What ensued was a pitched battle between the Huitznahua and the sacrificial victims. Although the Huitznahua had the upper hand, with quilted armor, spears, and clubs, Sahagún assures that there were deaths on both sides. In book 2 only, Sahagún comments that if the bathed ones captured any of the Huitznahua warriors, the captured warrior would be sacrificed in the field of battle on top of a teponaztli (horizontal log drum).[86] On the other hand, in book 9, Sahagún adds that if the warriors captured one of the slaves, they determined how much ransom should be demanded to return him to the merchant-bather for use in the upcoming sacrifice. The merchant-bather then had to pay whatever ransom was demanded. If he had no large capes with which to pay the ransom, the warriors would kill the slave there and then and consume some of his flesh.[87] In both texts, Sahagún emphasizes that this was not merely a ritual skirmish but a real battle. When the priest who supervised the battle saw that the image of Painal was approaching, he would cry out and stop the warfare, and the warriors would then all disperse. The sacrificial victims would fall in line behind the god bearer of Painal/Huitzilopochtli as he proceeded to the Templo Mayor.

Several different officials accompanied the image by this point. Leading the procession were young men who carried standards and two *tlachieloni* (special viewing devices) that were made of feathers with a hole in the middle. This device was particularly associated with Tezcatlipoca but appears in other contexts as well since it is related to warfare.[88] The Spanish text describes the tlachieloni as "two pieces of round featherwork, like a buckler [round shield], and they had a small hole drilled in the middle; these were like maces carried before the god, placed on staves, like lance staves."[89] The boys had to run very fast to lead the procession. As they approached the factions that had been battling, warriors would take the devices and standards away from the young men carrying the standards. Other warriors then also attempted to seize the ritual instruments. All the participants had to try to run as fast as they could to protect the devices. To the casual observer, it must have looked more like a relay race with the ritual devices being handed off from one set of warriors to another. This competition for the tlachieloni resembles something that Durán describes. The Dominican wrote that all along the route of the procession, people would chase after the tzoalli image to try to take it away from the teomama. Those who might succeed would gain favors from Huitzilopochtli.[90]

When the procession entered the *Quauhquijaoac* (Cuauhquiyahuac, "Eagle Gateway") of the sacred precinct, no one could try to take the implement away from the person who bore it. This location was also mentioned in the accounts of the final battle for the city between the Spanish and the Mexica. Sahagún describes it as "an eagle carved of stone, as tall as a man's height is tall; and flanking it was an ocelot on one side, and on the [other] side a wolf, likewise carved of stone."[91] A bit later,

Sahagún also implies that warriors competed to take hold of the amaranth image of the god, as Durán suggests. Durán adds that the entire route of the procession was decorated with triumphal arches with flowers, feathers, and banners. At each arch, there was music of drums, flutes, and conch shells.[92]

The last warriors to possess the tlachieloni ran up the stairway of the Templo Mayor into the sanctuary of Huitzilopochtli and cast the implements in front of the amaranth image of the god that had preceded them in the procession. The warriors collapsed on the floor of the place, exhausted from their efforts. They had to be revived by the priests, who cut their ears with a flint knife. Once recovered, the warriors descended from the temple, carrying pieces of the amaranth dough they had taken, particularly those who had seized control of the amaranth image. Sahagún adds that the image was, thus, indeed their captive. The participants then consumed the dough. They took some home to be shared with family and neighbors.[93] Torquemada explains that only males were allowed to consume the dough even though they might be only infants in the cradle.[94] Exactly when the amaranth image was broken into pieces is unknown. In book 2, Sahagún indicates that it was near the end of the ceremony of the Swiftness of Huitzilopochtli. In other places, he suggested that it took place at the very end of the sacrifices several hours later.

The route outlined by Durán was a shorter course than the one described by Sahagún, but they agree on the latter portions. A rough calculation indicates that the route of the ceremony according to Durán was about 28.4 kilometers (17.6 miles), which, if the runner took only two hours, would suggest a speed of more than eight miles per hour, a credible speed but less than modern marathoners, who run more than ten miles per hour and faster. The route described by Sahagún was longer, possibly some 35 kilometers (22 miles). Moreover, Sahagún suggests that the run took nearly twice as long, more than four hours, making it a more leisurely pace of five miles per hour. For his part, Torquemada argues that the course of the ceremony was some four or five leagues, approximately 16.9 to 21 kilometers (10.5 to 13 miles).[95] At the same time, one must remember that at least four sacrifices occurred along the route, which would have also added time to the circuit.

Durán also had a different description of how the dough image of the god was lifted to the sanctuary on top of the temple. Rather than having a single runner carry the image, Durán writes that it was carried on a litter by several men. When the procession of runners reached the base of the Templo Mayor, they set the litter down. The litter was tied with ropes, and then priests atop the temple hoisted it up to the sanctuary on top with great care while others helped from below, all accompanied by drums, horns, and other instruments. This had to proceed with great caution because the steps to the top were quite narrow, the incline was significant, and the litter could not be simply carried up without the image sliding off. Once the image reached the top, it was installed in a shelter made of flowers while others scattered flowers in front of and around it, stretching down the stairway and into the temple courtyard.[96] Nonetheless, Durán insists that the image was small enough to be carried by a single person during the Swiftness of Huitzilopochtli.

Durán continues his description with details that are absent from Sahagún. The young women who had crafted the dough image of the god then returned to the sacred precinct, carrying cakes made from tzoalli that had been fashioned to resemble large bones. They handed them to the young men, who carried the cakes to the top of the temple and placed them before the figurine of the god until there was simply no more room. There was a huge quantity of symbolic bones, more than four hundred according to Durán. These were given the name of "the bones and flesh of Huitzilopochtli."[97] The girls were prohibited from climbing the temple, let alone entering the sanctuary of the god. All the priests of Huitzilopochtli (whom Durán calls priests and deacons), wearing their most sumptuous robes, emerged from their house in rank order and processed around the temple. Also included in the priestly procession were several teixiptlahuan dressed in the attributes of the gods. The procession, with chanting, dancing, and prayers, consecrated the dough offerings, which were then considered to truly be the flesh and bones of Huitzilopochtli.[98] Durán continues to explain that all these ceremonies were merely a preface for the human sacrifices that were the central feature of the rituals to Huitzilopochtli in Panquetzaliztli.[99]

Durán places the run into a symbolic framework. He explains that the race of Painal was a metaphor for Huitzilopochtli. The ritual was called "the Swiftness of Huitzilopochtli" because "while the god was alive he was never caught, never taken prisoner in war, was always triumphant over his enemies, and, no matter how swift his foes, none ever caught up with him. He was the one who caught them. Therefore, this feast honored his speed."[100] The ceremony of the Swiftness of Huitzilopochtli was fraught with symbolism as will be seen in later chapters.

The Final Sacrifices

After the running procession had passed the battle of the Huitznahua, the surviving victims were lined up and led to the sacred precinct and arranged in rows in front of the Templo Mayor, according to Sahagún in the merchant section of the

Florentine Codex. They then processed four times around the temple and once again lined up in front.[101] At some point, it seems that the victims were undressed, their paper costumes stored away for their owners to keep.

Several structures and objects were aligned in front of the Templo Mayor leading west. The ball court was farthest away, then the skull rack, which was located closer. Immediately in front of the temple was the Coaxalpan, which had several small structures on it. Right up against the temple were two important objects. One was a bas-relief of the executed form of Coyolxauhqui, Huitzilopochtli's sister, whom he killed and dismembered. Also at the base of the temple was the *cuauhxicalco* (eagle bowl place), where the cuauhxicalli ("eagle bowl," a large basin used to receive sacrifices) was located.

As the image of Painal was taken up the temple, the chief priest of Huitzilopochtli brought down the sacrificial papers and placed them in the cuauhxicalli.[102] These were the ritual papers that had been rolled up just prior to the arrival of Painal. The priest raised the papers to the four directions before depositing them in the vessel. Another priest came down from the temple, carrying Huitzilopochtli's quintessential weapon, the xiuhcoatl. It looked like a burning pine torch, but instead it was a long paper snake decorated with red feathers to imitate the fire, and paper streamers a total of some twelve to eighteen feet long, which Torquemada describes as accompanying the entire procession route. The priest made the paper snake move as if it were real, even flicking its tongue. When he reached the cuauhxicalli, he raised the serpent to each of the four directions and then threw it on top of the sacrificial papers, where everything burned. The priest returned to the top of the temple and a shell trumpet sounded. The general public assembled in front of the temple to watch the spectacle. Everyone had been fasting for the day. As the sun was setting, people broke their fast before the slaves were sacrificed.[103]

The huey tlahtoani was seated on his *icpalli* (throne) in the courtyard, it seems, in front of the Templo Mayor. It was covered with wolf skin, placed on top of an ocelot-skin carpet, and from it he looked up to the temple of Huitzilopochtli. In front of him, they had placed an artificial tree made of reeds, sticks, and feathers, topped by a spread of quetzal feathers, with a mat of the same feathers at its base.[104] Trees, branches, and flags were all synonymous with Panquetzaliztli.

Painal then descended from the temple and began to escort the slave victims to their deaths on top of the temple. Painal was represented either by a priest ixiptla or a priest carrying the dough ixiptla of the god; the two descriptions provided by Sahagún differ on this point. The priest or god imitator passed beside the cuauhxicalli and then along the line of sacrificial victims. He then turned to lead the group as they all ascended the temple. In book 9, Sahagún specifies that the first victims to be sacrificed were warriors captured in battle, accompanied by their captors.[105] After them, the merchant-bathers accompanied their slaves to the sacrifice. As each died, a conch shell trumpet was sounded. The bodies of the sacrificial victims were rolled down the temple.[106] The priests who conducted the sacrifice wore short, sleeveless jackets, feathered fans on their heads, and paper pendants, and their cheeks were painted red with ocher. Four priests held the feet and hands of the victim while the main priest used a flint knife to open the chest and cut out the heart. This description closely matches the illustration that Sahagún provides in the *Primeros memoriales* and by Motolinia in his version.[107]

The heart was put in the sacrificial vessel in front of the image of the god while the body was tossed down the temple. If the victim was one of the men captured in battle, then the warrior who had captured him recovered the body, followed by the merchants recovering the bodies of the slaves. Since the war captives were sacrificed first, they became the foundation upon which the slave victims fell.[108] This all corresponds nearly exactly with the description by Motolinia, who also provides a detailed description of the actual sacrifice. During the description of the sacrifice, the Spanish text in the *Historia general* provides the Nahuatl name for the sacrificial bowl and the papers, which were rolled and offered at the same time: *tetepoalli* [*tetepohualli*] or *teteuitl* [*tetehuitl*].[109] These words, of course, appear in the Nahuatl text, but it is curious that Sahagún decided that they were important enough to repeat in the Spanish text.[110]

The merchants and their wives climbed up the temple to accompany their sacrificial victims. If a merchant had no wife, his uncles or other important close relatives might join him. Those who accompanied the slaves carried walking sticks decorated with quetzal feathers so that they looked like stalks of young corn. The walking stick was also emblematic of the merchants themselves. As they ascended, they would blow into their hands and then waft their breath over their own heads. Once on top of the Templo Mayor, they walked around the image of the god. After the sacrifice, they descended and arranged for help to carry the body of the sacrificial victims to their homes. Once at home, they quickly prepared the body of the victim for cooking. The flesh was placed in one pot, and corn was cooked in a different pot. Very small portions of the flesh were served on top of the cooked corn. The flesh was not seasoned with chilies but only with a little salt, and it was offered to all the merchant-bather's relatives.[111]

Durán's descriptions of the sacrifice are similar to those presented by Sahagún, although in this instance, the Dominican friar offers much more detail. Durán notes that six priests took part in the sacrifice, not the five described by Sahagún. The leader held the title of Topiltzin, or "Our Lord" (perhaps the Topiltzin Quetzalcoatl who initiated the running procession). The other assisting priests were called the *chachalmeca*, which Durán translates as "a minister of divine things."[112] Durán posits that the office of priest was of high social status and that it was passed down from father to son. The high priest wore a red mantle with green fringe, a headdress of green and yellow quetzal feathers, golden earplugs inlaid with green jade, and a blue stone labret. The other priests were smeared with black; they had curly hair and wore leather bands around their heads and black robes with white mantles. Before they set to work, they put down the colored paper shields that they had carried.[113] This description does not as closely represent the illustrations offered by Sahagún.

The sacrificial victims were nude, according to Durán, and were made to line up on a low platform beside the skull rack (tzompantli). As Sahagún notes, one of the priests descended from the sanctuary and processed along the line of victims, carrying a small image of the god. He then led the line of victims and climbed the temple. Similar to Sahagún, Durán records that the victims were brought to the top of the temple, where they were sacrificed, their hearts offered to Huitzilopochtli, and their bodies cast down from the temple, rolling down the stairway, since the sacrificial stone was close to the top of the stairway.

Durán continues to relate that the warriors who had captured victims in battle claimed the bodies, some forty or fifty of them. The bodies were taken away, prepared for eating, and then distributed. The blood of the victims was sprinkled on the dough image of the god and on the dough bones that had been prepared for the ceremony. At the conclusion of the ceremony, the young men and women again emerged into the courtyard and began to sing and dance in praise of the god. One of the songs was a call and response, with one part sung by the youths, the other by the priests, warriors, and elders. One of the dances consisted of forming a circle with some dancers in the middle. Throughout the day of the sacrifice, people could eat nothing but amaranth and honey (tzoalli). They could not drink anything, including water, until midday, when the sacrifices had ended. Even children were instructed not to drink anything after consuming the amaranth until after all the sacrifices had concluded.[114]

In a discussion of the god Yacatecuhtli, the patron of the merchants, in book 1 of the *Florentine Codex* Sahagún comments that the massive sacrifice at the Templo Mayor was not the only ritual sacrifice in celebration of Panquetzaliztli. In addition to their participation in the larger ceremony, the merchants also selected a sacrificial victim to be a teixiptla of their god, we assume Yacatecuhtli. After the victim was dressed, he was put on display. The ritual sacrifice was accompanied by singing, dancing, and feasting, probably in the neighborhood of the merchants, Pochtlan. In addition to the teixiptla, there may have been other sacrificial victims for this smaller celebration.[115]

The Denouement after the Sacrifices

In Sahagún's narrative in the *Florentine Codex*, after the sacrifices concluded, the merchant-bather continued to guard the ritual clothing he had provided for the slave victims, which had been stored away in a special box. Along with all the accouterments, the merchants also stored the bits of hair that had been cut from the tops of the victims' heads. Once the merchant-bather died, the box and its contents were burned.[116] Yet, in book 2, Sahagún writes that five days after the sacrifice, the paper clothes of the sacrificial victims were burned, marking their final departure from the earthly realm.[117] With the destruction of the victim's possessions after the death of the merchant-bather, Sahagún concludes his description of the Panquetzaliztli ceremonies in book 9 of the *Florentine Codex*.

Sahagún continues to explain more of the final acts of the ceremonial month in book 2. At the same time as the sacrifices at the Templo Mayor, there were also sacrifices in Huitznahuac, but only of victims associated with that neighborhood. Sahagún implies that the victims were actually from that neighborhood, but the Spanish text clarifies that the victims were slaves owned by residents of the neighborhood. None of the war captives were sacrificed in Huitznahuac, only slaves.[118]

While this was the end of the ceremonies associated with Painal and Huitzilopochtli, other rituals and ceremonies continued for at least another five days. In the appendix to book 2, where Sahagún also provides details about the amaranth-dough images and other performance aspects of the Panquetzaliztli celebrations, he suggests that the dough images were consumed at the very end of all the sacrifices. The tzoalli image of the god was ritually sacrificed, the sacrifice of the teixiptla. While the exact site for the ritual is unclear, in all likelihood it occurred in the sanctuary of Huitzilopochtli. The priest called Quetzalcoatl killed the image by plunging a flint arrow into its heart.[119] The huey tlahtoani, Moteuczoma, the principal priest of the Huitzilopochtli cult, the four assistant priests, four youth leaders, and some of the highest-ranking military leaders witnessed this ritual.

After this sacrificial death, the tzoalli image was broken into pieces and consumed. Moteuczoma received the portion that represented the heart. After that, the remainder, which resembled bones, was divided up. Two pieces were given to leaders from Tlatelolco, possibly the portions representing the buttocks. Two portions were given to the elders of the districts within Tlatelolco.[120] Similarly, parts were distributed to representatives from Tenochtitlan. In this manner, bits were given to two of the Tenochtitlan districts and the elders from two districts on a rotating schedule; in different years, different neighborhoods would be represented, since each city had several districts. As the pieces were divided and distributed, the portions quickly became quite small. In the end, the young men of the *calmecac* (temple school) associated with the Huitzilopochtli temple ate the remaining pieces. The portions given out were called *teuqualo* (*teocualo*), "the god is eaten," while those who consumed it were called *teopia*, "they keep (or hold) the god."[121]

At the end of this ritual, after consuming their portions of the image of the god, the men who had fasted and done the yearlong penance celebrated. One of the first activities mentioned by Sahagún is that the men who had been fasting now bathed, washing their heads with amolli soap. This implies that they probably had not bathed during their year of penance, or at least had not washed their hair.[122] After the bath, they ate festive dishes including fruit, fruit tamales, various stews, and dog that was specially prepared for the occasion. In addition, some got a little drunk on pulque. All this feasting and celebration demonstrated that they had successfully completed their fasts and penance, had consumed the god, and were ready to pursue the rest of their lives. They said that their burden had been lifted; they greeted the new day with joy and peace, each man returning to his occupation.[123]

After the main ceremony of the Swiftness of Huitzilopochtli, those involved in the performances engaged in feasting, drinking, singing, and dancing.[124] This part of the Panquetzaliztli celebrations actually occurred during the following month of Atemoztli. The great sacrificial ceremony at the Templo Mayor occurred on the last day of Panquetzaliztli and, in effect, concluded that month.

The morning after the sacrifice, on the first day of Atemoztli, people began to drink pulque and, in particular, a special type called blue pulque since it seemed to have a blue color when poured. This matches what Sahagún reports from Tepepulco. Food leftover from the previous day's ceremonies was distributed throughout the city. By and large, drunkenness in general and among young people in particular was considered a serious violation of the social order.[125] Consequently, those who engaged in drinking were old men and women, seasoned warriors who were married, men of marriageable age, and lords and leaders among the marriageable men. The leaders of the telpochcalli (young men's academies), who were no longer young themselves, also joined in the drinking but were very careful to do it secretly. If by chance they were discovered, people would punish them severely, beating them with sticks, cutting their hair, and kicking and dragging them, even to the point of death: "They beat them repeatedly with pine staves; they bruised their bodies sorely; and they shaved their heads like servants—they cut [the hair from] the heads of each one. They dragged each one; they went kicking them; on the ground they struck them repeatedly; they cast stones at them. Verily they afflicted them."[126] On the other hand, in the Spanish text, those who were discovered drinking surreptitiously were "punished, hit with clubs, had their hair clipped, dragged, kicked, and tossed them from there, being very badly treated."[127]

In addition to the drinking festivities, people gathered for singing in the homes of merchant-bathers, all seated on the ground, accompanied by drums, turtle shells, and gourd rattles. This was also an opportunity for gift giving. All the guests and servants were rewarded with gifts from the householder. The celebrations included the consumption of tobacco, chocolate, tamales, meat, and pulque, each given to someone who might particularly enjoy it. All the people who had worked behind the scenes making food, pulque, and tamales and helping out in the neighborhood also received gifts according to their tastes.[128]

They held the mock battle of Chonchayotl on the third day of Atemoztli, but it was still part of the Panquetzaliztli celebrations. One man took the role of the god Chonchayotl, with wild hair and blood on his body and generally appearing in disarray like a wild man. The priests who had served in the Panquetzaliztli rituals became one band supporting Chonchayotl while the young men of the telpochcalli became the opposition. The mock battle began at noon. The weapons of choice were fir branches, sticks, and reeds, with which they beat one another. Sometimes they tied up captives and proceeded to beat them. Occasionally, participants got hurt in the melee. If a young man happened to capture one of the priests, the boys rubbed the priest's body all over with broken maguey spines, causing horrible itching and burning. If the priests captured a young man, they would prick his ears, shoulders, chest, and other parts of his body with maguey spines until he bled. The two bands also took part in looting various buildings. The youths would steal chairs and drums from the palace while being pursued by the priests. The priests would steal mats, seats, and musical instruments from the temple schools (calmecac) while being chased by the young men. If members of either band entered the living quarters of a person from the other band, they looted it. All this ended at dusk on 3 Atemoztli.[129] Of course, this closely corresponds to the Chonchayotl ceremony described in Tepepulco, but the timing and several details seem to be different. In the regional capital, Sahagún describes it as occurring during Panquetzaliztli, not immediately after.

The final acts of Panquetzaliztli took place on 4 Atemoztli. The celebration was called *nexpixolo* (ashes are scattered). The belief was that the spirits of the sacrificial victims continued to walk the earth for four days. Thus, on that day, the slave owners took out the paper vestments that had been packed away in reed boxes immediately before the final sacrificial rites and burned them. The ashes were then scattered, allowing the spirits to depart to Mictlan, the place of the dead. All participants washed with amolli soap, then returned to their own homes after many days of feasting and celebration.[130]

In several other celebrations during the Mexica solar-year calendar, while many victims were sacrificed, one central victim in particular was frequently seen as a teixiptla, an impersonator of the god. This was especially true during the feast of Toxcatl, where one man was treated as a personification of a god throughout a whole year prior to his execution. In the case of Panquetzaliztli, however, most authors, including Sahagún, do not explicitly state that a specific impersonator was sacrificed. While Sahagún does not explicitly note it, all the sacrificial victims seem to have been ixiptlahuan of Huitzilopochtli since they were ritually dressed in paper garments that represented the array of the god.

Conclusions

The ceremonies and rituals of the month of Panquetzaliztli were extremely complex. They contained hundreds if not thousands of symbolic acts. Each movement, each gesture, each costume, was filled with symbolic import. Even with the assistance of cultural interpreters such as Sahagún, Durán, and Motolinia, it is impossible for scholars today to fully understand all the nuances. Nonetheless, it is important to look at each piece and attempt to understand its importance in the larger celebration and to understand whatever symbolic or historic meaning it might have in order to paint a fuller picture of the ceremonies' significance.

The Swiftness of Huitzilopochtli, the central ceremony on the last day of the month, was an exceptional feat for several reasons. Although the residents of the Central Basin of Mexico were fully acclimated to living in high altitudes, the Swiftness of Huitzilopochtli running ceremony took place at nearly 7,500 feet above sea level. The runner also carried an image of the god Huitzilopochtli, perhaps weighing ten pounds or more, making the task even more difficult. Lastly, according to some traditions, along the route onlookers sought to take the image from him and generally harassed him. The run was a feat of endurance that was marked by moments of great symbolism, especially at the moments in which the procession stopped along the way for human sacrifices. We do not know who officiated at the sacrifices, but it might well have been the teomama himself.

As has been observed by many scholars, the events associated with the Swiftness of Huitzilopochtli recapitulate the Mexica migration story and also contain elements of the mystical birth of the god Huitzilopochtli. According to legend, the Mexica departed from Aztlan and went through a series of adventures, the most important of which was the birth of the god Huitzilopochtli.[131] The ritual of the Swiftness took the participant and observer through these mythic events, culminating with the birth of the god and the sacrifice of the many victims who had been prepared throughout the month. Yet the month also symbolically related to many other features of Mexica myth, legend, and history. The rituals and ceremonies were adapted and modified by the Mexica to suit their own political agendas.

In essence, the procession of the Swiftness of Huitzilopochtli re-created in a symbolic manner the migration of the Mexica people from their primordial home of Aztlan (an island in the middle of a lake) to their new city of Tenochtitlan (an island in the middle of a lake). In the Swiftness of Huitzilopochtli, the procession left Aztlan but arrived at Tenochtitlan. Similarly, the ritual battle with the warriors of Huitznahuac symbolizes the birth of Huitzilopochtli and the battle with his brothers, the Centzon Huitznahua, and sister, Coyolxauqui. All these actions revolve around the Templo Mayor, which was symbolically the hill on which Huitzilopochtli was born, Coatepec.

In order to better understand many of the elements of the celebration, it is necessary to look at the cultural context in which they appeared and at other sources that can provide additional insight into the symbolism and import of the ceremonies and rituals. Fortunately, in addition to the texts that describe the rituals of the celebrations of Panquetzaliztli, pictorial documents—most copied shortly after the conquest but reflecting back on the precontact culture—also describe elements of the celebration. The next chapter will consider how Panquetzaliztli, Huitzilopochtli, and Painal are depicted in these pictorial manuscripts and other additional text sources. It will also look at other monthly celebrations that have similarities to Panquetzaliztli. All this is in an attempt to better understand the full symbolic import of the ceremonies and rituals of Panquetzaliztli.

Plate 1. Map of Tenochtitlan. *Codex Mendoza*, folio 2r, Arch. Selden A. 1, Bodleian Library, University of Oxford.

Plate 2. Huitzilopochtli. Bernardino de Sahagún, *Primeros memoriales*, folio 261r, Biblioteca del Palacio Nacional, Madrid, Spain, © Patrimonio Nacional España.

Plate 3. Painal. Bernardino de Sahagún, *Primeros memoriales*, folio 261r, Biblioteca del Palacio Nacional, Madrid, Spain, © Patrimonio Nacional España.

Plate 4. Huitzilopochtli. Bernardino de Sahagún, *Florentine Codex,* folio 10r, Biblioteca Medicea Laurenziana, Mediceo Palatino vol. 218.

Plate 5. Painal. Bernardino de Sahagún, *Florentine Codex,* folio 10r, Biblioteca Medicea Laurenziana, Mediceo Palatino vol. 218.

Plate 6. Panquetzaliztli. Bernardino de Sahagún, *Primeros memoriales,* folio 252v, Biblioteca del Palacio Nacional, Madrid, Spain, © 2018 Patrimonio Nacional de España.

Plate 7. Panquetzaliztli. *Codex Borgia*, p. 46,

Plate 8. Panquetzaliztli. Diego Durán, *Historia de los indios de la Nueva España,* Biblioteca Nacional de España, p. 681.

Plate 9. Huitzilopochtli. Diego Durán, *Historia de los indios de la Nueva España,* Biblioteca Nacional de España, p. 681.

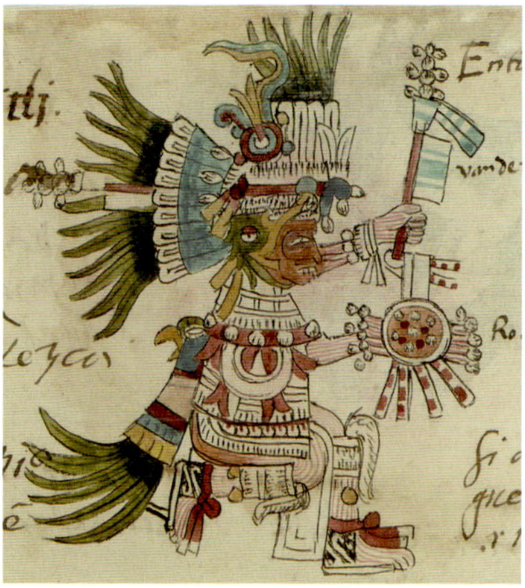

Plate 10. Huitzilopochtli. *Codex Telleriano-Remensis,* Bibliothèque National de France.

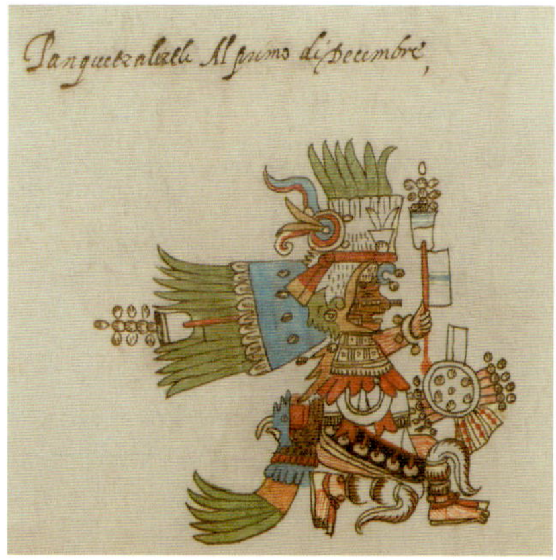

Plate 11. Huitzilopochtli. *Codex Vaticanus,* Vat. Lat. 3738, folio 49v, © 2018 Biblioteca Apostolica Vaticana, all rights reserved.

Plate 12. Huitzilopochtli. *Codex Magliabechiano,* Biblioteca Nazionale Centrale di Firenze.

Plate 13. New Fire. Ms. 1515, *Codex Borbonicus*, p. 33, Bibliothèque de l'Assemblé Nationale de France.

CHAPTER 4

OTHER CEREMONIES AND OTHER SOURCES

The descriptions of ceremonies presented thus far have focused largely on the accounts provided by Sahagún, Durán, and Motolinia. The pictorial manuscripts from outside the Central Basin of Mexico, along with those from communities outside Tenochtitlan, also give a unique view of the festivities. Yet several other types of materials can assist in further illuminating the rituals and ceremonies of Panquetzaliztli. These include other sections of the *Florentine Codex* that focus on specific rituals that were part of the larger month or that help to expand our knowledge of the month. Beyond that, within the xiuhpohualli, there are celebrations during other months that are cognate to or that help to better our understanding of the Panquetzaliztli rituals. Illustrations from the *Florentine Codex* can also expand our knowledge and further fill in details. There are also several more pictorial manuscripts from the Central Basin of Mexico that were produced in the last half of the sixteenth century that illustrate the feast, assisting modern scholars in understanding the nature and significance of the month.

For example, other sections of the *Florentine Codex*, and one part in particular, focus on the Panquetzaliztli ceremonies such as those in the calpolli of the feather workers. There are aspects of the Panquetzaliztli celebration in the rituals of Toxcatl as well as in several other months. Considering the similarities and their functions in the different contexts can provide insights into how the ceremonies and rituals served Panquetzaliztli. This is particularly helpful in understanding some of the subsidiary or component performances and rituals and seeing how they might relate to the larger themes of each individual month. The illustrations in the *Florentine Codex* provide yet another text with which we can gain a better understanding of the various rituals. Beyond these, some of the most important pictorial manuscripts are contemporary to the *Florentine Codex* and likewise reflect the ceremonial practices of Tenochtitlan. By analyzing their depictions of Panquetzaliztli, we can gain even more information about the practices of the month.

Descriptions from the *Florentine Codex*—Amantlan

Amantlan was the name of the calpolli housing the feather artisans. In book 9 of the *Florentine Codex,* Sahagún explores the activities of several artisan groups, including goldsmiths, lapidaries, and feather workers. Book 9 is also the section of his work where he looks more closely at the merchants and the specifics of their celebration of Panquetzaliztli, described in the previous chapter. In book 9, he devotes three chapters to the feather workers, the first of which explains their participation in some of the important ritual performances. For the feather workers, the months of Tlaxochimaco (also known as Miccailhuitontli, the ninth month) and Panquetzaliztli were the most important. Because Tlaxochimaco involved the sacrifice of small animals and birds, it was perhaps the more important of the two since the feather workers' trade was intimately linked to birds. Nonetheless, in chapter 19 of book 9 of the *Florentine Codex,* Sahagún provides some significant details about Panquetzaliztli as celebrated in one calpolli of the city of Tenochtitlan.[1]

The major difference between the performance of rituals in the feather workers' neighborhood and the celebrations in the rest of Tenochtitlan had to do with the ceremonies' focus and the absence of a running ceremony like the Swiftness of Huitzilopochtli. As we have seen, in Tenochtitlan the feast was tightly focused on the veneration of Huitzilopochtli, the Mexica's national deity. In Amantlan, the ceremony more generally venerated the god known as Coyotl Inahual (Coyote His Spirit Guide).[2]

Human sacrifice was still central to the celebration of Panquetzaliztli in Amantlan. If a warrior had been captured in battle or a slave had been secured from among captured warriors, the community would seek to use that person. Otherwise, the community held a fund-raising banquet to which they invited guests. Those who attended were expected to bring a large cotton cape in order to help purchase a sacrificial slave. Once acquired, through whatever means, the person who secured him or a representative of the community ritually bathed the slave. The slave then became the ixiptla of Coyotl Inahual. He received the insignia and ceremonial clothing of the god. The patron, if he was able, might present more than one victim. If this occurred, the other ixiptlahuan would represent other important gods of the community such as Yacateuctli (Lord Nose, patron of the merchants). For the ritual sacrifice, the elders of Amantlan gathered in the community temple, where they sang while holding vigil over the god impersonators. In order to lessen their anxiety, the slaves were given the "obsidian medicine," the draught that made the sacrificial victims more compliant and less fearful in the face of their sacrificial death.[3]

Since Amantlan was a calpolli of Tenochtitlan, it should come as no surprise that the Panquetzaliztli rituals performed in the neighborhood, broadly speaking, had a general similarity to those seen in the Templo Mayor. It is important to note that in Amantlan, there was no ceremony similar to the Swiftness of Huitzilopochtli. But in the festivities at both the Templo Mayor and Amantlan, the culminating ceremony involved the sacrifice of a captured warrior or slave. In both instances, the patron of the event bathed the victim. We can imagine that the patron took an active role in the care and feeding of the slave and accompanied him to the sacrifice, as was done in the Templo Mayor ceremony. In Amantlan, the slave victim became an ixiptla, not unlike the bathed ones who became ixiptlahuan of Huitzilopochtli.

Other Months with Elements Like Those of Panquetzaliztli

Several of the other twenty-day months of the Mexica xiuhpohualli feature rituals and performances that have echoes in the celebrations of Panquetzaliztli. Among the months, those with rituals most closely resembling those of Panquetzaliztli are Toxcatl and Tlaxochimaco.[4] The months of Hueymiccailhuitl (also known as Xocotlhuetzi) and Ochpaniztli also have some features that are reminiscent of those practiced in Panquetzaliztli.

The feast of Toxcatl, the fifth month of the solar year, was dedicated to the god Tezcatlipoca. The central ceremony of the feast was the celebration of a teixiptla: a man who lived for a year as the physical embodiment of the Tezcatlipoca, who was called Titlacahuan (We, His Men).[5] Titlacahuan was an aspect or avatar of Tezcatlipoca. Several of the early-colonial authors use the two names almost interchangeably in their descriptions of Tezcatlipoca. Sahagún, in book 2 of the *Florentine Codex*, describes the selection of the ixiptla in painful detail. The friar devotes scores of words to listing all the possible physical defects that should be avoided in choosing the imitator. He also comments that, in every respect, people treated the ixiptla as the deity. The ixiptla was given wives and the best food, drink, and clothing and was generally treated as the local embodiment of the deity.[6]

Two key features of the monthlong celebration of Toxcatl stand out when compared to Panquetzaliztli. An important ritual in Toxcatl was the peregrination of the god impersonator to various important sites. The travel lasted more than four days and occurred five days before the end of the month. This was no marathon run like the celebration of Panquetzaliztli. On the first day of the journey, the god impersonator and his entourage traveled to a place called Tecanman. They sang and danced in their procession and at the places where they stopped to spend the night. On the second day, they went to the temple dedicated to Titlacahuan, which was a critical stop. There, the ixiptla stayed in the home of the *calpixqui* (official in charge of the temple). The third day of travel included a boat trip to Tepetzinco in the middle of Lake Tetzcoco.[7] The fourth day involved a trip to Tepepulco. Sahagún notes that it was located near Tepetzinco, but in reality, it is not very close. Tepepulco is the same town where Sahagún began to elaborate his study of native culture. From Tepepulco, the ixiptla and his entourage returned by boat to Acaquilpan, or Caualtepec (Cahualtepec, possibly modern-day Acahualtepec), also near Tlapitzauhcan, where the ixiptla eventually met his death by sacrifice at the temple called the Tlacochcalco.[8] This site has been described as being near Chalco Atenco, to the southeast of Tenochtitlan.[9]

The month of Toxcatl took on special importance to the Spanish because of events that occurred during the conquest of Mexico. In June 1520, the Spanish forces had already peacefully entered Tenochtitlan as guests of the ruler, Moteuczoma II. Because of a threat from rival Spanish forces on the Gulf Coast, Cortés divided his army, leaving some of his men in Tenochtitlan under the command of Pedro de Alvarado while Cortés himself took the remaining men to confront their rivals. During Cortés's absence, Alvarado massacred the Mexica nobility during celebrations associated with the month of Toxcatl. Thus, Sahagún includes detailed descriptions of some of the celebrations of Toxcatl both in book 2, dealing with calendar rituals, and in book 12, dealing with the conquest.[10]

In Sahagún's additional narration of the Toxcatl festival, a statue of Huitzilopochtli was built in the temple of the Huitznahuac on a mesquite frame, using sticks with thorns. Fish-amaranth dough was added to this to replicate the flesh. It was decorated in the traditional manner, including the aneucyotl, which is described as being made of paper and feathers. The dough image then was adorned further with a sleeveless jacket decorated with severed human limbs and a cape of nettles and was embellished with eagle feathers. Once the image of the god was completed, young warriors, their leaders, and the young seasoned warriors would carry the figurine in procession from Huitznahuac to the Templo Mayor. They climbed the pyramid and deposited the image in front of the god. Feasting and dancing ensued.[11]

Torquemada clearly drew heavily from Sahagún for his description of the Toxcatl festivities. Together they provide an extensive description of how the figure of the god Toxcatl was constructed. Torquemada agrees that the figurine was placed on a litter, like a table or platform, decorated with serpents on each of the four legs. The framework for the figurine was made of mesquite sticks in the manner of bones. Torquemada offers the most complete description of the figure's adornment. He reports that it wore a cloth jacket or vest decorated with the image of human bones. It wore a distinctive hat made of paper that was wider at the top than at the brim so that it looked like a bowl and was decorated with feathers and a flint knife. Torquemada is unclear as to whether the flint knife was a real one or merely feathers or paper made to look like a bloody knife. On its shoulders, the image of the deity wore a blanket or cloak, called a *tlacuacuallo*, which was made of feathers and held in place with a golden clasp. At the base of the figure were placed bones made of tzoalli, called *teumumilli* (*teomomilli*, "divine bones"), which represented the god's power over death.[12]

Torquemada, drawing some from Sahagún, explains that the image and litter were carried on the shoulders of men, whom he describes as the bravest war captains. On the last night of Toxcatl, the warriors carried the litter to the temple, and it was then lifted with ropes to keep it level. In front of the litter, there was a large banner made of paper, more than 30 meters long and about 1.5 meters wide. It was decorated with the epithets and exploits of the god. Once the litter and image were installed in the god's sanctuary, some special rituals were performed. The ruler beheaded four quail in sacrifice and threw them at the base of the god. The warriors who accompanied him collected the quail, which were then salted and prepared for the monarch's meal. The god was also reverenced with incense from a clay censer shaped like a hollow spoon or gourd. Bits of clay were intentionally left in the clay body so that after the firing, the censer would rattle.[13]

This last celebration has provided more than a bit of confusion since many commentators could not understand why ceremonies involving Huitzilopochtli figured so prominently in Toxcatl, a month dedicated to Tezcatlipoca. Moreover, while this ceremony had some similarities to other devotions to Huitzilopochtli, it differed from the Panquetzaliztli celebrations particularly in that the participants did not run with the image of the god, and the image of the god may have been different: a human-size ixiptla of tzoalli on a wooden frame rather than a smaller doll-like image made entirely of dough. Nonetheless, the Spanish who witnessed it remembered the dancing and other celebrations that were part of the feast very well. One explanation holds that the amaranth image was actually that of Tezcatlipoca and that the Spaniards were mistaken. But this is not a detail that would have confused Sahagún's informants. Guilhem Olivier has provided the most cogent explanation. He posits that both gods were honored during these festivities. There were amaranth figurines of both, each had its own unique procession, and then both were worshipped together. In fact, an eyewitness, Diego Holguin, wrote after the conquest, "That idol Uchilobos [Huitzilopochtli] had an Indian tied on its back with a rope and another idol was in front of him with an Indian in the same manner."[14] For Olivier, the other idol was undoubtedly Tezcatlipoca.[15] Obviously, the Spaniards were not fluent in Mexica symbolism and had difficulty telling one god from another. Conceivably, some Spaniards might have known of the tradition of making a dough image of Huitzilopochtli during various celebrations such as Panquetzaliztli. When another dough image was used in Toxcatl, the assumption was that it must have been Huitzilopochtli as well. Nevertheless, Olivier's explanation that both gods were honored in this way resolves the confusion and validates the observations of the conquistadores.

Thus, to recapitulate, Toxcatl offered several similarities to the celebrations of Panquetzaliztli. Most importantly, both used tzoalli-dough figures of Huitzilopochtli as central elements of the final sacrificial rites. Both months also had important processions wherein an ixiptla was paraded through a major portion of the Central Basin. In Toxcatl, this occurred with a human ixiptla in procession and also by boat, covering the northeastern, eastern, and near-southeastern portions of the Valley. In Panquetzaliztli, the regions included the near-northwestern, western, and southwestern regions with a figurine carried by a priest. Yet, in many ways, they nearly perfectly reflect each other.

In the tenth month of the year, Xocotlhuetzi (fruit falls), the god Painal again played an important role.[16] The central ceremony of this month involved erecting a *xocotl* tree (a type of fruit tree, *Spondias purpurea*) in the sacred precinct. As in the celebration of Panquetzaliztli, figurines were made of tzoalli. In this celebration, the figurines represented the xocotl, the fruit of the tree, which is known as *jocote* in modern Mexico. As in Panquetzaliztli, warriors accompanied the prisoners they had taken in warfare. The captives would eventually be sacrificed, but in a slightly different ceremony from Panquetzaliztli's. Ceremonial dancing, dressing with ceremonial paper garments, and fasting were also features of the month. As with Panquetzaliztli, in which a lock of hair and the paper garments were taken from the victims and stored by the owner, during Xocotlhuetzi, the warriors cut a lock of hair from their captive's head, which was then stored in a small coffer. Similarly, before the sacrifice, the victims were lined up beside the skull rack. Their paper garments and the banners that they had carried were then burned in the eagle vessel at the base of the Templo Mayor. The ceremony awaited the arrival of Painal, the messenger. As in the Panquetzaliztli sacrifice, the god imitator supervised the process whereby each warrior grabbed his captive to take him to sacrifice. In Xocotlhuetzi, the victims were drugged using a powder called *yauhtli*.[17]

The process of sacrifice in this festival was perhaps one of the more gruesome practiced by the Mexica. The victims, after being drugged, were tossed onto the burning paper in the eagle vessel until their skin blistered. While still alive, they were pulled from the fire and then suffered heart extraction. The hearts were offered to the god of fire, Xiuhteuctli (Turquoise/Fire Lord).[18] It is not clear whether Painal was represented by a god imitator or through a figurine, because at one point, Sahagún writes, "And [as for] Painal, his old men carried him. They went encircling him, they went crowding about him."[19] Later in the month, when the tree erected for the month was ready to be taken down, young men would climb the supporting ropes, hoping to get pieces of the amaranth figurine that had been placed on top. Pieces of this would eventually be distributed.[20] Similarly, in Izcalli, the last month of the vague solar year, Painal also accompanied sacrificial victims to their fate.[21]

In the rituals for the feast of Ochpaniztli, the eleventh Mexica month, running also played an important role. As part of the larger series of ceremonies honoring the goddesses Teteo Inan (also known as Toci and Tlazolteotl), a young woman impersonated the goddess in a series of ritual dances and skirmishes. Eventually, she was sacrificed and then flayed. A priest, who became an ixiptla, wore her skin for the remainder of the month. A large piece of skin from her thigh was handed to a runner, who carried it to Pochtlan, the neighborhood of the merchants. There awaited another god impersonator representing her son, Cinteotl. The skin was then placed on his face as a mask.

While the thigh skin was being carried to Pochtlan, the priest who wore the skin of the ixiptla, who was now himself an ixiptla named Teccizquacuilli, descended from the temple. Nobles and warriors waited at the bottom, and they then began to run, beating their shields, and engaging in a ritual of mock warfare in a ceremony called *çacacali* (*zacacalli*, "they fight with grass"). In addition to shields, they carried grass brooms with which they beat one another, causing many small cuts and tears of the skin. In the end, participants were covered with blood, their own and that of their mock enemies. Finally, the god impersonator and her entourage confronted the warriors and drove them away.[22]

Later in the cycle of ceremonies for Ochpaniztli, the god impersonator of Cinteotl ran away from Tenochtitlan in order to deposit the thigh-skin mask in enemy territory. Strong and agile warriors accompanied him. They ran to a place called Popotl Temi (Full of Straw) on the slopes of Iztac Tepetl (White Mountain),[23] a region considered to be enemy territory. If they encountered enemies, they would fight. Upon arrival at the place, the skin was stretched on a wooden frame and left on display in commemoration of the event. In all likelihood, this ritual symbolized the birth of Cinteotl. The thigh-skin mask was symbolic of his emergence from his mother's womb. It was taken to enemy land just as the umbilical cord of newborn boys was to be buried on a battlefield to give them strength in battle.[24] As the month of Ochpaniztli continued, another ritual involving running took place. In particular, at one point the warriors blazed a path for the god impersonator of Toci by running from the sacred precinct to the place called Tocititlan (the Place beside Toci).[25] The ceremonies of this month have been considered expiatory, having to do with the rejection of filth and the maintenance of balance.[26]

In the seventeenth month, Tititl, there was a very minor running ceremony. In this instance, priests congregated at the base of the Templo Mayor. The ritual involved running up the temple as quickly as possible, grabbing flowers arrayed atop it, and then descending, dropping the flowers into the sacred vessel, where grain had also been deposited and was burning. This ritual accomplished, the priests simply left as quickly as they had appeared.[27]

Perhaps the ceremonies most strikingly reminiscent of Panquetzaliztli occurred during the nemontemi, the five days that followed the last month of Izcalli before the first month of Atl cahualo. In particular, Sahagún suggests that these days may have provided an opportunity for intercalary days, that is, leap days. The friar notes that in the first three years of a cycle, nothing extraordinary happened during this period between calendars. But in the fourth year of the cycle, there were sacrifices of ixiptlahuan of Xiuhteuctli who were dressed as Ixcozauhqui, the yellow-faced manifestation of the fire god. This ritual had many similarities to the sacrifices in Panquetzaliztli. Both men and women captives and slaves were selected for sacrifice. They were adorned with the paper garments in the raiment of Xiuhteuctli/Ixcozauhqui. The slaves and captives were both bathed with water (tlaaltilti) and also with sand (xalaquia). The hair on the tops of their heads was cut and saved. Feathers were pasted in their place. They were taken to Xiuhteuctli's temple, known as the Tzonmolco, and paraded to the top, where they walked a circuit, then were brought back down. The paper clothing was collected, and the victims were imprisoned the night before the sacrifice. In the morning, they were made to sing and dance in the forecourt of the temple until they were hoarse. Once the sun had passed the zenith, the impersonator of Painal descended the temple and then led the victims back to their fate on top. As in Panquetzaliztli, the war captives died first, followed by the bathed ones, the slaves who had been purchased for the purpose.[28] The presence of Painal, the representative of Huitzilopochtli, marked this festival as a critical one since otherwise the month was dedicated to fire.[29]

The idea that this ceremony might have been used as a pretext for adding days to the calendar has more to do with what followed. For the next eighteen hours, the Mexica nobility, led by the emperor, danced and consumed prodigious amounts of pulque. Children had their earlobes pierced, and feathers were inserted as adornments. Warriors, respected women, and others were sought out and given gifts of clothing and food such as the drink pinole. Children were held briefly over a fire containing incense and had their hair singed. Everyone, including the children, drank pulque. Parents would also grab their children by the neck and pull upward, encouraging them to grow tall. It has been suggested that all these ceremonies, from the sacrifices to the consumption of pulque, occupied forty-eight hours, but it was counted as a single day both in the xiuhpohualli and the tonalpohualli.[30]

The Tzonmolco temple of Xiuhteuctli might have had a role in the New Fire ceremony. Certainly, the priests of that temple were charged with keeping the fire burning at all times, except for when it was extinguished before the New Fire.[31] Also, the Tzonmolco neighborhood was one of the sections of Tenochtitlan traditionally associated with the merchants.[32] Thus, all these discrete elements have cognates in the Panquetzaliztli festival and its associated ceremonies.

Looking at Sahagún's descriptions of the eighteen months of the xiuhpohualli, a few other cognates with Panquetzaliztli also emerge. The use of the Aiauhcalco appears in the first month, Atl cahualo; the sixth month, Etzalcualiztli; the thirteenth, Tepeilhuitl; and the sixteenth, Atemoztli.[33] In most of these instances, it was a venue for ritual bathing or some other preparatory ritual for sacrifice. In several other months, the victims were also bathed prior to their sacrifice. In the fourteenth month, Quecholli, the pulque makers bathed victims for the gods Tlamatzincatl, Izquitecatl, Mixcoatl and his consort, Yehuatl Icue.[34] In the last month, Izcalli, ceremonially bathed victims were sacrificed to Xiuhteuctli.[35] The ritual of xalaquia also can be found in other monthly celebrations. In the eighth month, Hueytecuilhuitl, after a procession that included four stops, one of which was Xolloco, the sacrificial victims were cleansed by the sand bath.[36] In addition to ceremonial water bathing in the last month of Izcalli, the victims also engaged in the xalaquia.[37] While a distinctive feature of Panquetzaliztli was the raising of branches such as fir branches, in the month of Teotl eco, the twelfth month, fir branches were raised on temples and in homes.[38] Moreover, the presence of banners, from which Panquetzaliztli takes its name, appeared in other months, especially in the context of ritual sacrifice.[39]

Several details of the Panquetzaliztli rituals also figure in descriptions of other months. For example, the wearing of paper garments and the cutting of a tuft of hair from the victim to be either guarded or burned afterward appeared in several celebrations. In spite of Sahagún's long protestations about the absence of drunkenness in Mexica society, the ritual consumption of pulque, even to the point of inebriation, occurred in many of the monthly ceremonies, just as the consumption of blue pulque played an important role in Panquetzaliztli. The use of amaranth dough to make figures of the gods, replica bones, or even physical features such as mountaintops and the deities they represent were frequent parts of the monthly rituals.

Thus, several of the major elements seen in Panquetzaliztli have analogues in other months. Toxcatl included both a ritual procession and tzoalli images of the gods, including Huitzilopochtli. Running and processions were very common features and were seen in Ochpaniztli and Tititl. Various aspects of the selection of sacrificial victims, their dress, the clipping of their hair, and the storage of their possessions in reed boxes appeared in Xocotlhuetzi and the nemontemi. Painal himself made appearances in Xocotlhuetzi and Izcalli. In this way, we can begin to appreciate the application of different rituals to different monthlong celebrations.

Pictorial Manuscripts

Illustrations from the Florentine Codex

The *Florentine Codex* consists of three texts. As noted earlier, much information is provided in the Nahuatl- and Spanish-language texts, the latter forming the *Historia general.* But in addition, Sahagún also provides illustrations to expand on the textual information. By and large, the images in the *Primeros memoriales* can be considered somewhat closer to preconquest prototypes than those in the *Florentine*

Fig. 7. Panquetzaliztli, presentation of a slave. *Florentine Codex.* Bernardino de Sahagún, *Historia general,* ed. Francisco del Paso y Troncoso, vol. 5.

Codex. The precontact depictions tend to be somewhat flat, the figures in profile with little suggestion of roundness. Even the *Primeros memoriales* illustrations have already begun to depart from that style. The drawings from the *Florentine Codex* are slightly more like a European model: the figures are at three-quarters profile and seem more rounded, and some hint at gestures. The figures seem to be depictions of real people, not flat images (see figs. 7 and 8).[40]

Unfortunately, despite the richness of the description of the Panquetzaliztli ceremony in the *Florentine Codex,* Sahagún provides very few pictures. The two images that he does include are equivocal and can be interpreted any number of ways. The first figure (see fig. 7) is of a man standing, wearing only a breechcloth and a heart pendant around his neck. The front flap of the breechcloth is split in a manner reminiscent of the split tongue of a snake.[41] His hair is disheveled. On either side of him are two well-dressed men, wearing traditional breechcloths and long capes, which are open because the two men are gesturing toward the central figure. This probably illustrates when the merchants presented their best slaves for sacrifice.

Fig. 8. Panquetzaliztli, student melee. *Florentine Codex*. Bernardino de Sahagún, *Historia general*, ed. Francisco del Paso y Troncoso, vol. 5.

The second illustration (see fig. 8) is of four figures engaged in a speaking or shouting battle. It probably serves to illustrate the ritual battle of Chonchayotl in the *Florentine Codex*. The drawing consists of two registers. In the upper register, two men with their capes wrapped around their left forearms and holding clubs in their right hands are in a shouting match, which is depicted by the double speech glyphs coming out of their mouths. The capes wrapped around their forearms might well be an attempt to protect themselves from the blows of the other. In the lower register, one man lies on his back while his opponent grabs him by the hair and seems ready to attack him with a maguey thorn. In the battle of Chonchayotl, priests and students would have a mock battle and shouting match. If one were captured, he would be pricked with maguey thorns until he bled.[42]

Illustrations in Durán

Durán also provides an illustration that accompanies his writing regarding Panquetzaliztli (see plate 8). In the principal drawing that depicts the month of Panquetzaliztli, Durán shows a group of five figures seated indoors on a mat (petlatl). It is a mixed group with at least one woman and four men. Two figures are not clearly shown to be male or female but seem to be seated as males and lack the distinctive female hairstyle. The group is partaking in a ritual meal, with the central figure dipping into a basin, while the female figure on the viewer's right offers what seem to be tortillas, although the food is colored red. This probably illustrates the midnight meal taken by people during the four days' fast. Floating above this more domestic scene, we find a male figure holding a flag in his hands. The flag is the constant symbol for the month. The illustration does not refer at all to the runner carrying the dough figure, but the seated figure does resemble the depiction of Painal seen in both the *Primeros memoriales* and the *Florentine Codex*.

Durán also offers a drawing of the god Huitzilopochtli (see plate 9). It is unlike any of the ones supervised by Sahagún. It shows a man wearing the array of the god. Like the illustrations of Painal provided by Sahagún, Huitzilopochtli is seated. Unlike those, he appears on a low platform. He has a gold stripe on his face and one on his forehead. He wears the hummingbird headdress with a golden beak associated with the god. In addition, the figure wears a feather headdress that may or may not be part of the hummingbird regalia or the aneucyotl. He has a feather cape around his body. In his right hand, he holds the snake staff that is iconic of the god. In his left hand, he has the shield with tufts of eagle feathers along with darts without points and a flag. Another flag is tacked onto his back. This is part of a larger image that also includes the symbol for Tenochtitlan along with aquatic beasts found in the lake and another seated figure.

Clearly, the illustrations offered by Durán are much more in the European vernacular than even the *Florentine Codex* illustrations of Sahagún. These are paintings in which figures interact with one another and are placed in natural-looking surroundings. They are rooted in a very specific physical environment. Only the one image in the Panquetzaliztli illustration floats above the domestic scene to which it is symbolically linked. All of these are unlike preconquest depictions in which the gods were completely isolated from any other context in a manner similar to illustrations of the deities found in the *Primeros memoriales* and *Florentine Codex*.

Tezcatlipoca Iconography

The relationship between Huitzilopochtli and Tezcatlipoca has emerged in several of the texts considered. As noted, Tezcatlipoca was a god of war (Yaotl) but was also associated with many intangible or evanescent characteristics. One of these was a trickster, playing with human foibles. He was known by two tonalpohualli signs: 1 Death and 2 Reed.[43] In his study of the deity, Olivier has identified forty-four iconographical elements used to depict the god. Some of the more common ones include the following:

Striped face painting
Square design under the nose
Square ear pendant
Short-cropped hair
Heron-feather headdress
Feather-balls headdress
Yellow feather-ball headdress
Mirror on chest, back, or at temple
Collar with jingle bells
Basket with flowers
Loincloth
Jingle bells on arms or legs
Knotted sandals
Mirror or animal foot in lieu of foot
Shield
Flag/Banner
Atlatl (spear thrower)[44]

Clearly, many of these overlap with Huitzilopochtli, as seen in the analysis in chapter 1. The use of the shield and spear thrower is common. The mirror disk on the chest or in the headband is also common to both. Even items like the feather-down balls, closely associated with Huitzilopochtli's birth, are shared by both deities. As noted earlier, the missing foot that is replaced by a mirror or animal foot can also be found as an attribute for both gods, although it is much more closely associated with Tezcatlipoca.

Other Pictorial Manuscripts

In order to appreciate the similarities between the differing descriptions offered in various narrative accounts and to better discern the differences among them, other contemporary or near-contemporary descriptions of the feasts are helpful. Fortunately, there are several other accounts of the feasts of the xiuhpohualli in addition to those seen in chapter 2. They offer some details about Panquetzaliztli ceremonies, and most of them come from the Central Basin of Mexico. Of those to be considered here, all date to the last quarter of the sixteenth century and are contemporaneous to Sahagún and Durán.

Codex Telleriano-Remensis

The *Codex Telleriano-Remensis* offers a rich source of information about the preconquest past. In all likelihood, native artists in the middle of the sixteenth century, around 1562–63, possibly in the Tlatelolco district of Tenochtitlan, drew the work after the Spanish conquest. Among other illustrated manuscripts of early-colonial Mexico, it has much in common with the *Codex Vaticanus A*. The *Vaticanus A* might well be a later copy that has a common source with the *Telleriano-Remensis*. The style of the drawings and the fact that the glosses are in Italian have led scholars to conclude that it is a copy of some other, possibly lost manuscript, the possible prototype of both it and the *Telleriano-Remensis*. Certainly the *Vaticanus A* includes some information absent in the *Telleriano-Remensis*. Important for this study, the *Telleriano-Remensis* contains a great deal of material on life in preconquest times. Furthermore, the illustrations are frequently accompanied by glosses in Spanish that were inserted at some point after the illustrations were completed. The authors of the annotations are unknown, but one is believed to be Fr. Pedro de los Rios. The commentaries describe the events and rituals depicted in the drawings. The work contains images for both the ritual 260-day tonalpohualli and for the 365-day xiuhpohualli. The page illustrating the month of Panquetzaliztli is especially rich with three different sets of commentaries.[45]

The panel for Panquetzaliztli consists of a figure dressed in a costume that, at first glance, has multiple different significances (see plate 10). In particular, the figure has the obsidian mirror, which was associated with Tezcatlipoca but was also fairly common with Huitzilopochtli, tucked in the white feathers of his headdress. In his left hand, he holds the banner that is emblematic of the month. Another feature common to several deities is a white, circular pectoral.[46] Nonetheless, his headdress, the quetzal-feather back ornament, and the "buckle" on the back of his belt might be identified as indicative of Huitzilopochtli.[47] Regardless of the details of the symbolism of the costume, it clearly is not a simple representation of either Huitzilopochtli or of Tezcatlipoca but is in many ways a hybrid. Taken as a whole, however, based on the iconography presented in chapter 1, the figure has more in common with Huitzilopochtli.

Scholars have determined that six separate people annotated the manuscript in Spanish and Nahuatl to clarify and explain the images. Of these, four provided the bulk of the additional information on Panquetzaliztli. They are identified as Hands One through Four.[48] The first explicitly identified the figure as that of Tezcatlipoca, who, the commentator notes, was celebrated three times during the year.[49] Probably because of the equivocal image, the first commentator notes that Tezcatlipoca was not depicted with his snake foot, one of the unique symbols of the god, because the depiction was from a time before he had sinned, an action through which he lost his foot. This depiction was of the time when he was in the heavens. As a result of the war of the heavens, Tezcatlipoca came down to earth. Guilhem Olivier has studied this aspect of Tezcatlipoca and offers some tentative conclusions. The act of sinning referred to by the commentator probably had to do with illicit sexual relations or drunkenness, or possibly both. At the same time, the mutilation of the god is also related to the production of fire and lightening. In many of the myths of Mesoamerica, lightening and fire are associated with a one-legged or mutilated god.[50]

Hand Three observes that the feast of Panquetzaliztli began on about the first of December and that the two key symbols of the god's costume were the banner and the shield that he carried. The shield strongly resembles the shield carried by Huitzilopochtli in the *Primeros memoriales*, although the shield here is red and not white (as Huitzilopochtli's was) or turquoise (as Painal's was). It also contains seven down puffs and not the five usually associated with the god. Nonetheless, the figure wears the striped pants and sleeved tunic that are also associated with Huitzilopochtli

Hand Two writes that the feast received its name from the banners that were raised in celebration. The feast was also a time of warrior sacrifices; captains and warriors would sacrifice a few men they had captured. This commentator then links the feast to the national god, Huitzilopochtli, noting that the god was the first captain and warrior of the Mexica. Quite importantly, he notes that the feast was celebrated differently in Chalco, where their captain was Tezcatlipoca, and that sacrifices were offered to him instead.[51] The commentator then explains that bread was made from amaranth seeds, called tzoalli, mixed with honey. The bread was blessed and then broken into pieces. The priest would place some of these into sacrificial vessels. As people came forward, the priest would use a maguey spine to transfer some of the bread into the mouths of the faithful. Of course, this particular observation might not truly reflect the preconquest ritual since it bears more than a passing similarity to the distribution of the consecrated host in the Christian Eucharist.

Hand Two goes on to write that during the month, the Mexica also celebrated the god of fire, Xiuhteuctli. That commentator describes the ceremony as involving four priests who came down from the top of the temple, each carrying a burning firebrand of pinewood. They executed various rites to the four cardinal directions. Later, at noon, they put their firebrands into the ceremonial vessel at the base of the temple where the fire burned for a whole day and night, obviously with additional wood added. It thus provided illumination for the night and day. This commentator does not include the paper sacrifices that are mentioned in other accounts of this festival, such as the one found in the *Florentine Codex*.[52] The ritual involving the four fire priests is absent in Sahagún's extensive treatment of Panquetzaliztli. Their presence is, however, strongly suggestive of the illustrations and narratives found in several manuscripts concerning the New Fire ceremony, which will be considered more fully later.

It seems clear that the image of the month of Panquetzaliztli in the *Codex Telleriano-Remensis* repeats the uncertainty regarding the divine patronage of this festival. While the image more closely resembles Huitzilopochtli, some attributes are consistent with Tezcatlipoca. One of those who provided annotations recognized this confusion and assisted in clarifying by noting that different places celebrated different deities during the festival. Although the commentator does not state it explicitly, the implication is that in Tenochtitlan, Huitzilopochtli was the focus of these festivities. Yet elsewhere, such as in Chalco, the month was dedicated to Tezcatlipoca.

Codex Vaticanus A

As noted above, the *Codex Vaticanus A* is closely related to the *Telleriano-Remensis* and the *Magliabecchiano* (below), although each contains some discrete information not contained in the other. All date from the middle to late sixteenth century, come from the Central Basin, and cover similar materials associated with the Mexican calendars. The section of the *Vaticanus A* that discusses the feast of Panquetzaliztli is illustrated in a manner very reminiscent of the *Telleriano-Remensis*. In most aspects, the two are nearly identical, even down to the figure half-kneeling on his right leg in both manuscripts (see plate 11). Unlike the other works, the glosses in the *Vaticanus A* are written in Italian rather than the Spanish or Nahuatl found in the other early painted manuscripts. The description indicates that the feast was dedicated to Huitzilopochtli and that individuals captured in battle were sacrificed to honor him. It also notes that the dough figurine of the god was later broken up and distributed in a manner not unlike communion in the Christian Eucharist.[53]

Codex Magliabecchiano

Perhaps the most recent of the pictorial manuscripts in the pre-Columbian style to include information regarding the feast of Panquetzaliztli is the *Codex Magliabecchiano* held at the Biblioteca Nazionale Centrale of Florence. Dating to the last quarter of the sixteenth century (and thus roughly contemporaneous with the *Florentine Codex*), the *Magliabecchiano* has illustrations and descriptions of the two calendars, the tonalpohualli and the xiuhpohualli, and their components. While not all the months of the solar year are included, there is an illustration and commentary on the feast of Panquetzaliztli. The image is a full-color drawing of the god Huitzilopochtli (see plate 12). The illustration depicts a figure in the costume of the god. Because the turquoise cape is so long, the legs and feet are not visible. It might be a depiction of a seated figure, such as those of Painal. Boone has concluded that this representation of the god is, in fact, a representation of the figurine made of amaranth dough for the celebration of the feast.[54]

The image closely resembles those found in the *Borgia*, *Telleriano-Remensis*, and *Vaticanus A* codices. In the *Magliabecchiano*, the face of the god impersonator is striped blue and yellow. He wears a red headdress topped by what seem to be quetzal feathers. Out of the middle of the headdress, we can see the banner that is indicative of the feast of Panquetzaliztli. The banner is colored blue-green and topped with a flint knife like the one used in sacrificial rites. There are also tufts of eagle down along the pole holding the banner, on the top of the flint, and the on corner of the banner. These symbols taken collectively evoke Huitzilopochtli.

Unlike any other image of the god, this one has what might be deer antlers on the headband at the base of the headdress, although the depiction of Painal in the *Florentine Codex* also had equivocal ornaments on the headband. It is possible that this object was, in fact, the artist's attempt to draw the hummingbird or the blood bird that was frequently found on the god's headdress. The other possibility is that the artist copied another rendering that had a smoking mirror in the headband, and the antlers are the remnants of smoke coming from the mirror. As with several of the other illustrations, he holds the tehuehuelli, the special shield, ornamented with the same down tufts found in his headdress. Behind the shield, there seems to be another banner, also topped with a flint knife and additionally adorned with quetzal feathers. On his chest, he has the circular pectoral decorated with a wide red ribbon tied in a bow, similar to the one seen in the *Primeros memoriales* and other illustrated manuscripts. On his back, he might well have the quetzal-feather ornamentation seen elsewhere.

The commentary for Panquetzaliztli in the *Codex Magliabecchiano* stresses that this feast was specifically dedicated to Huitzilopochtli, who is described here as a demon. The commentator characterizes Huitzilopochtli as a friend of Tezcatlipoca. According to the commentator, the feast took its name from a wide *texutli* (*texotli*, "blue") object called a panitl (banner) that was placed in the headdress of the god. The figure of the god was dressed in painted paper and held a leather shield in his hand. During this feast, the commentator concludes, the Mexica performed the largest number of human sacrifices of prisoners from Tlaxcala and Huexotzingo.[55] This observation is consistent with what Durán describes for the feast.

The pictorial manuscripts, taken as a group, provide significant information not contained in the narrative accounts of the first missionaries. Through the illustrations, modern scholars can better understand how the festivals were celebrated in general terms, relying only on iconography and limited verbal descriptions. The month of Panquetzaliztli was closely associated with the New Fire ceremony, as will be explored in chapter 5. While in Tenochtitlan, the month was dedicated to Huitzilopochtli, clearly that was not the case in other places. Tezcatlipoca played a very important role in several of the pictorial descriptions of the month. What was common among all was the presence of the raised flag, which gave the month its name. The flag, as has been noted, was associated with human sacrifice, and thus the month itself was seen as a time for specific human sacrifices. The sources also agree, generally, that it corresponded to late November and early December in the European calendar. All also place it as the fifteenth month of the cycle, except for the Tovar Calendar (seen in chapter 1), which mistakenly places it as fourteenth.

Although much information can be drawn from the narrative and pictorial descriptions of the month of Panquetzaliztli, by looking at the specific rituals of the month and then considering analogs found in other months, we can begin to understand the nature and impact of those rituals. Thus, the next section will propose what the essential elements of Panquetzaliztli were as celebrated prior to the rise of the Triple Alliance and outside the area of direct Mexica control.

Protocelebration of Panquetzaliztli

Descriptions of the rituals associated with the month of Panquetzaliztli that come from areas outside Tenochtitlan tended to ignore some of the key features of the celebration that Sahagún and Durán reported for the imperial capital. In particular, the two unique features for Tenochtitlan were the runner carrying the tzoalli-dough image of Huitzilopochtli and the feasts and rituals involving the merchants. Consequently, one can theorize that the celebration of Panquetzaliztli outside the area of Mexica control had different features.

Looking at all the descriptions of other celebrations associated with the month, a few common features stand out. The month had a common name, which was stable throughout the Nahuatl-speaking world, namely Panquetzaliztli. It was the fifteenth month of the xiuhpohualli. All authors agreed upon the act of raising banners as a ceremonial aspect of the month, as the signature ritual of the feast. The dedication of the month to Huitzilopochtli is tentative, since in some places, Tezcatlipoca was equally important. At the same time, images of Huitzilopochtli were also made in Tenochtitlan during the month of Toxcatl, which was dedicated to Tezcatlipoca.

Looking at all the descriptions, we can assume that the month of Panquetzaliztli was dedicated to war and things martial. Perhaps, broadly among Nahuatl speakers, the month originally had been focused on Tezcatlipoca in his role as god of war. But in Mexica territories, and in Tenochtitlan in particular, Huitzilopochtli took on a leading role, as the national god and as a god of war. Several commentators suggest that the month of Panquetzaliztli was dedicated to war. It marked the full onset of the dry season during which armies could be prepared for war. Even among the Mexica, the month was the initiation of the warring season. Crops had been harvested, the dry season was well established, and city-states had the opportunity and the manpower to engage in warfare.[56] If we focus on a central theme of the celebration of war, then many aspects of the celebration fall into place. The month included feasts and rituals that involved warriors. The warriors and their captives seem to have been at the core of the celebrations, with the merchants and their slaves added on. Many of the sources indicate that the key feature of the month was the sacrifice of war captives. Indeed, the very symbol of the month, the flag or banner, represented sacrifice in Mexica iconography.

A slightly smaller number of authors report the use of dough images, tortillas, or other items that were consumed as part of the ritual. Looking at all the accounts, there seems to be a feasting element that included either large tortillas or dough made from amaranth and honey that was part of the rituals. Lastly, a few accounts detail drinking one or more types of pulque as an important feature of the celebration. Unfortunately, one must be very cautious about ascribing ritual value to the distribution of food and drink in the context of ritual sacrifice, since this was exactly the sort of parallel that the friars would frequently identify as precursors of the Christian Eucharist, for good or for ill.

The Mexica, then, used a wide repertoire of rituals to venerate their principle god, Huitzilopochtli, that had cognates in many other months. These included ixiptlahuan, human sacrifice, bathing in water and sand, processions and running, dough images, and many others. These elements would have been necessary to give the aura of sanctity and veneration to the larger ceremony. In the case of Panquetzaliztli, however, it was the juxtaposition of running and the use of the dough image of the god along with the participation of the merchants that gave the celebration much of its unique character in Tenochtitlan. Perhaps unique to Panquetzaliztli was the combination of a runner with one who bore the god, a combination of two elements of Mexica history and statecraft: people who ran to bear messages and persons who carried the god and other burdens.

Stripped of all its complex rituals, then, in its most basic form, Panquetzaliztli served as a monthlong celebration of war. Thus, it can come as no surprise that the sacrificial victims would be chosen from warriors captured in battle. In other areas, both in the Central Basin of Mexico and beyond, some sources indicate that the patron of Panquetzaliztli was Tezcatlipoca, the Nahua god of war. This makes sense. Huitzilopochtli was the god specifically associated with the Mexica, and very little evidence for him exists prior to their rise. In a calendar month dedicated to warfare, it would be reasonable to assume that the god being honored was the god of war. Prior to the rise of the Mexica, this would have been Tezcatlipoca. After the rise of the Mexica, especially in areas dominated by them, patronage for the month would have fallen to Huitzilopochtli. By the time the Spanish arrived, especially in the areas from which they drew their information, the month had become closely associated with the Mexica national god. Moreover, many of the discrete rituals within the monthlong celebration had more to do with addressing issues unique to the Mexica condition than to the older veneration of a month associated with the celebration of war and war making.

CHAPTER 5

THE TRANSFORMATION OF PANQUETZALIZTLI

Sahagún characterizes many of the months as "the feast and debt paying," "*yn ilhujtl, yoān in nextlaoaliztli*" (*in ilhuitl, ihuan in nextlahualiztli*).[1] The acts of sacrificing and honoring the gods as debt payment were essential elements of the months of the xiuhpohualli.[2] As a result, each month was dedicated to one particular god and also responded to a specific set of circumstances over the course of the ceremonial year. These celebrations seem to have been closely related to the changes in seasons and the cycles of the agricultural year. In many ways, Panquetzaliztli was similar to the other months in that it was dedicated to a particular god, Huitzilopochtli in Tenochtitlan, and it responded to a specific element of the natural environment, the formal beginning of the dry period that inaugurated the season of war making.

The ceremonies and rituals described by Durán and by Sahagún in the *Florentine Codex* for the month of Panquetzaliztli in Tenochtitlan differ from Sahagún's first impressions collected in Tepepulco and from suggestions about the celebration gleaned from other sources. Quite simply, they stand at odds with descriptions of the ceremonies in other places, described earlier as the "protocelebration." This chapter will carefully consider the symbolism and details of the performances in Tenochtitlan and compare them to the protocelebration. By also considering similar rituals from other monthly performances in the xiuhpohualli, as seen in the previous chapter, we can also better understand the symbolic power of the rituals. Lastly, this chapter will analyze the major divergences between the Tenochtitlan ceremonies and those found elsewhere and will consider the forces behind the changes. Tepepulco and Tenochtitlan had very different histories, and thus one would expect the ceremonial life of each to reflect local traditions and customs. However, Tepepulco was a modest town while Tenochtitlan was a massive city, possibly the largest in the world at that time. Clearly, the ceremonial life of a large capital city would differ significantly from that of even a regional capital.[3]

The feast of Panquetzaliztli existed long before the Mexica's rise and the establishment of the Triple Alliance. As seen in the previous chapters, in all likelihood, prior to the rise of the Mexica, the month was dedicated to Tezcatlipoca, not Huitzilopochtli. As a celebration of war, the ceremonies and rituals involved warriors and the larger cult of war: captives and sacrifice. Other common themes between the Tenochtitlan rituals and those found elsewhere include the ritual that gave the month its name: the raising of banners. Consumption of pulque and amaranth dough were also fairly ubiquitous, not just in the Panquetzaliztli celebration but in veintena rituals in general. Also, aspects of the Chonchayotl revelry can be seen in the signature ritual of the Swiftness of Huitzilopochtli, although Chonchayotl himself figured in the celebrations both in Tepepulco and Tenochtitlan.

In contrast, the Mexica celebration of the month included many unique features. There are no suggestions that merchants were part of the celebrations outside Tenochtitlan. Their addition to the celebrations must be considered a Mexica innovation. In the waning years of the Mexica Empire, the signature ritual of the Mexica Panquetzaliztli celebration was probably the run of Painal, which also seems to be a somewhat recent innovation. While the battle of the Huitznahua might be associated with Chonchayotl and his cutting of people's ears, the scale of the battle and its symbolism was unique to the Mexica. Moreover, the feast was used by the Mexica as one of four celebrations during which they required subject peoples to bring their tribute to the capital.[4] Under the Mexica, the cycle of rituals and celebrations during the month underwent a transformation within a few decades before the arrival of the Spaniards.[5] The Mexica used the month to celebrate the birth and exploits of their national god, Huitzilopochtli. In order to better understand the symbolism of the Panquetzaliztli celebrations, we must look into the cult of Huitzilopochtli, the legends surrounding the god, and his special relationship to the Mexica. This chapter will first consider the similarities in the ways the various communities celebrated Panquetzaliztli in order to look for common themes. It will then focus on the differences between the manner of the month's commemoration in Tenochtitlan and in other areas of central Mexico.

Similarities in How Panquetzaliztli Was Celebrated

Because of the vary dramatic events that occurred during the month of Panquetzaliztli in nearly every place it was celebrated, some of the more mundane and private rituals tend to be overlooked. Yet a careful analysis demonstrates that there was a substratum of common ritual, especially at a personal or household level. Because these devotions were private, the colonial observers did not pay as much attention to them. Some were common to other monthly celebrations; some were featured only, or largely, in Panquetzaliztli.

Perhaps the most important of these lesser rituals was the one that actually gave the name to the month: the raising of banners. Sahagún's informants in Tepepulco do not explain why the month was named the way it was. But in Tenochtitlan, they note that the underlying ritual behind all the celebrations of the month consisted of the cutting of fir and pine tree branches. These were laid on altars on mountaintops and then carried into the city.[6] In other depictions of the month, one or more figures are shown holding a banner, such as in the Boban and Tovar calendars. Durán discusses the cutting of fir branches and the placing of banners in trees. He also notes that this practice was especially common in the regions of Chollolan, Tlaxcala, and in the basins to the west and south of Tenochtitlan.[7] Unfortunately, the significance of this practice is not clear. As has been noted before, banners iconographically symbolized sacrificial victims. So, at a very general level, the raising of banners signified the month in which an exceptional number of sacrifices were to occur.[8] But fir branches are not banners. The iconography of the month usually shows paper banners, not branches. At the same time, the use of branches and the presence of flags were ubiquitous among nearly all local celebrations.

Looking specifically at the cutting of fir branches, there might be more to the practice than simply decorating with greens. In the *Primeros memoriales,* Sahagún details a ritual known as "Laying Fir Branches" (*acxoyatemaliztli*). In this small ritual, the devotee gathered fir branches and then arranged them as an offering. This arrangement of branches would then become a place where individuals could place thorns that had been used for personal sacrifice and thus were covered with blood.[9] In the *Florentine Codex,* Sahagún writes of the cutting for fir branches with the word *acxoiatlaliaia* (*acxoyatlaliaia,* "laying down fir branches"). The two terms are closely related, with the word *acxoyatl* common to both. Generally, this word means "branches used in penitential rituals, fir."[10] In the description from the *Primeros memoriales,* Sahagún uses a noun form of the word meaning something like, "the laying down of branches," which is built on the stem *acxoyatl* and the stem *tema,* which is a verb meaning "to fill in or place something." In the description from the *Florentine Codex,* Sahagún creates a past progressive verb meaning "he was laying down branches," adding the noun stem from *acxoyatl* to the verb *tlalia,* which means "to set something down on the ground." So, while the two words appear to be quite distinct, they have a similar semantic content.

For his part, Motolinia describes many acts of personal bloodletting associated with the month of Panquetzaliztli. He writes that the natives pierced their tongues, chests, earlobes, thighs, and other parts to draw blood. The blood was either absorbed on strips of paper, which were then burned, or it was smeared on the image of the god using fingers.[11]

The raising of banners and the cutting of fir branches had symbolic meanings related to sacrifice. The banners reflected sacrificial victims in large-scale public displays of human sacrifice. In the *Historia general,* Sahagún notes that the banners carried by victims "were the signal that they had been sentenced to death."[12] In the *Codex Telleriano-Remensis,* in the section that presents Mexica history as a time line, periods of extraordinary human sacrifice are noted with small figures wearing distinctive costumes and carrying banners.[13] On the other hand, the fir branches indicate a smaller, mundane devotion having to do with mortification and bloodletting as a personal sacrifice. Thus, taken together, they indicate the range of sacrificial devotions common among Nahua peoples. Thus, the month of Panquetzaliztli would become a month par excellence of sacrifice, ranging from the personal level to large-scale imperial displays.

Closely related to the theme of sacrifice, most of the descriptions of the ceremonies of Panquetzaliztli also mention that key participants were required to undergo a period of abstinence lasting from as long as four months (eighty days) to as few as one to five days. In Tepepulco, Sahagún reports that the abstinence included cessation of bathing (either with soap and water or in steam baths) and the denial of sexual relations. Eventually during the month, everyone in the community joined in a fast, even if for only one day.[14] In Tenochtitlan, Sahagún found a similar discipline. While he does not include references to fasting in his central long description of the ceremonies, in the brief introduction in the first part of book 2 of the *Florentine Codex,* Sahagún notes that the priests involved in the celebration fasted and performed penance for two months (forty days) prior to ceremonies of Panquetzaliztli. The penance consisted of going naked to the mountains while carrying branches.[15] Sahagún suggests that the merchants and their households prepared themselves ritually for the events of the month. In the Spanish version of his account, the *Historia general,* Sahagún observes that the participants in the sacrifices, the merchants and their households, and the elders of the neighborhoods fasted for five days before the final hecatomb.[16] In the *Florentine Codex,* Sahagún expands on this to add that they also abstained from sexual relations during these four days.[17] Clearly, the merchants suffered a rather significant outlay of money in the purchase of hundreds of gifts along with food and drink for hundreds of people. Other sources are a bit more descriptive in discussing the fasting and abstinence involved in the celebration. Durán indicates that everyone who wished to participate in the Swiftness of Huitzilopochtli underwent a daylong fast. After consuming some tzoalli at midnight, they fasted for a full day, eating and drinking nothing. He called the fast *netenhuatzaliztli,* which he translated as "drying up or removing moisture from the mouth."[18]

Singing and dancing played important roles in the rituals associated with Panquetzaliztli in most descriptions of the month. Singing the hymn to Huitzilopochtli, the "Tlaxotecayotl," opened the celebrations of the month. It continued to be sung throughout the month. There are numerous references to the use of native conch-shell trumpets along with drums to accompany both the singers and the dances that followed. Dancing played an important role in the celebrations according to all sources. The central dance of the month was called the serpent dance (coanecuiloa). The participants included the sacrificial victims, the bathers, the assistants, and others.[19] In Tepepulco, the singing and dancing were more widespread and included the whole community. They offered young men and women a chance to be together. Moreover, Sahagún suggests that they might have been part of the eighty-day preparation for the feast.[20]

In Panquetzaliztli, celebrants consumed octli (fermented maguey sap), known in modern times as pulque, along with tzoalli. The drinking occurred only after the sacrifices had been completed.[21] Only blue pulque is mentioned when Sahagún describes the drinking associated with the feast in Tenochtitlan, but the description from Tepepulco is more detailed in that Sahagún discusses two different types of pulque: blue pulque and fivefold pulque. Furthermore, the consumption of pulque seems to have lasted for many days, perhaps including the eighty days of preparation leading up to the festival.[22] While Durán mentions the drinking of pulque as part of the rituals, he does not offer any elaboration and merely notes that offerings of the beverage were made.[23] Clearly, the consumption of pulque is at odds with other observations that the participants spent much time in penance and abstinence. Unfortunately, some of the emphasis on the drinking of pulque might be an exaggeration by the friars who observed the practices, since they routinely also lamented the reputed drunkenness of the natives.

The eating of amaranth dough was also a common part of the rituals in all of the descriptions. In Tepepulco, Sahagún mentions, the dough was made as an offering, but he stops just short of writing that it was then eaten.[24] All the sources describing the celebrations in Tenochtitlan agree that the distribution of the amaranth dough was a critical part of the larger ceremony. Durán uses his description to launch into a diatribe that the distribution of the amaranth dough was a diabolical violation of the Christian Eucharist in which consecrated bread was distributed to the faithful.[25]

In the *Primeros memoriales* and in the *Florentine Codex,* Sahagún includes the rituals surrounding the character of Chonchayotl. None of the other sources mention this figure. Sahagún calls the appearance of this figure by the same name in both locations, Chonchaiocacalioa (Chonchayocacalyoa), or "the Mock Battle of Chonchayotl." In Tepepulco, a priest arrayed in the image of Huitzilopochtli, called Chonchayotl in this ritual, went out to the streets and byways to seize passersby.[26] In Tenochtitlan, Chonchayotl was relegated to a minor role in the overall celebration. The ritual pitted forces from the two schools for young men, the calmecac and the telpochcalli, against one another.[27] Both these celebrations are a form of ritual warfare in which sectors of society fight one another for greater social cohesion.

The figure of Chonchayotl is enigmatic. Other than his participation in the Panquetzaliztli festival, little is known of him. At the same time, Graulich argues that he represents the dead Huitzilopochtli returned to life but converted into a Tzitzimitl, a devilish creature of the night. As a Tzitzimitl, Chonchayotl could be related to Tezcatlipoca.[28] It is possible that the mock battle of Chonchayotl, as practiced in Tepepulco and, one assumes, elsewhere, eventually became the battle of the Huitznahua in the Tenochtitlan celebrations. In Tenochtitlan, they may have opted to also keep something of the original Chonchayotl mock battle per se because it was fun and an opportunity for social reversal in which students would battle one another and get their teachers involved. Because Chonchayotl, at least in Tepepulco, roamed the streets to punish the unaware passerby, he can be considered a trickster. In this function, he might be related to Tezcatlipoca and suggest an older origin for this particular bit of ritual. The battle was relatively important in Tepepulco and was still practiced in Tenochtitlan, although it came later in the cycle and in a slightly different manner.

Thus, several activities were common to Panquetzaliztli wherever it was celebrated. There were sacrifices including both personal blood sacrifices as well as large-scale human sacrifice. Abstinence also played an important role: fasting, the cessation of bathing, and the denial of sexual relations. Perhaps the opposite side of abstinence is feasting and drinking, for food, feasts, and the consumption of pulque were also important components of the celebration in all locales according to the authors. Singing and dancing likewise played a central role in the celebration of the feast, although evidence for this is stronger from Tenochtitlan than in outlying areas. Lastly, the enigmatic presence of Chonchayotl also linked to the celebrations of Tepepulco and Tenochtitlan. Other than this last element, one could posit that the remaining rituals and practices could be found in every series of rituals and celebrations for all eighteen months of the Mexica year.

Templo Mayor as Coatepec and the Birth of Huitzilopochtli

The Templo Mayor was the focal point for the celebrations of Panquetzaliztli in Tenochtitlan, just as the temple to Huitzilopochtli was in Tepepulco. But the Templo Mayor was envisioned as more than just the largest religious building in the sacred precinct of Tenochtitlan. It also figured as a symbolic representation of the mythical mountain Coatepec (Snake Mountain). That locale played a central role both in both the mythic birth of Huitzilopochtli and the Mexica migration story.[29]

One of the origin myths for Huitzilopochtli was intimately linked to the origin myth of the Mexica people themselves. The deity and the people were joined in deep ties of reciprocity.[30] As was discussed earlier, one of the central myths describing the birth of Huitzilopochtli reinforces his role as a solar god. Huitzilopochtli was born to Coatlicue (Snake Her Skirt) on top of Coatepec (Snake Mountain). He emerged fully armed and killed his sister, Coyolxauqui, and brothers, the Centzon Huitznahua, who had plotted to kill him. Because Huitzilopochtli had no known father, one of his epithets in Nahuatl was Tetzahuitl, "Something Scandalous or Frightful." Sahagún expands on this, adding, "For no one appeared as his father."[31] His brothers were clothed in paper armor that he ignited with his Fire Serpent. He beheaded and dismembered his sister, Coyolxauhqui, and threw her body parts off Snake Hill.[32] In the famous sculpture of the dismembered Coyoxauhqui found at the base of the Templo Mayor, one can clearly see the wounds of her death (see fig. 1). Lying naked, she is beheaded and dismembered. She also carries symbols of her name in the bells that adorn her cheeks. On her forehead are the balls of down, which were also representative of Huitzilopochtli since that was the mechanism whereby his mother was impregnated.[33] She also has snake "garters" tied around each of her limbs just below the point of dismemberment, probably in recognition of her mother: Coatlicue.

Analyzing this birth myth, scholars have noted that if Huitzilopochtli was considered the solar deity, then Coyolxauhqui would be the representation of the moon, while the Huitznahua were the stars. The coming of the sun inevitably drives away and defeats the moon and stars.[34] The xiuhcoatl has been interpreted as the burning rays of the sun or possibly a thunderbolt or a meteor.[35] Lastly, the Templo Mayor was considered to be Coatepec, the place where Coatlicue was impregnated and where Huitzilopochtli was born.[36] While many understood that it was a symbolic relationship—that the pyramid was not the actual hill or mountain—this distinction was perhaps not as widespread in the popular imagination. The origin myths place the physical location of the original Coatepec somewhere to the northwest, possibly in the region of Tula.

All sources since Sahagún agree that the Templo Mayor symbolically represented Coatepec. The Coyolxauhqui stone was discovered at the base of the Templo Mayor, symbolically reinforcing the myth of her destruction by Huitzilopochtli and the relationship of Coatepec with the Templo Mayor. The sanctuary to Huitzilopochtli shared the pinnacle of the Templo Mayor with that of the ancient rain god, Tlaloc. Huitzilopochtli's sanctuary was on the south, Tlaloc's to the north. The relationship between the Templo Mayor and Coatepec was so close that when the temple was rededicated after a major renovation in 1487, the ceremonies of rededication were timed to occur during the month of Panquetzaliztli.[37]

Templo Mayor/Coatepec had important astronomical implications. Research has demonstrated that while the temple is not strictly constructed in a north-south or east-west orientation, it is astronomically oriented. It also was aligned with the surrounding mountains and with several astronomical events. The Templo Mayor faced in a generally east-west configuration, so that an observer standing in front of the temple would be looking generally east; in fact, it faces about seven degrees south of east. The gap between the two temples atop the Templo Mayor lined up with a low spot, or pass, between two peaks in the eastern range of the Central Basin. The mountain called Tlaloc was to the north and Yeloxochitl/Telapon to the south. After complicated calculations, Anthony Aveni and his colleagues posited that from an observation point on the Templo Mayor, the sun would rise over Yeloxochitl/Telapon on the first day of Atl cahualo, the first month of the vague solar year. The first day of Tlacaxipehualiztli would see the sun in the pass, while Etzalcualiztli and Panquetzaliztli would host the solstices.[38] Looking at two details of the ancient complex, they found that the Coyolxauqui stone was on an exact east-west axis with what would have been the plinth holding the image of Huitzilopochtli in the later phases of the Templo Mayor.[39] The orientation of the temple was so important that Aveni has noted that when Moteuczoma Ilhuicamina was informed that the building was out of alignment during the feast of Tlacaxipehualiztli, the ruler wanted to rebuild and correct it immediately.[40]

Because the structure underwent several reconstructions, the sanctuaries at the top of the temple were at a different point in space each time the temple was elevated. The cleft between the sanctuaries of Tlaloc and Huitzilopochtli moved higher and slightly to the east while the sanctuary to Tlaloc moved slightly north. The south wall of the sanctuary to Huitzilopochtli moved south, and the temple as a whole took over more of the forecourt to the west. There was, thus, a stable point somewhere in the middle of the temple. Priests used the cleft between the sanctuaries for astronomical sightings. In all likelihood, the temple was oriented to provide for a clear line of sight to the cleft in the mountains to the east on the day of the equinox.[41] The cleft in the mountains and the cleft between the sanctuaries were important as symbols of creation and birth. The notch between the two temples represented fecundity—birth. Huitzilopochtli was born on Coatepec. His xiuhcoatl, a phallic symbol, destroyed the female power of Coyolxauhqui. According to the *Histoyre du Mechique*, man was created from a half man/half woman who emerged from a cleft in the mountains caused by an arrow that the sun shot from the sky.[42] In this story we can also appreciate that the arrow was a symbolic phallus, the cleft a symbolic vagina.

The Mexica national origin myth inserted a bit of circularity into the birth myth of Huitzilopochtli. According to their origin story, the Mexica came from an island home called Aztlan. In this account, the Mexica discovered the god, Huitzilopochtli, in a cave as they set out on their migration (see fig. 2). He was carried by one of their leaders, who became a teomama, and he led them on their path (see fig. 3). Eventually the migration reached Coatepec, where Huitzilopochtli was born of Coatlicue.[43] This version of the myth is necessarily circular, since the god existed before he reached Coatepec. This seeming impossibility is explained in a sixteenth-century collection of myths. It narrates the migration of the Mexica from Aztlan to Coatepec (spelled "Cuauhtepec" in that version). Because Huitzilopochtli both accompanied the migrants and was born at the location, that variant explains, "She became pregnant without assistance of a male, and Huitzilopochtli was born of her, in addition to the other times when he born, since he was a god, he could do and accomplish what he wanted."[44] This account has Coatlicue as a virgin, thus suggesting that Huitzilopochtli was her first child. The four hundred opponents who sought to kill Huitzilopochtli had been made by Tezcatlipoca, were killed before the start of the epoch, and then were resuscitated. Lastly, the author notes that the birth of Huitzilopochtli and the death of the four hundred opponents was celebrated annually, which is a reference to the feast of Panquetzaliztli.

Some of the legends and several modern scholars hold that Huitzilopochtli was a man who was deified: an elder called Huitzilin (Hummingbird), who led his people on their migration. His name was significant because, according to belief, warriors who die in battle become hummingbirds who accompany the sun on its daily course.[45] As a leader, he was infused with the power of the deity Tetzauhteotl (Frightful or Scandalous God), a god of fisher people who had presented himself as a wizard and manifestation of the moon, not unlike Tezcatlipoca.[46] Thus, the deity who directed the migration was an avatar of Tezcatlipoca speaking through the medium of a leader named Huitzilipoch, or Huitzilin.[47] During the migration, Huitzilin died and underwent an apotheosis, born as Huitzilopochtli, according to the legend, at Coatepec, where the Mexica had stopped on their migration.[48]

Eduardo Matos Moctezuma offers a cogent analysis of the seeming circularity of the migration and the finding of Huitzilopochtli, who is later born at Coatepec. He posits that the Mexica were part of a larger group of migrants, whom he calls the Huitznahua. Upon arriving at a place called Coatepec, a large faction under the leadership of a woman warrior, Coyolxauhqui, disobeyed the commands of the leader. Female leadership was not unknown among the Mexica. The pictorial manuscript showing the migration includes one woman in a leadership position serving as one of the god bearers, a woman identified as Chimalma (see fig. 3). In response to the rebellion of the Huitznahua, the Mexica leader called Huitzilopochtli attacked them and, in the process, killed their leader then dismembered and decapitated her. The remaining leaders were sacrificed.[49] David Carrasco largely follows this same logic, but he notes that before the birth of Huitzilopochtli, Coyolxauhqui acted like a berserker, inciting her brothers to fight, egging them on into ever more vicious and warlike paroxysms of anger. But upon his emergence and slaughter of Coyolxauhqui, Huitzilopochtli became the berserker, fighting with increasing bloodlust as he pursued each of his enemies until all were totally destroyed.[50]

María Castañeda de la Paz posits that the Mexica, upon leaving their island home, worshipped the god Mixcoatl, the god of the hunt, as represented in his signature weapon the *amimitl* (water arrow).[51] The story of the migration, then, is also the story of how the Mexica came to choose and be chosen by Huitzilopochtli as their national god. One of the leaves of the *Tira de Peregrinación* depicts the sacrifice of three persons on barrel cacti and thorn trees. For Castañeda, this is a representation of the creatures of Mixcoatl, the four hundred mimixcoa, created to hunt for the sun in his daily passage. The mimixcoa would lie in trees and cacti in order to be fed by eagles. The drawing signifies that three of the leaders of the group were elevated to the rank of great warriors. This was also the moment in which Huitzilopochtli, shown in the form of an eagle, gave the Mexica bows, arrows, and woven baskets to annihilate the mimixcoa, the servants/children of Mixcoatl. In this way, Huitzilopochtli supplanted Mixcoatl.[52]

Another interpretation of the birth of Huitzilopochtli sees the conflict as a battle between peoples who pursue hunting and gathering against sedentary agriculturalists. In this interpretation of the myth, the Mexica were the hunters and gatherers. The Huitznahua and Coyolxauhqui represent the sedentary agricultural people of central Mexico. Although the Mexica, led by their ruler/god Huitzilopochtli, defeat the Huitznahua eventually, they also accept the settled life of agriculturalists.[53] As noted earlier, the defeat of Coyolxauhqui and the Centzon Huitznahua signifies the triumph of the sun over the moon and stars each day at dawn. In this interpretation, Coyolxauhqui is the embodiment of the moon while the Four Hundred Southerners represent the countless stars of the sky, all of which cede dominance of the sky to the rising sun.[54] Regardless of the historic or symbolic roots of the strife between Huitzilopochtli and his siblings, the battle between the sacrificial victims and the warriors of the Huitznahuac neighborhood of Tenochtitlan during the celebrations of Panquetzaliztli can be interpreted as reenacting this event. It is possible that the battle was a precedent for the mock battle of Chonchayotl.

The legend of Huitzilopochtli's birth at Coatepec is of central importance in the study of Panquetzaliztli because most scholars have concluded that the central ritual of the month, the Swiftness of Huitzilopochtli, recapitulated the migration history of the Mexica. The final hecatomb of sacrificial victims, starting with the ritual battle in Huitznahuac and continuing through the immolation of the victims at the Templo Mayor, was a re-creation of the events of Huitzilopochtli's birth, which occurred precisely on Coatepec, now represented by the Templo Mayor.[55] Symbolically, during the final Panquetzaliztli ritual, the ixiptla coming down with the xiuhcoatl was Huitzilopochtli reborn, just as his amaranth ixiptla was "killed." The runner, upon returning to the Templo Mayor, ascended the staircase and entered into the sanctuary, and the god impersonator emerged. The sanctuary represents a cave that, in turn, represents the womb of the goddess Coatlicue from which the god emerged fully formed and armed.[56] He descended the staircase and set fire to the paper in the cuauhxicalli just as Huitzilopochtli burned his brothers, who were then ritually sacrificed in his honor. At his feet was the sculptural representation of the defeated Coyolxauhqui. It was a ritual rebirth and recapitulation of the mythic events.

In addition to the battle with the Huitznahua, in the final rituals of Panquetzaliztli, the victims circled the Templo Mayor several times, just as Huitzilopochtli chased the Huitznahua and killed them.[57] After the victims had been killed atop the Templo Mayor, their bodies were tossed down just as Huitzilopochtli dismembered and threw down the body of his sister Coyolxauhqui, beside which the sacrificial victims were required to walk.[58] Indeed, their bodies probably landed near the monumental sculpture of the goddess at the foot of the temple.

The only element seeming to be missing from the symbolic re-creation of the Mexica migration and battle of the Centzon Huitznahua was the sacrifice and dismemberment of Coyolxauhqui. It is possible that the sacrifice of the two warriors in the ritual ball court at the outset of the Swiftness of Huitzilopochtli symbolically represented the death of Coyolxauhqui. According to Eduard Seler, the ball court as a ritual space was identified with the moon just as Coyolxauqui's death by Huitzilopochtli represented the defeat of the moon by the rising sun.[59] Consequently, the two figures sacrificed at the start of the Swiftness of Huitzilopochtli, could represent Coyolxauqui. In the version of the origin myth cited by Seler, Huitzilopochtli ordered that a ball court be built proximate to Coatepec. There, he killed Coyolxauqui in the very middle of the ball court, cut off her head, and tore out her heart. Matos Moctezuma posits that when the sacrificial victims were beheaded and thrown off of the temple, they represented Coyolxauhqui.[60]

As seen in earlier chapters, sixteenth-century sources indicate that the ceremonies of the month of Panquetzaliztli were in commemoration of the birth of the god. Thus, the re-creation of the Mexica migration and Huitzilopochtli's miraculous birth at Coatepec formed part of the core ritual performances for the festival of Panquetzaliztli. While the birth of Huitzilopochtli was central to the celebration, the events of the migration played an important role in understanding the symbolism of the ritual of the Swiftness of Huitzilopochtli as celebrated during Panquetzaliztli.

The Mexica Migration

In the Swiftness of Huitzilopochtli celebration in Panquetzaliztli, the Mexica were ritually reenacting their migration. The Mexica migration began in a temple located on an island in the middle of a lake. The Swiftness of Huitzilopochtli traced a similar route from the Templo Mayor, located on the island of Tenochtitlan, to Tlatelolco, over to the western shore of the lake, near Chapultepec, then returning to the Templo Mayor/Coatepec from near Coyohuacan. In all this, Huitzilopochtli was carried by a teomama, just as, in the migration, the god was similarly carried.

Looking at the *Florentine Codex* account of the ritual, there seem to be at least four sacrifices (ball court, Nonoalco/Tlatelolco, Popotlan, Izquitlan/Chapultepec). These sacrifices could represent the four New Fire ceremonies that the migrating Mexica performed en route to Anahuac.[61] At the same time, the number four is also an important number for completeness among the Nahua. Many altepeme had four calpolli (neighborhood districts), including Tenochtitlan itself. For example, there had been four creations prior to the current fifth sun, the primordial couple had four sons, and there are many more examples of four.

The various stops in the ceremonial circuit would have been equally filled with symbolism. The first stop was at the Teotlachco within the sacred precinct. There, either two or four warriors were sacrificed, and their bodies were dragged through the sand to leave trails of blood. Burr Cartwright Brundage and Eduard Seler have posited that this symbolically represented the killing and dismemberment of Coyolxauqui, the sister of Huitzilopochtli.[62] The text provided by Sahagún calls these sacrificial victims by the names of two gods: Amapan and Huapatzan, while in other versions, he merely notes that the victims were sacrificed to these gods. Torquemada adds that quail were sacrificed and that two warriors were tied by their heels and sacrificed. He further explains, however, that many other victims were also killed at the ball court, implying a larger sacrifice. Clearly, the sacrifice in the divine ball court was an initiatory ritual to establish the theme of the performance and prepare the runner for the path he was to take. Moreover, it resembles the sacrifice made by the gods at Teotihuacan in order to start the sun and moon moving in their courses. This blood sacrifice might have provided the spiritual energy to allow to the ixiptla to follow his course.[63] As will be seen later, the trajectory of Painal as he ran the circuit also imitated the movement of the sun, according to Nahua cosmology.

The next set of sacrifices occurred at Tlatelolco/Nonoalco. There, Painal/Huitzilopochtli was joined by his brother Cuahuitl Icac. Cuahuitl Icac, one of the Centzon Huitznahua (the brothers of Huitzilopochtli), chose not to join his brothers in their attempt to kill the unborn Huitzilopochtli but instead passed information of the attack to the Huitzilopochtli. The sacrifice performed at Nonoalco probably provided the energy necessary to vivify Cuahuitl Icac to allow him to accompany Painal/Huitzilopochtli on his journey. According to the legend, as the Centzon Huitznahua approached Coatepec, Cuahuitl Icac relayed the information to the unborn Huitzilopochtli. On their way to Coatepec, the four hundred brothers passed by Tzompantitlan, Coaxalpan, and Apetlac.[64] These place names also refer to the divine geography of Tenochtitlan. Tzompantitlan is "Beneath the Skull Rack," Coaxalpan is "the Snake Sand Place," and Apetlac is "the Place of the Water Mat." Thus, Tzompantitlan was the spot within the sacred precinct where the divine skull rack was located. The Coaxalpan is associated with the cleansing ceremonies involving sand, the xalaquia, in the forecourt to the Templo Mayor. And the Apetlac was the place immediately at the base of the temple where the sacrificial victims were bathed during the course of the month.[65]

According to Motolinia, the next sacrifices occurred outside Azcapotzalco, at a shrine named Acolman. There, he specifies that four captives fell victim to the sacrificial knife. Sahagún places these sacrifices at Popotlan. In all likelihood the two spots were either the same or quite near to one another. Quite unassociated with the Mexica migration, this general location had some historic significance. Early in their history, the Mexica benefitted from being subject to Azcapotzalco, the capital of the Tepaneca Empire. Yet, eventually, the Mexica began to chafe under the control of their more powerful neighbors. They began a series of skirmishes and wars to eventually gain their independence. The final battle that resulted in the death of the Tepaneca war leader Maxtla occurred somewhere between the city and Tlatelolco.[66] On the other hand, there is no event or place in the migration stories that might correspond to Popotlan or Acolman.

The fourth sacrifice occurred alongside the hill of Chapultepec, at Izquitlan. As has been noted, Izquitlan was the name of one of the original neighborhoods of the city. Chapultepec had tremendous historic importance for the Mexica. They had settled near the springs and outcropping of Chapultepec when they first arrived in the Central Basin. Furthermore, in the later years of the Triple Alliance, the rulers had their images carved into the living rock of Chapultepec. The place called Izquitlan could not have been more than a few hundred meters away. Consequently, the sacrifices at this spot might well have been ritual commemorations of Mexica history and reminders of their first entry into the Basin.

The final set of sacrifices occurred at the Templo Mayor after the return of

Painal/Huitzilopochtli. The victims were dressed as ixiptlahuan of Huitzilopochtli himself. At the temple, the sacrificial victims were ritually attacked with the Fire Serpent then made to walk around the temple and scale its heights to their own demise. After death, their bodies were tossed to the ground, just as Coyolxauqui and the Centzon Huitznahua were killed and thrown off Coatepec. While some of the stops and sacrifices along the route of the Swiftness of Huitzilopochtli can potentially be linked to events during the Mexica migration, one cannot link every event. Quite simply, there was no canonical version of the migration story but rather a variety of legends. Most agreed on a few basic points, but there was much divergence among them all.

On one level, then, the celebration of the Swiftness of Huitzilopochtli corresponds closely to the events of Huitzilopochtli's birth story. But in other details, it also represents the Mexica migration story. The journey began in the sanctuary of the temple of Aztlan, as depicted in the *Tira de Peregrinación*. In that migration story, the lords of the Mexica carried Huitzilopochtli. Over the course of the migration, they endured hardships. According to tradition, the migration took some two hundred years, during which the Mexica celebrated four New Fire ceremonies. The four sacrifices made along the route of the Swiftness of Huitzilopochtli could represent the sacrifices made in the migration. Quite simply the signature celebration of the month of Panquetzaliztli, the Swiftness of Huitzilopochtli, was also a ceremonial reiteration of the migration story of the Mexica.[67] Thus, upon closer analysis, we find that within the celebrations of a month dedicated to war, the Mexica inserted their own history as a people and the symbolic birth of their special god.

Movement in the Swiftness of Huitzilopochtli

The Swiftness of Huitzilopochtli ceremony in Panquetzaliztli generally moved counterclockwise from the Templo Mayor to Tlatelolco, Tlacopan, Coyohuacan, and back to the Templo Mayor. The route of the god encompassed the southwestern quarter of the Central Basin (see map 2). The runner took a path that generally kept the Templo Mayor to his left, the side favored by Huitzilopochtli, whose name means "Hummingbird on the Left." It also kept the heart of the god, in the left side of the body, closest to the heart of the empire. Elizabeth H. Boone also observes that in some of the migration manuscripts such as the *Mapa Sigüenza*, the migration journey took place in a counterclockwise fashion.[68]

Brundage argues that this movement also replicated the movement of the sun itself, moving from east to west, then dropping down (to the south) to then return to its starting place in the east again.[69] Not only did the general path outline the daily route of the sun, the larger course imitated the sun's annual movement. As the ceremony began, the runner moved north, tracing the sun's rise on the eastern horizon from the solstice to the spring equinox. The first half of the circuit then proceeded to the west, tracing the course of the sun in the heavens. It then moved southward, as the sun does from the summer solstice to the equinox, and then the second half of the ceremony moved generally from west to east, as the sun passes through the underworld to prepare to rise yet again.[70] Thus, the association of Huitzilopochtli/Painal with the solar disk was also reinforced by the runner's movement.

One would imagine that within the ritual calendar there would be a need for ceremonies that similarly covered the four other regions of the Central Basin, just as the Swiftness of Huitzilopochtli covered the southwestern circuit. Looking at the series of monthlong celebrations of the xiuhpohualli, we can also see that there were four months (Atl cahualo, Toxcatl, Ochpaniztli, and Panquetzaliztli) in which processions from the center to the periphery, like that found in the Swiftness of Huitzilopochtli, play an important role.

The first year of the xiuhpohualli was Atl cahualo (Water It Stops). This month was dedicated to the rain gods, the Tlaloque. It consisted of numerous sacrifices of small children around the metaphysical environment of the Central Basin. The children selected were ones with a double cowlick in their hair. Part of the ceremonies included putting up paper streamers that had been stained with rubber. The children sacrificed were called "human paper streamers."[71] As part of this ritual, Sahagún mentions eight or nine places where the children were sacrificed: Quauhtepetl, Mount Yoaltecatl, Tepetzinco, Poyauhtlan, Pantitlan, Cocotl, and Yiauhqueme. Either Tepetzinco or Pantitlan seems to have been the central or crucial sacrifice. As the children were sacrificed, their tears were thought to mimic and encourage the rain. Earlier in his discussion, Sahagún wrote that the sacrifices took place on mountaintops, and thus we might assume that all these locations were mountains. He explicitly states that Yoaltecatl was a mountain. In the *Historia general*, Sahagún clarifies the locations. Quauhtepetl was designated as a hill or mountain and was located near Tlatelolco. Yoaltecatl was to one side of what is now the Shrine of Guadalupe. Tepetzinco, which means "little hill," was a small hill in the lake on the border between Tlatelolco and Tenochtitlan. Poyauhtlan was a mountain in the eastern part of the basin, beyond which was the altepetl of Tlaxcala. Pantitlan means "Beneath, or Beside the Flag" and was a whirlpool to the south and east of Tenochtitlan in Lake Tetzcoco.[72] Cocotl was a hill located in the region of Chalco Atenco. Yiauhqueme was a hill, since Sahagún describes the sacrifice as taking place on top of it (*icpac*), and it was located near Atlacuihuaya.[73] These sacrificial sites occupy nearly all compass points in the basin, with the possible exception of due west: from Yoaltecatl in the north-northwest to Yiauhqueme in the west-southwest. Unlike the Panquetzaliztli procession and sacrifices, the sites for Atl cahualo processions did not seem to be linked to one another but acted more like destinations for sacrifices, with each procession nominally beginning in the sacred precinct. If they were linked, then the general direction of the ceremonies might violate a counterclockwise ritual movement, beginning in the north, then moving to the east and south before passing through to the west and southwest.[74]

In the month of Tlacaxipehualiztli (the Flaying of Men), after the death of a captive warrior in gladiatorial combat, the man who had captured the warrior filled a bowl with the victim's blood. The captor then visited all the major temples of the city and placed some of the victim's blood on the lips of the gods' images. Yet Sahagún does not provide an exact itinerary. Nor does there seem to have been a fixed route taken by the captor; it was simply one that included all the important sanctuaries.[75]

Just as the runner in the Swiftness of Huitzilopochtli visited various symbolic places in the western and southern sections of the Central Basin, during Toxcatl, the ixiptla visited sites in the north and east, thus making the two celebrations nearly mirror images of each other. In Toxcatl, rather than running, the god imitator embarked on a leisurely journey over the course of four days, going as far as Tepepulco. While the Swiftness of Huitzilopochtli included sacrifices at the Teotlachco, Nonoalco, Izquitlan, and the Templo Mayor, the celebrations of Toxcatl had the procession stop at four specific locations: Tecanman, Titlacauan, Tepetzinco, and Tepepulco. From Tepepulco, the god impersonator went to Acaquilpan or Cahualtepec, where he was sacrificed.[76] Thus, the Toxcatl procession did not return to the Templo Mayor.

The ceremonies of the month of Ochpaniztli also involved runners and processions. One of the early runs was from the temple of Tlazolteotl (Teteo Inan, Toci) to the Templo Mayor and then to Pochtlan.[77] While the exact location of Pochtlan is not clear, in Nahuatl, a person from there would be a pochteca, which was the term for the long-distance merchants. Thus, we can assume it was a calpolli in the altepetl of Tlatelolco where the merchants were concentrated and thus was located to the north of the Templo Mayor.

In the Ochpaniztli celebrations, a seasoned warrior took the thigh-skin mask and began to run. Other strong warriors and fast runners accompanied him. The group raced to the foot of the snow-capped peak known today as Iztaccihuatl (White Woman). There, they buried the mask at a place known as Popotl Temi (Straw It Is Full). The narrative provided by Sahagún suggests that this was outside Mexica and Aztec control, because enemies set upon the runners. The runners were forced to fight the enemies, with both sides suffering deaths.[78]

Later in Ochpaniztli, following a ritual sowing of grain, a group of warriors began running a route that was seemingly within the sacred precinct. Sahagún observes that even the huey tlahtoani Moteuczoma participated in the run. The priest who wore the skin of the goddess impersonator, Toci, also joined in the race, but the runners and crowd kept her separate from the main group. As the run continued, participants dropped out of the group until only a very few remained. At last, only the priest was left as he reached the temple of Tocititlan (Beside Toci).[79] Durán describes this part of the ceremony as being a mock battle in which two groups skirmished between the Templo Mayor and the temple at Tocititlan.[80] This temple was located at the very southern end of the city of Tenochtitlan. As one entered the city from the south, it was on the right, that is, to the east.[81] This would be closer to the Templo Mayor than the place known as Acachinanco and probably very near to the modern Pino Suárez Metro station.

Based on the details provided by Sahagún and other commentators, we cannot clearly determine the exact route taken by runners and processions during the feast of Ochpaniztli. Nevertheless, they concentrated on the eastern and southeastern sectors of the city and basin. The calpolli of Pochtlan was probably in the northern altepetl of Tlatelolco, but the temple to Toci was located on the southern edge of the city. Iztaccihuatl/Iztactepetl is in the southeastern corner of the Central Basin. Thus, two of the main processions, ceremonies, and running routes focused on the south and southeast.

Taken as a whole, one can see that the feasts of Toxcatl, Ochpaniztli, and Panquetzaliztli involved processions and ceremonies that inscribed routes in three of the four cardinal regions of the city and basin. Toxcatl focused on the north and northeast. Ochpaniztli engaged the south and southeast, while Panquetzaliztli predominantly traversed the west and southwest. One might posit that another of the monthly festivals had the north and northwest as its focus of attention, thus completing the circuit of possible destinations in all four quadrants. Images such as the one on the foundation page of the *Codex Mendoza* that describe the political subdivisions of the city would lead us to assume that such a conceptualization of the ritual space surrounding Tenochtitlan also existed.

Tezcatlipoca versus Huitzilopochtli

As is suggested by Motolinia and in the *Codex Telleriano-Remensis*, the month of Panquetzaliztli was probably dedicated to the god Tezcatlipoca rather than Huitzilopochtli, especially prior to the rise of the Mexica and in regions outside Mexica dominance.[82] To more fully consider this possibility, we can look at the myths surrounding the two gods and the contexts in which one or the other takes a central role in celebrations. On the surface, the two have much in common. Both are associated with war. Both have some celestial aspects. Both figure as supreme deities under certain circumstances. The two gods vied for primacy among the gods in the monthlong celebration of the creation of the gods, Teotl eco, which was thought of as the birthday of the gods. While Tezcatlipoca had generally been given the recognition as the first god to appear, by Aztec times, this was contested, and the privilege passed to Huitzilopochtli.[83]

In addition to Huitzilopochtli's birth from Coatlicue on Coatepec, there are other traditions about his origin. According to one story, which was copied in the sixteenth century, probably by another Franciscan, Andrés de Olmos, two primordial gods existed from before all time in the highest level of heaven: Tonacateuctli and Tonacacihuatl, Our Lord of Flesh and Our Lady of Flesh. The couple engendered four sons. Each was associated with a different color and one of the cardinal directions, and all were known by a common name of Tezcatlipoca (Smoking Mirror). The first-born was Tlatlauhqui Tezcatlipoca (the Red Tezcatlipoca), who was the lord of those from Huexotzingo and Tlaxcala and was also known as Camaxtli, the god of the hunt. His color was red because he was red at birth. The second was Yayauhqui Tezcatlipoca, both the best and worst; he ordered the others when he could. His color was black. When early sources refer to the deity Tezcatlipoca, they mean the Black Tezcatlipoca. The third was Quetzalcoatl, also called Yohualli Ehecatl (Night Wind), who was possibly associated with the color white. The last and smallest was Omiteuctli (Bone Lord), also known as Maquizcoatl (possibly "Serpent Bracelet"), who was associated with the color blue. Among the Mexica, he became Huitzilopochtli because he was left-handed. Huitzilopochtli could thus be known as the Blue Tezcatlipoca. The account is clear that Huitzilopochtli was born without flesh. For many centuries, he was only a skeleton.[84] The rest of creation proceeded from these four demiurges. Also, each of the four had several avatars or manifestations. Because of this fourfold nature of Tezcatlipoca and the identification of one of his manifestations as Huitzilopochtli, some scholars hold that the Hummingbird god began as an avatar or alternate manifestation of the Smoking Mirror god.[85]

As with siblings anywhere, there were conflicts among the four gods. In general, the tales tend to focus on the duality and rivalry of Tezcatlipoca and Quetzalcoatl. On one level, they represented opposites in the color spectrum, black and white.[86] They also represented two distinct personality types. Tezcatlipoca was a war god whereas Quetzalcoatl was a god of civilization and order. The antagonism between the two was also seen as an aspect of the fall of the great mother civilization of Tula. In that story, Tezcatlipoca used a two-sided mirror to defeat Quetzalcoatl, the ruler of Tula, in a civil war.[87]

The rivalry between Tezcatlipoca and Huitzilopochtli was more subdued. There were two important aspects of the competition. One consists of myths in which Huitzilopochtli was substituted for Quetzalcoatl. While the names were changed, the broad outlines of the stories remain essentially the same. Another group of myths simply depict a direct confrontation between Tezcatlipoca and Huitzilopochtli, with no parallel found in the corpus of stories about Quetzalcoatl, as will be seen later.

There is no doubt that Tezcatlipoca was an important god among the Mexica in his own right. Yet, among other groups, historic and contemporaneous, Tezcatlipoca was nearly unequivocally recognized as supreme. The ancient legends held that the Toltecs, residents of mythic Tula, revered Tezcatlipoca as their supreme god, as did the Acolhua of Tetzcoco, who considered themselves the heirs of the Toltecs.[88] The legends held that the fall of Tula came as a direct result of the rivalry between Tezcatlipoca and Quetzalcoatl.[89]

In his discussion of the celebrations for the month of Panquetzaliztli, Michel Graulich posits that Huitzilopochtli's most important competition was not with Tezcatlipoca but rather Quetzalcoatl. He bases this position on Quetzalcoatl's identification with the sun. Graulich argues that Panquetzaliztli is a celebration of the return of the sun, and thus, for the Mexica, it was the celebration of the birth of Huitzilopochtli as a manifestation of the sun. Yet Graulich also writes extensively that the Mexica did not have a method of keeping the solar calendar aligned with the solar year for lack of a leap day or other mechanism. This meant that the feast was not necessarily celebrated at a time in which the sun had either reached its apex, such as June, or its nadir, such as December, but made a slow progression through the seasons. In short, Graulich suggests that by identifying Huitzilopochtli with the sun, the Mexica had, in effect, proclaimed that their arrival coincided with a new sun, a new era in human events, not just a seasonal recognition such as the winter solstice.[90] Consequently, he argues that the rivalry between Quetzalcoatl and Tezcatlipoca was modified to be one between Huitzilopochtli and Tezcatlipoca. Many scholars disagree with Graulich regarding the supposed absence of leap days, as will be discussed later. Nonetheless, he does clearly establish the essence of many of the rivalries among these gods.

Perhaps one of the clearest examples of Huitzilopochtli appearing in a story also associated with Quetzalcoatl is the birth story of the god. As noted, upon hearing that his brothers, the Centzon Huitznahua, were plotting with his sister, Coyolxauqui, to murder him at birth, Huitzilopochtli then emerged ready for battle, wielding his famous xiuhcoatl, and killed them all. This story is similar to the battle between Quetzalcoatl and the Centzon Mimixcoa (Four Hundred Cloud Snakes). An outsider, Quetzalcoatl, confronted the Mimixcoa and his uncle, Apanecatl, all of whom he defeated to become lord of Tula, just as Huitzilopochtli, an outsider, confronted his sister and brothers, whom he defeated to emerge as the national god of the Mexica.[91] In the one tale, Quetzalcoatl, as the morning star, defeated the stars of night as the dawn broke. As noted earlier, in the case of Huitzilopochtli, the god, as the new sun, defeated the stars and moon to establish his rule and power. In some legends, Tezcatlipoca was the creator of the Centzon Huitznahua, who attempted to kill Huitzilopochtli before his birth, presaging the eventual rivalry and conflict between the two deities.[92]

The Mimixcoa provide yet another important link between the deities. In several accounts, they were to hunt for the sustenance needed to move the sun, Tonatiuh. The ixiptlahuan of the festival of Tlacaxipehualiztli (Flaying of Men) were dressed as the Mimixcoa. When one looks at the iconography of the Mimixcoa, in several contexts, they are shown as sacrificial victims carrying banners.[93]

While all Mexica monthly feasts involved human sacrifice, in Panquetzaliztli, the number of victims was larger, and the symbolism of the victims was more important. The victims chosen for sacrifice in the month came from among the men captured in war. The use of war captives had its origins in the pre-Mexica celebrations of Panquetzaliztli, when the feast would have been dedicated to Tezcatlipoca as the god of war. The Mexica subtly modified this older tradition to celebrate Huitzilopochtli as the patron of war.

The ceremonies of Panquetzaliztli culminated in the final acts of the last day, which celebrated the birth of Huitzilopochtli and the Mexica migration. The day on which this ceremony occurred corresponded, at least in the early sixteenth century, to a day very near the winter solstice (about December 21, Gregorian), when many cultures celebrated the birth of the sun. For example, both the Roman festival of Sol Invictus and the Christian Nativity of Jesus fall near the winter solstice. At least in the years immediately prior to the conquest, the birth of Huitzilopochtli fell near the shortest day of the year, from which point the sun would continue to increase. In the late spring, the Mexica celebrated the feast of Toxcatl, a monthlong series of ceremonies dedicated to Tezcatlipoca. The symbolism employed by the Mexica also found a parallel in Christian symbolism. Christians celebrate the feast of Saint John the Baptist on June 24. Based on Biblical texts, the liturgies for Christmas and Saint John the Baptist imply that as John diminished, Jesus increased. Thus, the importance of the two figures was tied to the waxing and waning of the sun. The Mexica viewed the rivalry between Tezcatlipoca and Huitzilopochtli in a similar manner.[94]

Other scholars have noted a general trend among the Mexica to appropriate some of the aspects of Tezcatlipoca to Huitzilopochtli and even to posit that Huitzilopochtli was a transfiguration of the older god.[95] Prior to the rise of the emperor Itzcoatl and the defeat of the Tepaneca of Azcapotzalco, Huitzilopochtli was at best a minor god, intimately associated with the Mexica. With their rise to power, the Mexica began to transform him into a solar/celestial divinity. Huitzilopochtli came to share a similar set of powers and attributes with Tezcatlipoca, and eventually he became almost interchangeable with the sun god, Tonatiuh.[96] The timing of the Panquetzaliztli ceremonies and the winter solstice would then tend to reinforce the association of Huitzilopochtli with the solar disk.

While Huitzilopochtli might share some aspects with these other gods, they were different, and each had its own unique place in the divine scheme. Tezcatlipoca was a supreme god, a manifestation of the immanence of the divinity, as is reflected in several of his epithets: Tloque Nahuaque (Lord of the Near, Lord of the Close By), Ipalnemoani (He through Whom We Live), and Necoc Yaotl (Enemy on Both Sides).[97] In her translation of Durán work, Doris Heyden notes that even these epithets were appropriated by the Mexica for their god.[98] In the last years of Mexica rule, Huitzilopochtli was characterized as the Tezcatlipoca of the south, and he was identified with the young sun as it rose and fought its way westward.[99]

Both Tezcatlipoca and Huitzilopochtli were associated with the sun, fire, and war.[100] In different instances, both gods were embodiments of the ideal young warrior. Tezcatlipoca appeared as Telpochtli (the Youth) and Yaotl (War) and manifested profound links to the cult of war.[101] Huitzilopochtli was seen as leading the Mexica in their war against rival tribes. His lieutenant, Painal, a key figure in the Panquetzaliztli ceremonies, was considered a war captain. Just as different cities dedicated Panquetzaliztli to Tezcatlipoca, different traditions had Tezcatlipoca as their principal deity, as in the case of the Tetzcoco-centered accounts of Alva Ixtlilxochitl and Durán.[102]

The rivalry between Huitzilopochtli and Tezcatlipoca to be the deity of the sun parallels one of the Nahua creation legends. In the aftermath of the fourth sun's destruction, as the gods created the world yet again, they gathered at Teotihuacan, the ancient altepetl that predated the Mexica and most of their Nahua cousins, the ruins of which were still visible in the north of the Central Basin. The gods built a large bonfire in order to illuminate the world. They asked that one of their number sacrifice himself in the fire to create the new sun. Two deities stepped forward: Tecuciztecatl and Nanahuatzin. Tecuciztecatl was richly attired, wealthy, and handsome. When he did penance, it was with the finest materials. Nanahuatzin was pimpled, dressed in rags, and had to make do with whatever he could in order to do his penance. But Nanahuatzin was courageous. When the time came for them to be transformed by fire, the gods called first to Tecuciztecatl. Four times he approached the blaze but was unable to muster the courage to leap into the flames. Finally the gods called on Nanahuatzin, who leaped into the fire and was transformed into the sun. Upon seeing this, Tecuciztecatl gained the courage and also jumped into the fire and was transformed into a sun. But with two suns, there was no darkness, so one of the gods grabbed a rabbit and threw it on the face of Tecuciztecatl, diminishing his glow.[103] The story helps to explain why, when looking at the moon, natives of central Mexico see a rabbit in the mixture of dark and light areas. The tension, then, between Huitzilopochtli and Tezcatlipoca that developed by the Mexica in their calendar celebrations had a mythic basis in the battle between Nanahuatzin and Tecuciztecatl to be the principal solar deity.

Even the depictions of Huitzilopochtli had some elements of Tezcatlipoca. Previous chapters list common iconographical elements associated with each god. Based on the two lists, the gods share several symbols. Many of these are common to a large number of different deities or supernatural beings in the Nahua world. Both have feather headdresses, but of course, nearly every other deity or supernatural being wears a headdress, frequently of feathers. Tezcatlipoca wears heron feathers while Huitzilopochtli normally sports quetzal or blue-green feathers. Both have striped face painting: Tezcatlipoca's is black, and Huitzilopochtli's is blue. But Huitzilopochtli also has a black star design around his eyes that can look like a black stripe. Again, many other supernatural deities also have striped face painting. As warriors, both the gods also carry spear throwers, although Huitzilopochtli's is frequently in the shape of a serpent. Banners appear in the array of both gods. Huitzilopochtli sometimes carries a sacrificial banner topped with a flint knife while Tezcatlipoca might simply carry a banner.

Although the smoking mirror is associated most closely with Tezcatlipoca, the device is also found in many depictions of Huitzilopochtli, at his temples, on his chest, or sometimes even as a foot. Tezcatlipoca carries his round shield with feather balls and paper flags, and Huitzilopochtli has his special shield, the tehuehuelli, which also has feather balls, in this case, down puffs. Nonetheless, down puffs also appear at various places in the array of Tezcatlipoca.[104] In one of the descriptions of Huitzilopochtli's birth, the god emerges with some other attributes of Tezcatlipoca. Perhaps the most striking is the deformed left leg of Tezcatlipoca, who frequently appears with one foot amputated or replaced with a mirror, bird, or animal foot. This is also found in some pictures of Huitzilopochtli. Describing the array of Huitzilopochtli at birth, Sahagún notes the following: "And on his one thin foot, his left, he had the sole pasted with feathers."[105]

While the descriptions of the Panquetzaliztli celebrations suggest that the Mexica supplanted reverence for Tezcatlipoca with Huitzilopochtli, there are other indications of competition between the two gods. We can also see vestiges of an older Tezcatlipoca-focused celebration in the intimate rituals involving the merchants and their bathed slaves. During the ceremonies in the guild house in Tochtepec, after the merchant placed his offerings before the image of the god Yacateuctli and conducted other rituals, he would withdraw to a private room. Depending on how many slaves he planned to offer in the forthcoming sacrifice, the merchant would then decapitate the same number of quail and throw their bodies into the fire.[106] While quail sacrifice was ubiquitous in Mexica rituals, the quail was considered one of the main animals sacrificed to Tezcatlipoca because both the bird and the god were associated with the earth and night.[107]

If Huitzilopochtli became the sun, then the role played by Painal was that of the planet Venus. Just as Venus appears to be the harbinger of the sun in its role as the morning star, so then did Painal, who was the messenger, precede Huitzilopochtli.[108] In fact, in the central ritual of Panquetzaliztli, Painal ran the entire solar circuit, from east to west, then through the underworld and back to the Templo Mayor in anticipation of the arrival of the god Huitzilopochtli. As the messenger or harbinger of the sun, Painal would become Tlahuizcalpanteuctli

(Lord of the Morning Sky) and was associated with Venus as the morning star. As noted above, Quetzalcoatl was also associated with the planet Venus, further complicating the rivalry.

Merchants and Panquetzaliztli—The Military-Commercial Complex

In his description of Panquetzaliztli in Tepepulco, Sahagún notes that the ceremonies resembled those of Tlacaxipehualiztli, the rituals dedicated to the god of regeneration, Xipe Totec. Nonetheless, the two were quite different in that during Panquetzaliztli, the victims were sacrificed in the normal manner by having their hearts cut out of their chests. In addition to heart sacrifice during Tlacaxipehualiztli, victims were flayed, that is, their skin was removed. Yet there is an important similarity between the two festivals, namely, both were celebrations of war and warriors. In both months, large numbers of captive warriors were sacrificed.[109] Panquetzaliztli celebrated the beginning of the war season.[110] But while Panquetzaliztli depended upon the sacrifice of captured warriors from other states, and leading Tenochca warriors took part, merchants also participated in a very public and prominent way.

The generic Panquetzaliztli celebration revolved around the celebration of warfare and the sacrifice of warriors who had been captured in warfare. But in Tenochtitlan, while it was a celebration of war and warriors, and that theme was given primacy in the formal celebrations, the efforts of the warriors were augmented if not eclipsed by the merchants. Certainly, Sahagún leaves the distinct impression that the merchants had become the prime movers of the celebration; they provided most of the funding for the feasts and rituals and served as patrons of many of the sacrificial victims. Nearly all of his narrative meticulously details the rituals and performances of the merchants throughout the month.

The merchants' rise to a status nearly equal to the warriors tells us a great deal about Mexica statecraft. While the Mexica—with their allies, Tetzcoco and Tlacopan—enjoyed great power thanks to their military prowess, the use of merchants as spies, intelligence gatherers, and subversive agents cannot be diminished.[111] As the empire expanded, the merchants also played a crucial role in linking the vast territories through trade while the officials of the state bound the jurisdictions together using tribute and military force. Thus, the very essence of the Mexica Empire linked trade and tribute, merchants and military might. The empire was maintained through an alliance of militarism and statecraft, all supported by the Mexica merchants. In return, the Triple Alliance offered the merchants protection. If a merchant working for the state was captured or killed, the military would seek retribution. The successful merchants were accorded prestige nearly equivalent to that of the most powerful warriors, as is seen in the Panquetzaliztli rituals. In the time of Moteuczoma II, the last years before Spanish arrival, merchants had come to gain a status equal to that of the most seasoned warrior thanks to their statecraft and work as spies and informants. It was even said that the huey tlahtoani considered them like sons: "*in iuhquima ipilhoan quinchioaia*."[112]

As agents of the Triple Alliance, the Mexica were the most important merchants in Mesoamerica. They roamed from the deserts of the northwest to the jungles of Central America. They were the most obvious representatives of the Mexica state in many, many places. Knowing this, the rulers of Tenochtitlan used the long-distance merchants as gatherers of information. The merchants reported on the roads, defenses, and political conditions throughout the region. If an enemy state wished to attack the Mexica, that enemy state could easily capture and kill Mexica merchants. The Mexica used these incidents so many times and over such a wide area that Ross Hassig posits that it was not so much a reason for war as a pretext for war. Such incidents were handy surrogates if the leaders of outlying states wished to send a message of hostility or peace to the Mexica.[113] It should, then, come as no surprise that in Tenochtitlan, the merchants were given a place of importance during the celebration of the month that was dedicated to the Mexica national god, warfare, and the sacrifice of captives of war. By adding the merchants, the Mexica demonstrated that their empire was as much about economics as politics. To manifest this, they packed it all into a religious ceremony.[114]

Merchants, generically, were known as pochtecah (pochtecatl, singular). They were divided up into several categories, including the oztomecah (vanguard merchants), nahualoztomecah (disguised vanguard merchants), teyahualoanimeh (disguised merchants), and tecoanimeh (slave merchants) among others.[115] At the lowest end of the spectrum were individuals who might best be characterized as peddlers, who generally sold their own produce or were limited in their activity to minor purchases and sales within their own neighborhoods. The large-scale religious activities such as those found in Panquetzaliztli were reserved to members of the merchants' guild and only to the leading members at that. The guild was self-governing.[116] There was an expectation that individual merchants would gain positions of increasing authority and responsibility within the civil and religious hierarchy of the guild as they matured. Each position required a greater and greater expenditure in order to provide gifts and banquets for the other members of the guild.[117] Participation in the sacrifices of Panquetzaliztli became an important method whereby an influential merchant could distinguish himself from others and gain access to the highest ranks of the guild.[118] The expenditures served as a method of income redistribution in that the wealthiest merchants spent lavishly on the celebration and gave gifts to hundreds of participants. Yet it was also, perversely, a form of conspicuous consumption. Only the very richest merchants could spend the huge amounts needed to pull off the celebration even though Mexica proverbs admonished the merchants against public displays of their wealth. The merchants' support of the Panquetzaliztli celebrations also assisted the state in imposing its dominance and power. Thus, the merchants' participation clearly demonstrated that they were on a par with the seasoned warriors as twin pillars of the Mexica state.

The preliminary ceremonies of Panquetzaliztli had the effect of drawing the warriors and merchants together since the latter put on banquets to honor all participants in the ceremonies. This activity would have reinforced whatever political and social ties already existed between the two groups. The merchants also gave lavish gifts to warriors and others in the days leading up to the final sacrifice, thus participating in some income redistribution. Yet it is also quite possible that the warriors continued to feel some animosity toward the merchants. After all, the merchants had only become an active part of statecraft, at least partially supplanting the military, by the mid-fifteenth century, which was fairly recent. Consequently, the festivities of Panquetzaliztli as practiced in Tenochtitlan might have also been a method of defusing possible antagonism between the two groups just as the Chonchayotl battles could appease the students of the calmecac and the telpochcalli.[119]

In a somewhat subtler way, the route of the Swiftness of Huitzilopochtli, at least as recorded by Sahagún, also reflects this alliance between the warriors and the merchants. After the sacrifices at the divine ball court in Tenochtitlan, the runner carrying Huitzilopochtli first went to the city of Tlatelolco. As noted earlier, Tlatelolco had begun its existence as an independent city-state, occupying an island adjacent to Tenochtitlan. Some of the leadership of Tlatelolco had come from among the merchant groups, and the city was the center for trade in the Central Basin. But in 1473, the Tenochca, under huey tlahtoani Axayacatl, declared war on their sister state of Tlatelolco, ultimately defeating it. Nonetheless, it was necessary to cultivate close ties with the Tlatelolcan leaders, especially with the long-distance merchants. Thus, they came to have a place of great importance during the celebrations of Panquetzaliztli.

The central role of the merchants in Sahagún's description of the ceremonies and rituals can also be attributed to the fact that many of the friar's informants resided in the merchant quarter in Tlatelolco, where the Franciscan college and friary were located. While the College of the Holy Cross, Colegio de la Santa Cruz, drew young men from throughout the colony, it was heavily influenced by its neighborhood. Thus, living and working in Tlatelolco, Sahagún came to draw more heavily on the recollections and experiences of that neighborhood's residents, who may well have been more closely associated with the merchants than any other social group.

The merchants were not subject to the same tribute system as commoners. In addition to other privileges largely secured after the defeat of Tlatelolco in 1473, merchants gave large gifts to the huey tlahtoani instead of paying tribute. This also included direct financial support for the solar-year festivals. Consequently, the merchants' important role in Panquetzaliztli could also be a sign of their financial support for the state and for one of the most important religious ceremonies of the year.[120]

Tribute Payment at Panquetzaliztli

The month of Panquetzaliztli was one of the four times a year in which tributary states of the Triple Alliance were required to present their payments to their overlords. The other months were Tlacaxipehualiztli, Etzalcualiztli, and Ochpaniztli. The placement of these dates in the solar year was important because they corresponded to periods in the agricultural cycle. This created a sequence of payments alternating between eighty and one hundred days. The timing was such that it also guaranteed that representatives of the subject states would witness some of the most impressive and grisly celebrations of the Mexica ritual calendar.

Tlacaxipehualiztli (the Flaying of Men), the second month of the solar year, fell in the hot dry season of the Central Basin in late March, near the beginning of the spring planting season. Symbolically, the central ritual, wherein victims were sacrificed and then had their skin removed to be worn by a priest, represented the earth taking on its new verdure in the spring. Unlike many months, where the rituals of the month built up to a final culminating celebration, as in Panquetzaliztli, Tlacaxipehualiztli's sacrifices occurred at the beginning of the month, allowing the priests and warriors to celebrate other rituals throughout the month while wearing the skin of the victims.[121]

Etzalcualiztli (Eating of Beans) was the sixth month. As the name of the month indicates, it was the time when the first fruits of the season would be harvested in

June, ending roughly near the summer solstice. Eating a porridge made from the first corn and beans for the season was a central ritual of the month. Many captured warriors were sacrificed in honor of the rain god, Tlaloc. Their bodies were then thrown into the whirlpool that was frequently active in Lake Tetzcoco. During the festival, priests who had transgressed did their penance through ritual bathing. Those who had seriously violated priestly norms were nearly drowned and left for dead.[122]

The eleventh month was Ochpaniztli (Sweeping), and it fell in late September and early October. Thus, it was closely associated with the fall harvest. The month was dedicated to Toci and was celebrated with ritual bathing, sweeping, and human sacrifice. The highlight was the sacrifice of a god impersonator (ixiptla) of the goddess, who was then flayed, and a young man would wear her skin. He then led four sacrificial victims to the Templo Mayor, and many more captives were sacrificed. The emperor also greeted new warriors and invested them with the insignia of their rank.[123]

As has been seen, in Panquetzaliztli, the ceremonies revolved around the sacrifice of captive warriors and slaves in what some have indicated were prodigious amounts. It also marked the celebration of the mythic birth of Huitzilopochtli and was a commemoration of both the Mexica migration and their rise to power under the guidance of their national god. Thus, it was a particularly appropriate time to invite representatives of subject states to witness the symbolic celebration of Mexica history and prowess. Furthermore, it marked the absolute end of the agricultural season: the end of the harvest and the conclusion of field preparations for the winter fallow. With the closing of the agricultural cycle, the period for warfare began, dictated by the absence of rain and the availability of manpower that was not actively engaged in agriculture.[124] Taken as a group, these four months represented important moments in the agricultural and ecological calendar. Three of the four, Tlacaxipehualiztli, Etzalcualiztli, and Ochpaniztli, marked important moments in the planting and harvesting cycle. Panquetzaliztli stood outside that group since it corresponded to the dead of winter.

The tribute delivery cycle also took into account the fact that different crops ripened and developed at different times in different places. Scattering the tribute payments throughout the year maximized the supply to Tenochtitlan and drew on a wide variety of products. Many of the tribute items were not agricultural but manufactured goods, such as cloth, blankets, and armor. Thus, the distribution of their collection around the calendar also smoothed out the supply to the Aztecs and gave the subject people an opportunity to stagger their manufacture, spreading it out over a longer period.

It is possible that the Mexica adopted the tribute payment schedule from their predecessors. The leadership role of the Mexica in the Alliance was of fairly recent origin, since, for at least a century, until the defeat of the Tepaneca of Azcapotzalco in 1427, they themselves had been tributaries, not overlords. There are indications that under the Tepaneca, subject cities brought in their tribute on a rolling basis, whenever crops were ripe and the manufacture of goods completed. Tetzcoco, for example, paid tribute to the Tepaneca on a semiannual basis, while Cuauhnahuac, for its part, paid tribute to Tetzcoco six times yearly. It was not until the reign of Moteuczoma II that the new quarterly schedule was implemented.[125]

The tribute payment system had deep roots in the Central Basin, which the Aztecs merely tapped into. The Aztecs might have enhanced this tribute-payment schedule by developing even more symbolic and imposing ceremonies when tributaries were known to be arriving in the city. Quite simply, the schedule, whatever its origins, offered a moment in which the Aztecs could impress and cow their tributaries through a show of power: military, financial, and divine. The celebrations of Panquetzaliztli were just one means of vividly demonstrating the power, authority, and ultimate terror of Huitzilopochtli and his chosen people.[126]

The arrival of foreign dignitaries in Tenochtitlan was not an uncommon event. Thus, they might have entered the city ahead of their tlamama (porters) carrying the tribute. It is possible, however, that these leaders were given the cloak of anonymity by being allowed to dress as locals. This occurred during the accession ceremonies when Ahuitzotl became huey tlahtoani, which Durán describes. Writing about the leaders from enemy states—Tlaxcala, Huejotzinco, and Chollolan—the friar says, "Their customary garments were changed in favor of those of the Aztecs [*sic*] and, in order to disguise them further, they were made to hold flowers, branches, and rushes, as though they were men who were coming to adorn the temple and the royal house." After the tribute had been presented, the sacrifices ensued. The result was that "the guests, seeing such wealth and opulence and such authority and power, were filled with terror."[127] During the reign of Moteuczoma II, leaders of these enemy states were invited three to four times a year to witness specific celebrations, one of which was the Panquetzaliztli festival, in addition to the tribute delivery days.[128]

Conclusions—Rewriting History

One of the more dramatic events in Mexica history occurred following the defeat of the Tepaneca of Azcapotzalco by the Mexica and their allies, which established the basis for the hegemony of the Triple Alliance. In the wake of that victory, the new huey tlahtoani, Itzcoatl, destroyed some of the old histories and painted manuscripts.[129] While the details of the book burning are lost to the mists of time, the consensus among modern scholars is that the event marked a turning point in Mexica culture. What had begun as a migrating group of hunters and gathers had become a powerful city-state. The Mexica credited the efficacy of their god Huitzilopochtli for this success and rise to power . As Durán summarizes it, "This vocation of war had been given to them by their god Huitzilopochtli, who promised them his favor and assistance."[130] In keeping with their new status as the leading power of the Central Basin, the Mexica drew an end to their earlier time, destroyed some of their records, and stepped into a new and dominant role.[131]

Part and parcel of this new status was the elevation of Huitzilopochtli to the status of supreme deity. Just as the Mexica had come to dominate the other Nahuatl-speaking groups of the Central Basin, Huitzilopochtli came to dominate the pantheon of Nahua deities. As part of this process, many of the roles and celebrations that had been ascribed to Tezcatlipoca were now given to Huitzilopochtli, the most important of which were the celebrations associated with the month of Panquetzaliztli.

CHAPTER 6

LOOKING AT HISTORY THROUGH PANQUETZALIZTLI

Looking at the celebration of Panquetzaliztli, it is clear that over the course of time, many features of the celebration changed. The festival in all likelihood began as a celebration of war and was dedicated to Tezcatlipoca. The rituals as described in Tenochtitlan exhibited many details that were absent in other places. High among these was the nearly central role played by the merchants. The festival also became a focal point of power and authority that the Mexica, in turn, required tributaries to attend. Indeed, the festival took on such importance that the celebration of the New Fire ceremony, that is, the binding of the years that took place once every fifty-two years, was moved in order to coincide with the celebration of Panquetzaliztli. Yet, while these changes can be documented or extracted from the accounts and narratives, there are no clear indications as to precisely when these changes occurred. This chapter will consider the changes and evaluate the probable moments in which they were implemented in Tenochtitlan or will at least point to the historical precedents that inspired them.

Mexica Innovations

The dedication of the Panquetzaliztli celebrations to Huitzilopochtli coincided with the rise of the Triple Alliance. As noted earlier, the preexisting celebrations focused on Tezcatlipoca as the god of war. Because the month fell at the beginning of the long dry period of Mesoamerican winter, it was also a traditional time of warfare. Thus, the dedication of that month to a war god makes perfect sense.

The Mexica have been credited with various innovations to the preexisting Nahua culture, especially after their rise as part of the Triple Alliance. When the Mexica first entered the Central Basin of Mexico, they discovered a densely settled city-based political structure. As weak newcomers, they eventually became subservient to Azcapotzalco. Azcapotzalco, the altepetl of the Tepaneca people, had been the most important city-state of the Central Basin of Mexico for many years, with both Tetzcoco and Tenochtitlan subject to it. Nonetheless, those latter two cities allied themselves, along with renegade Tepaneca of Tlacopan, in order to confront Azcapotzalco. The uprising was successful, and the victors used their alliance to conquer other, smaller cities of the Central Basin, including Xochimilco, Cuitlahuac, and finally Chalco.[1]

After defeating their longtime overlords of Azcapotzalco, the Mexica rulers Itzcoatl and Moteuczoma I, with the advice of their kinsman Tlacaelel, initiated a widespread series of political and religious reforms to consolidate power. This moment of victory was also celebrated by the famous, though possibly apocryphal, burning of records by Itzcoatl sometime after 1427. The destruction provided the Mexica leadership with the opportunity to rewrite history.[2] It also allowed them to modify other things, like the calendar and religious ceremonies, while creating a new narrative regarding their rise to power.

Preconquest Central Mexican civilizations generally considered that the world had gone through three creations and destructions and that the current existence of the world was the fourth. The number four was powerful, relating to the four cardinal directions. Many groups had four (or a multiple of four) calpolli. Yet the Mexica modified this very traditional view of existence to insist that the world was in its fifth creation and that they were the de facto rulers of that epoch. Their cosmology held that there had been four incomplete and defective previous creations of the world. Each of these creations was called a sun, had been governed by a calendrical sign and deity, and had ended with a cataclysm. The length of each of these previous epochs was a number of years divisible by fifty-two—that is, periods between New Fire ceremonies, also known as the xiuhmolpilli (binding of the years), which marked completed calendrical cycles. This also implied that the current epoch would end at the completion of some yet-undetermined period. In the traditional cosmology inherited by the Mexica, each of the three previous epochs had lasted 676 years (thirteen cycles of fifty-two years), for a total of 2,028 years. When they modified the system, the Mexica kept the total at 2,028 but simply divided one of the previous epochs roughly in half so that one had six cycles and the other had seven.[3]

Ending the suns at the completion of a fifty-two-year cycle placed great emphasis on the New Fire ceremony because it marked the end of a way of life after a sufficient number of years had passed. Prior to the Mexica, the end of the world was predictable: it fell after thirteen cycles. But when the Mexica divided one cycle into two unequal parts, it set up a situation in which no one knew exactly when the end might come. Under the four-sun regimen, one could assume that the fourth sun would end after it completed thirteen bindings of the years, just as the previous three had. Adding a fifth sun and changing the length of two of the epochs added a great deal of uncertainty into the system. Although previous suns had ended after six, seven, or thirteen bindings, the doubt remained that any given binding of the years might bring the final cataclysm that would destroy the sun. This also meant that it was an especially important time to sacrifice in order to nourish the gods to assure that the cycle of days and years continued.

Further investigations into this cosmology have indicated that the reform probably occurred nearer to Spanish arrival rather than early in the rise of the Mexica. The cosmology had not yet taken on a canonical form early on. Some of the accounts collected after the conquest note that the middle two suns were the shortened ones; others report that the last two suns prior to the current age were short. The different accounts also mention different deities as ruling the four epochs. They only agree on the contemporary epoch, ruled by Nahui Ollin (Four Movement). Two well-known sculptures of the Mexica bear that image: the Sunstone, popularly known as the Aztec Calendar, and the piece known as the Temple of the Sacred War. For a variety of reasons, scholars have assigned both of these to the reign of Moteuczoma II. Consequently, the conclusion is that the innovation from four suns to five dates from the reign of the last huey tlahtoani, Moteuczoma II (1502–20).[4]

One of the legends, collected by Sahagún, further helps to explain some of the tensions that are present in the ceremonies of Panquetzaliztli and the importance of nourishing the gods in the binding of the years. The story of the fifth sun's creation at Teotihuacan and of the competition between Tecuciztecatl and Nanahuatzin also sets the example of the gods sacrificing themselves for the creation of the sun. In return, humans needed to sacrifice to nourish the gods in order to keep the sun in its course. On a metaphorical and symbolic level, this story has come to provide many insights into Mexica thought.

Huitzilopochtli

The rise of the Mexica as part of the Triple Alliance also allowed them to insert Huitzilopochtli into the traditional stories. Huitzilopochtli came to take a more important role in civic and religious life under the Mexica. Miguel León-Portilla posits that the primacy of Huitzilopochtli and the effort to raise him above all other Nahua gods was a policy formulated by the famous royal adviser Tlacaelel beginning after the Triple Alliance's victory. The supremacy of Huitzilopochtli was secured with the defeat of Azcapotzalco.[5]

Beyond what has been outlined above, there was a religious aspect to the war with Azcapotzalco, which can be seen in an event that occurred just prior to the outbreak of the war. The Mexica had been so worn down and overburdened by their Tepaneca overlords that, as a final gesture of submission in order to improve their lot, they handed the image of Huitzilopochtli over to the control of the Tepaneca. On the one hand, it symbolized abject subjugation. But on the other hand, Durán suggests, putting it in a positive light, that the very presence of Huitzilopochtli might "put fear and terror into the hearts of those people [the Tepaneca]."[6] The close relationship of a people with their patron deity was clearly a part of statecraft in the Central Basin of Mexico in the fifteenth century. Consequently, upon the rise of the Mexica, the logical corollary was to then place their god in a superior position over the patron deities of their subject polities.

The rise of the imperial cult of the Mexica in relation to their strategy has been the focus of much research over the last half century. León-Portilla advanced thinking greatly when he focused on the religious and political reforms instituted under Itzcoatl, Moteuczoma I, and Tlacaelel. These reforms linked the solar deity (Tonatiuh) with Huitzilopochtli. In order to nourish the sun, prodigious amounts of blood were required through human sacrifice. At the same time, the Mexica attributed some if not all aspects of the solar deity to Huitzilopochtli. In order to provide the victims that were needed to nourish the sun, a strong and aggressive military was required, which would, in turn, extend the dominion of the god. This resulted in the initiation of the *Xochiyaotl*, or *in xochitl in yaotl* (Flower War), in which participants vied to capture their foes on the field of battle. Tlacaelel characterized the field of battle as a marketplace where Huitzilopochtli could get his desired food, and he compared the sacrificial victims to "hot maize cakes from the griddle—tortillas from a nearby place." These captured warriors would be offered to nourish Huitzilopochtli, "as though he were eating warm breads, soft and tasty, straight out of the oven."[7] One can argue that one of the effects of this policy was to shift Panquetzaliztli into a month dedicated to Huitzilopochtli rather than Tezcatlipoca. This is also crucial to our understanding of the celebration of the month because of the importance of large-scale human sacrifice, which propitiated the gods but was also as a tool of terror against potential foes. Thus, the month of Panquetzaliztli celebrated warfare and also provided a physical manifestation of Mexica might and power.

Huitzilopochtli did not completely dominate the calendar. On the one hand, he appeared in several of the veintena (monthlong feasts), such as Toxcatl and Panquetzaliztli, but he did not appear as one of the deities in the tonalpohualli (the 260-day ritual calendar) or as one of the Lords of the Day or Night in the trecena almanacs.[8] While the various religious reforms of the Mexica potentially began some seventy years prior to Spanish arrival, clearly they had not all pervaded the religious and calendrical system. Thus, Huitzilopochtli had come to reign supreme among Mexica deities and had been granted lordship in several of the monthlong festivals of the xiuhpohualli but had not broken into the ritual calendar. This is clear from his absence among the lords of the hours in the days and night of that calendar.

Perhaps there was no greater symbol of Huitzilopochtli's power and dominance in the Mexica world than the Templo Mayor itself. The imposing structure occupied the very center of the Mexica world. The sanctuaries atop this structure were dedicated to Huitzilopochtli and Tlaloc, as they were in Tlatelolco, the Mexica's other city on the central island. These deities represented the two essential elements needed for life: Tlaloc was the god of rain while Huitzilopochtli came to represent the sun. At their very core, the Mexica identified themselves with Huitzilopochtli, and their rise saw a rise in the importance of their deity. He became the embodiment of their power. Throughout their artistic production, from about 1460 onward, the Mexica depicted Huitzilopochtli more and more as the superior god and replacement for Tezcatlipoca.[9]

The Merchants and Civil War with Tlatelolco

Not all colonial observers report the merchants' participation in the extensive Panquetzaliztli celebrations. Durán is silent on the issue and does not even report that the Swiftness of Huitzilopochtli went to Tlatelolco, the area most clearly associated with the merchants. Sahagún, however, gives his fullest description of the Panquetzaliztli ceremonies in conjunction with the merchants' participation. It is nearly impossible to discover the cause of this discrepancy. Nonetheless, Durán collected much of his information in Tetzcoco, not in Tenochtitlan, and thus his informants might not have been as intimately aware of all the nuances associated with the celebration. Likewise, Sahagún was living in the Franciscan monastery in Tlatelolco when he interviewed elders and others about preconquest traditions.

Thus, he had a larger concentration of individuals with intimate knowledge of that particular part of the ceremony. Lastly, it is possible that the participation of the merchants was a late addition to the overall celebration of Panquetzaliztli, and thus only those intimately associated with its rites and rituals would recall it.

We might imagine that merchant participation was probably added after the defeat of Tlatelolco by Tenochtitlan in a civil war in 1473 as a means of placating the leadership of the defeated altepetl. The Tlatelolco war was a turning point in relations between the two altepeme, and repercussions continued for decades to come, if the ceremonies of Panquetzaliztli bear witness. The war pitted the twin cities of Tenochtitlan and Tlatelolco against one another. These two altepeme were both founded by the original Mexica migrants who, according to legend, had left Aztlan and were later adopted by Huitzilopochtli. Upon finally settling on deserted islands in the middle of the lake in the Central Basin of Mexico, they formed two city-states. Tlatelolco, as has been noted, was the home to the merchants (pochtecah). Because they were both descendants of a single tribal group, the leadership of the two cities was closely related by marriage. In the early 1470s, the tlahtoani of Tlatelolco was the brother-in-law of Tenochtitlan's huey tlahtoani.

Ostensibly, the civil war began as a fight between the two ruling houses. In some accounts, the ruler of Tlatelolco, Moquihuix, was married to the older sister of the Tenochtitlan's ruler, Axayacatl. The latter was a member of the imperial clan, a grandson of Moteuczoma I and great-nephew of Itzcoatl. Axayacatl's election came as a surprise to many since he was relatively young at the time, about twenty, and had at least two elder brothers who were passed over in his election, though the brothers, Tizoc and Ahuitzotl, would eventually become rulers of the altepetl. At the time of Axayacatl's election, the Mexica elders approached Tlacaelel to see whether he was interested in serving as ruler, and he politely declined.[10]

In the lead-up to the civil war, Axayacatl protested his sister's treatment at Moquihuix's hands. According to other sources, some young men of Tenochtitlan abducted and raped some girls from Tlatelolco. This required Moquihuix to protest to the ruler in Tenochtitlan. Regardless of the actual triggering event, the war seems to have been manufactured by the Tenochca. As these two triggering incidents reflect, though, it became highly charged with a sexual symbolism.[11] It also occurred shortly after the death of the tlahtoani of Tetzcoco, Nezahualcoyotl, whom many describe as the arbiter of disputes among Triple Alliance members. The death of the Tetzcocan leader closed one pathway to a peaceful resolution of whatever disputes may have arisen between Tenochtitlan and Tlatelolco.[12]

Nonetheless, after formally declaring war on his kinsman, Axayacatl led troops into the neighboring city-state. The two sides engaged in some limited skirmishes, after which each party sent a messenger seeking a resolution to the hostilities. Durán suggests that the Tlatelolca sought allies from outside the Central Basin, from Tlaxcala or Huejotzinco.[13]

When the preliminary advances, skirmishes, and attempts to seek allies or mediation were all completed, the battle was joined. The Tlatelolca advanced, probably seeking control of the Templo Mayor of Tenochtitlan, the symbolic heart of the city. But the Tenochca parried the attack and pushed their foes all the way to the great market of Tlatelolco. Then the Tlatelolca launched one of the most curious of all offenses. The women of Tlatelolco disrobed and ran naked through the streets of the twin cities, distracting the Tenochca warriors. Some expressed breast milk and sprinkled it on their foes. Naked boys, with their faces painted black and feathers in their hair, followed the women, seeking to confuse and disrupt the invaders. These extraordinary measures were to no avail, and the Tenochca captured the Templo Mayor of Tlatelolco and threw Moquihuix to his death.[14]

In the aftermath of the war, the Tlatelolca were subjected to a military ruler and were forced to pay tribute to their sister city. They were prohibited from having a sanctuary for their tribal god, Huitzilopochtli, on their Templo Mayor, though it should be repeated that the Tlatelolca shared the deity with Tenochtitlan since all were equally Mexica. The Tenochca also subjected the Tlatelolca to other indignities.[15] Yet this harsh treatment had the potential to undermine the integrity of Tlatelolco and interfered with the success of the merchants who made up the principal classes of the city. The harsh military rule was replaced by a more benign approach. The city was still under the control of a military governor, but the merchants were accorded positions of honor. In the aftermath of the war, the merchants were used even more extensively as an extension of the military in foreign campaigns, and the city was relieved of its tribute responsibilities. Now it merely needed to provide "gifts" to the huey tlahtoani of Tenochtitlan and to defray the costs of the monthly feasts and festivals of the solar calendar.[16]

The civil war is one of the most curious events of Mexica history. The traditional accounts explain it in rather personal terms: a family feud, insults of one polity against the other, disputes caused by two groups living in close proximity with one another. But there was undoubtedly an underlying cause for the hostility. This probably had to do with the Tlatelolcan merchants' role in alliance statecraft. While the merchants were ethnically Mexica, they were not directly subject to the Tenochca Mexica huey tlahtoani, the person generally recognized as the primus inter pares of the leadership of the Triple Alliance. The chronicles tell of situations in which Tlatelolco pursued its own diplomatic and military policy, not always in accord with that of Tenochtitlan. Thus, it seems reasonable that, shortly after having acceded to the Tenochca throne, Axayacatl decided to bring the whole of the Mexica polity directly under his rule and abolish the political independence of Tlatelolco.[17]

Emily Umberger proposes an equally plausible explanation. Looking at the narrative and pictorial accounts of the war, she proposes that the Tenochca attacked the Tlatelolca in order to punish them for an expansive building campaign, one part of which was the expansion and embellishment of the Tlatelolca Templo Mayor. As in Tenochtitlan, the Templo Mayor was the physical representation of Coatepec, the mythical place of Huitzilopochtli's birth. It would have been an intolerable insult to the Tenochca to have their brothers and sisters in Tlatelolco claim to have the "true" Coatepec, housing the "true" Huitzilopochtli. In the aftermath of the war, the Tlatelolca Huitzilopochtli was removed and probably installed in the temple of the Huitznahuac neighborhood of Tenochtitlan, since the *Codex Mendoza* notes that the upkeep of that temple fell to the merchants.[18] Thus, the battle at the end of the Swiftness of Huitzilopochtli, in which the sacrificial victims battle the Huitznahua, could also be a symbolic replication of the defeat of the Tlatelolca by the Tenochca. The Tlatelolca Templo Mayor was ordered destroyed, and the great market came to occupy some of its space. We thus might well explain the civil war as an attempt on the part of the Tenochca to assert their Templo Mayor as the true and only Coatepec. Umberger also notes that the actions of Axayacatl in defeating Moquihuix have a striking similarity to Huitzilopochtli's defeat of Coyolxauhqui and her brothers, paralleling the mythic events of Coatepec.[19] This interpretation is also consistent with the depiction of the event in the *Codex Mendoza,* which shows Moquihuix falling from atop the Templo Mayor (we assume of Tlatelolco) as Coyolxauqui was thrown from Coatepec. The *Codex Mendoza* also depicts the sanctuaries on top of the temple on fire, a symbol of military defeat.[20] We must note that by the time of Spanish arrival in 1519, Tlatelolco had regained its Templo Mayor. The conquistadores describe it, and it was the last refuge of the Mexica defenders during the conquest.

Because of the critical role played by the merchants as spies and vanguard informants, the rulers of Tenochtitlan needed to keep the merchants in their good graces. Thus, in a revision of the Panquetzaliztli rituals, leading merchants were called upon to play a significant role, right behind that of the most important warriors. The merchants, of course, also got to spend time with the warriors and ruling elite during all the preparations and banquets that preceded the final sacrificial rituals.[21]

One additional bit of assistance in dating possible changes to Panquetzaliztli is the reference that during their preparations for the ceremonies, the merchant-bathers travelled to Tochtepec to the guild house to perform certain rituals. As a member of the Triple Alliance, the Tetzcocan leader Nezahualcoyotl (ruling circa 1420–72) conquered this region of what is now the State of Veracruz. Depending on which source is to be believed, the area came under Mexica control under either Moteuczoma I (ruling 1440–69) or Axayacatl (ruling 1469–81). The best evidence points to conquest in around 1455, probably under Nezahualcoyotl or possibly Moteuczoma I.[22] This, however, does not mean that forces did not have to return to that frontier from time to time to reconquer or reestablish Aztec dominance. While the conquistadores do not mention it as a trading outpost, it did have an Aztec garrison of some significance by the time of Spanish arrival.[23] Consequently, the pilgrimage of the merchant-bathers to Tochtepec had to have begun after 1455, and was probably much later.

The New Fire Ceremony

One important way in which the Panquetzaliztli celebrations of Tenochtitlan differed from those in other regions and from the celebrations in early Nahua history was their coincidence with the New Fire ceremony.[24] In order to better understand the nature of the ceremony and its importance in Nahua thought and religion, we must look again at the very nature of the xihuitl, the vague or solar year.

The xihuitl consisted of eighteen months of twenty days each; five days, called the nemontemi, were left over each year and were generally considered to be unlucky. Because the solar calendar contained 365 days and the actual length of the solar year is approximately 365.25 days, the solar calendar would slowly move through the seasons. European calendars solved this problem through the addition of leap days. Scholars have sought to discover whether the Nahua had the equivalent of leap days or whether the calendar continued to slide through the seasons. Scholars have also wondered whether the calendar was periodically brought back into line using some mechanism other than leap days. Several leading scholars believe that there was such a process, but it is unclear how it operated. Nonetheless, looking at all the months of the year, and the ceremonies associated with each, there is a clear indication that the months were tied to the seasons.

Toxcatl marked the end of the spring dry season. Etzalcualiztli celebrated the first fruits and was when corn and bean porridges were made. Panquetzaliztli marked the end of the harvest in the fall and the beginning of the dry period of early winter.[25]

Using both the xiuhpohualli and the tonalpohualli, the Mexica kept track of years within the larger fifty-two-year cycle by naming them according to the date in the 260-day calendar on which the specific solar calendar year began, and that date was called a year bearer. Because of the mathematics, only four of the symbols would appear as year bearers. These were Rabbit, Reed, Flint, and House. The cycle of years traditionally started with 1 Rabbit, followed by the next year of 2 Reed, 3 Flint, 4 House, and then 5 Rabbit, etc. This scheme also meant that the fifty-two-year period was divided into four thirteen-year periods, each starting with a year one: 1 Rabbit, 1 Reed, 1 Flint, and 1 House.

The New Fire ceremony, when the xiuhpohualli and the tonalpohualli calendars again came into initial alignment, was an important festival marked by human sacrifice and other rituals destined to assure the continuation of the calendar and the movement of the sun. The details of the New Fire ceremony are particularly evocative.[26] In anticipation of the ceremony, all fires throughout the Central Basin of Mexico were extinguished. Women cleaned their homes thoroughly. Old clothing and household utensils were discarded. On the night of the ceremony, sacrificial victims were taken to a hill in the Central Basin of Mexico a few miles east of the Templo Mayor named Huixachtepetl or Huixachtitlan ("Hill of the Thorn Tree" or "Beside the Thorn Tree"; it is now known as Cerro de la Estrella). The ceremony was to be conducted when the Pleiades reached their zenith in the local sky. In a small temple at the summit of the hill, the fire priest and four assistants placed the victim on the sacrificial stone. This was a special victim, generally someone well born who had been captured in battle and who had a name that contained the word *xihuitl*. At the appointed moment, the priest thrust the obsidian dagger into the victim's chest, cut it open, and removed the still-beating heart.[27]

The priest, too, was specified. According to custom, he was the chief priest of the temple to Huitzilopochtli found in the neighborhood of Tzonmolco (also known as Copolco). This was one of the traditional neighborhoods of the merchants.[28] The priest then quickly took a fire-starting bow and kindled a flame in the chest cavity of the victim. Spectators throughout the valley strained their eyes to see when the flame emerged, thus ushering in a new calendar cycle and guaranteeing the rising of the sun once again. Also participating in the ceremony was a group of ixiptlahuan in costumes of the major deities: Quetzalcoatl, Tlaloc, and others. This group was called the Teunenemi (Teonehnemi, "Walking gods").[29] These are depicted in the *Codex Borbonicus* (see plate 13).

According to Sahagún and others, five days of preparation (the nemontemi) preceded the New Fire ceremony. As noted above, in most early-colonial discussions, these days, also called "useless days," were not formally part of any month but were required to fill out the count of days each year. They fell at the end of one solar year before the beginning of the next.[30] The ceremonial observances of the nemontemi began with a general housecleaning, during which people threw out rubbish, got rid of broken pottery, and discarded old images of deities in wood or stone as well as the three stones used to elevate pots in the hearth. All fires were extinguished, and families had to eat cold food for the five days. On the night of the sacrifice and the kindling of the new fire, women and children donned maguey-leaf masks. Women were locked away in granaries. Children were also confined to their homes and were forced to stay awake through the night. A legend was told that children who fell asleep would be transformed into mice. Everyone performed small acts of penance, pricking their ears to draw drops of blood. Adult males then climbed to their rooftops to watch for the first glimmer of light from the new fire.[31]

Once the new fire was kindled, the fire priest lit a large torch from which fire was then passed through the ritual cohort. One runner took up the flame and ran as quickly as possible to the temple of Huitzilopochtli on the Templo Mayor. After the fires were started on the Templo Mayor, runners with torches passed throughout the city and valley, spreading the new fire to everyone. Messenger runners stood by to carry the fire to outlying settlements, using the relay posts set up to foster communication in the empire.[32] The people received the fire, lit their hearths, and engaged in small personal rituals. As before, each person cut his or her earlobe for a bit of blood. Even babies had their earlobes cut. Then everyone ate a bit of amaranth-dough cake.[33]

Several elements of the New Fire ceremony are consistent with elements found in the ceremonies of Panquetzaliztli. Central to both was the performance of a runner. In the veintena feast, the runner followed a circuit in the valley carrying a dough image of the god. In the New Fire, he carried the newly kindled fire from Huixachtepetl to the Templo Mayor, where others picked it up and distributed it throughout the city. Both rituals symbolically celebrated the birth of the sun. In Panquetzaliztli, it was the victory of the sun over the forces of darkness. In the New Fire, it was the celebration of the start of a new calendar cycle, perhaps using sympathetic magic to move the heavens along. Both rituals featured the power of fire. In the New Fire, it was the single most important element and the focus of the celebration. In Panquetzaliztli, fire was used to purify the sacrificial victims as they witnessed the burning of the ritual paper and then walked by the burning brazier as they ascended the temple. Lastly, both ceremonies focused on sacrificial victims. In the case of the Panquetzaliztli ritual, between one hundred and two hundred victims were killed. In the New Fire, though all attention was focused on one victim, in all likelihood, many others were also sacrificed.

The New Fire ceremony had an effect of aligning the cosmic and terrestrial powers at a specific moment in time. One way of thinking of it was that the stars came into alignment. Directly under the Pleiades, the fire was kindled, creating a vertical axis of power. Then the fire was distributed horizontally by means of the runners, bringing the horizontal plane into alignment with the vertical. The whole cosmos was then infused with power, the locus of which was the flame in the chest of the sacrificial victim.[34]

Sources (written, pictorial, and sculptural) from the Central Basin of Mexico uniformly record 2 Reed as the year in which the New Fire ceremony occurred. Nonetheless, the designation of 2 Reed as the date for the celebration of the New Fire ceremony was an odd choice. Since the essence of the ceremony was to mark the completion of the fifty-two-year cycle of the tonalpohualli and the xiuhpohualli and the beginning of another, logically this would have occurred between the end of each of the component calendar cycles and the beginning of the next cycle for both. Consequently, it should occur on a day numbered one in the tonalpohualli, specifically 1 Rabbit, 1 Reed, 1 Flint, or 1 House, since they were the year bearers. Many neighboring cultures used the date of 1 Rabbit for the day of the ceremony.[35] Yet, for the Mexica, it fell on the ritual day of 2 Reed. This strongly indicates that the Mexica changed the date of the ceremony for some reason. They seem to have moved the date of the celebration an entire ritual year. One explanation has been that 1 Rabbit recalled a previous year of that name that suffered a deep and devastating famine.[36] Whatever the cause, it is clear that by the time of Spanish arrival, the New Fire ceremony had become inextricably associated with the month of Panquetzaliztli and was held in a year designated 2 Reed.[37]

Looking at the xiuhpohualli, we would assume that the celebration of the New Fire ceremony would occur at the end of one year and the beginning of another. This would have meant that the ceremony would fall at the end of the nameless days, the nemontemi, or on the first day of the New Year, the first day of Atl cahualo (the Ceasing of Water). But as noted above, by the early sixteenth century, it occurred in the month of Panquetzaliztli, the fifteenth of eighteen months, not in the spring but at the onset of winter. The sixteenth-century observers offer no explanation for this odd occurrence. Nor does this shift seem to be related to the presence or absence of leap days that might have kept the xihuitl coordinated with the solar year and the changing seasons.[38]

Lacking a simple or mechanical explanation for the move of the New Fire ceremony from February/March to December, one might assume that the ceremony was tied to an important astronomical event. Indeed, Sahagún writes that the ceremony occurred when the Pleiades had reached its zenith. Hassig points out that holding the New Fire ceremony at the end/beginning of the xiuhpohualli is incompatible with timing it with the Pleiades at zenith. The constellation reaches zenith in the late fall or early winter, not in the early spring, when the Mexica calendar is believed to have begun.[39] Yet, by celebrating it between late November and mid-to-late December, the Pleiades could be the central celestial marking event. As it turns out, the month of Panquetzaliztli generally occurred within a few weeks of the winter solstice, which falls routinely around December 21 in the Gregorian calendar. Thus, it would occur near the nadir of the sun's progress, the point at which it appears to be lowest in the sky, and corresponds also to the zenith of the Pleiades.[40]

The move of the New Fire from 1 Rabbit to 2 Reed was a response to one set of variables. A second series of arguments is needed to explain moving the ceremony to December. Quite simply, this allowed the Mexica to take advantage of proximity to the winter solstice and preexisting celebrations that had formerly been dedicated to Tezcatlipoca and then to appropriate all the symbolism inherent in that month to their national god, Huitzilopochtli. Most of the descriptions of Panquetzaliztli note that the month was a celebration of Huitzilopochtli. The Mexica, in modifying the calendar and moving the New Fire, proclaimed their support of their national god as the supreme solar deity.[41]

Moving the New Fire Ceremony to Panquetzaliztli also helps to explain why the *Codex Borgia* illustration for that month stands in such distinct contrast to the illustrations found in other manuscripts in the native style. Quite simply, the page does not illustrate the Panquetzaliztli celebration at all. It is a picture of the New Fire ceremony, which was celebrated in conjunction with the month. The central actor on the page is Quetzalcoatl, in keeping with the important role he plays in the rest of the manuscript. He performs the New Fire ritual in the chest cavity of Xiuhteuctli, the god of fire. The figures in the temples on either side would thus be Quetzalcoatl and Tezcatlipoca rather than Xiuhteuctli and Tezcatlipoca, as Milbrath claims.[42] The role of Tezcatlipoca in the Panquetzaliztli ceremony persisted in regions outside of direct Mexica control, as manifest by the images from the *Codex Borgia* and others. But because the *Codex Borgia* was produced outside the region of Mexica control, Huitzilopochtli did not take the central role in the New Fire ceremony; rather, Tezcatlipoca and Quetzalcoatl did.[43] One complicating factor is that there is little other evidence that the New Fire ceremony was celebrated in the Tlaxcala region. Thus, the illustration is of a generic fire ceremony, not specifically the New Fire.

As noted, several pictorial manuscripts and sculptures document the New Fire ceremony. One of the most important of these is found in the *Codex Borbonicus* (see plate 13). The pictorial manuscript is made of folded native paper, amate, some fourteen meters long. It is a *tonalamatl*, or divinatory daybook, giving information on both the twenty thirteen-day periods of the tonalpohualli and illustrating some important ceremonies from the xiuhpohualli. Page 34 of the manuscript illustrates the New Fire ceremony. The central image is of the four *tletlenamaque* (fire priests) kindling their firebrands in the newly created fire. Along the bottom and left side, we can see the procession of the ixiptlahuan impersonating the Teonehnemi. On the lower-right side, women and children wear maguey masks, while in the middle of the three images, a woman has been placed in a granary. Along the top are three important glyphs that place the ceremony in time and space. On the far right is the glyph for Huixachtepetl, the location of the temple and ceremony, surrounded by the glyph for the new fire, which is a drilling stick embedded in its support. To the left of that is a small temple topped with a banner, conveying the message that the ceremony occurred during the month of Panquetzaliztli. This is confirmed by the presence of an image of Huitzilopochtli just to the left of that, standing on the base of the temple. It is clearly Huitzilopochtli because he has the quetzal-feather headdress, the hummingbird back device, the starry-sky eye mask, and the blue-striped face, and he carries both his shield (without down puffs) and his snake atlatl. Lastly, to the left of that is a cartouche with the date glyph of 2 Reed.[44] Clearly, this image illustrates the New Fire ceremony that took place in Panquetzaliztli in the year 2 Reed on Huixachtepetl. Nonetheless, it does not demonstrate in which of the possible fifty-two-year cycles it might have occurred, although, since the manuscript was produced at about the time of the conquest, one might imagine it referred to a recent one, such as 1507.

What is not clear in any discussion of the New Fire ceremony and its move into Panquetzaliztli is whether the nemontemi also moved. The descriptions continue

Fig. 9. Xiuhmolpilli. Museo Nacional de Antropología, Mexico. Drawing by Kendra Farstad.

to imply that the Few Fire ceremony occurred after the nemontemi. In the *Codex Borbonicus,* the figures on the right include women and children in masks being hidden away, elements of the last day of the nemontemi. Because of the ceremonies and practices leading up to the New Fire, the nemontemi were an integral part. Yet, in order to incorporate these into a Panquetzaliztli feast, the five useless days would have to have migrated to the period between Panquetzaliztli and Atemoztli, at least in New Fire years.[45] They might well have remained between Izcalli and Atl cahualo in ordinary years. Possibly, some days with similar activities might have been inserted into Panquetzaliztli in New Fire ceremony years. Yet most of the accounts from the early-colonial period continue to discuss the nemontemi as falling in the spring, not late fall. Consequently, we must assume that the nemontemi remained fixed in the xiuhpohualli, and only the actual New Fire ceremony moved into Panquetzaliztli. Exactly when in Panquetzaliztli this ceremony was inserted remains a mystery.[46]

The celebration of the New Fire ceremony in 2 Reed is well documented in other ways beyond Sahagún and the *Borbonicus.* One of the most famous artifacts commemorating the binding of the years is a stone representation of a xiuihmolpilli, a bundle of reeds representing a bundle of years (see fig. 9). Several date glyphs on it, helping to place it in time, have caused a great deal of speculation.

Fig. 10. Teocalli de la Guerra Sagrada, Museo Nacional de Antropología, Mexico. Drawing by Emily Umberger.

It has a 2 Reed glyph, referring to the year for the binding of the years, but also 1 Death and 1 Flint. In one of the earliest analyses, Seler concludes that these latter two refer respectively to Tezcatlipoca and Huitzilopochtli as lords of the celebration of the New Fire.[47]

Precisely when the New Fire ceremony was moved from 1 Rabbit to 2 Reed is hotly contested. While many accounts written shortly after the conquest mark the New Fire ceremony as having occurred on 2 Reed as many as hundreds of years prior to Spanish arrival, the consensus of opinion places the reform during

Fig. 11. 2 Reed glyph, Teocalli de la Guerra Sagrada, Museo Nacional de Antropología, Mexico. Drawing by Emily Umberger.

the reign of Moteuczoma II, such that 1507, which was the last ceremony prior to Spanish arrival, was probably the first to be celebrated in 2 Reed.[48] The other possibility is that because of the drought and famine in 1454, the ceremony was delayed a year to 1455 with the hope of a more propitious climate.[49] Nonetheless, many of the extant sculptural items related to Moteuczoma II tend to suggest that he was responsible. At the very least, the sculptures simply document that he reigned during a New Fire ceremony in 2 Reed.[50] Three pieces in particular stand out.

One is a large sculpture called the Teocalli de la Guerra Sagrada (the Temple of the Sacred War). The monument is in the shape of a stepped temple pyramid and was found in Mexico City near the palace of Moteuczoma II. It consists of a temple with thirteen steps, with engravings that include the glyphs for 1 Rabbit and 2 Reed on either side of the stairway (see fig. 10). The piece could even be a partial replica of the Templo Mayor itself. The date glyphs for 1 Rabbit and 2 Reed are large and prominent on the base. Looking closely (see fig. 11), the 2 Reed glyph seems to be bound with a rope, implying the binding of years, another name for the New Fire ceremony. On top of the temple, on the sides of the sanctuaries,

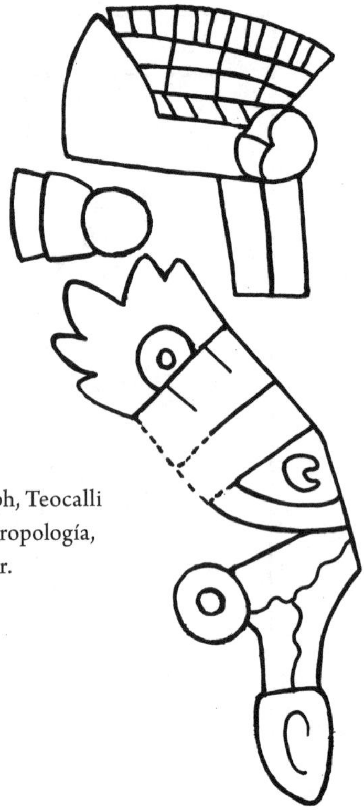

Fig. 12. Moteuczoma Xocoyotzin personal glyph, Teocalli de la Guerra Sagrada, Museo Nacional de Antropología, Mexico. Drawing by Emily Umberger.

are glyphs for 1 Flint and 1 Death. There is a solar disk atop the temple with the glyph of 4 Movement, the name of the current creation of the universe, the fifth sun, commemorating that reform as well. On the platform on top of the stairs, lying in front of the solar disk, is the figure of Tlalteuctli, the Earth Lord. On either side are deities, identified as Huitzilopochtli on the left and Tezcatlipoca on the right. Huitzilopochtli manifests the typical hummingbird headdress but has other attributes of Tezcatlipoca and Xiuhteuctli. The Tezcatlipoca, however, also has a name glyph identifying him as Moteuczoma II. The personal glyph (see fig. 12) consists of the ruler's crown (*copilli* or *xiuhuitzolli*), a nose or lip plug, and a speech glyph, which some have interpreted as the sign of the sacred war, *atl tlachinolli* (water-fire). There are images of warriors on either side below the date glyphs for 1 Death and 1 Flint. On the back, there is the image of the eagle on the cactus, documenting the founding of Tenochtitlan. The warriors, the Death and Flint glyphs, and the foundational eagle all have the atl tlachinolli glyph. This is a dense text, and since its discovery in 1926, many scholars have worked to interpret all its meanings. The piece also carries the name of "Montezuma's throne."

Critical analyses of the piece since its discovery have generally agreed that it commemorates the New Fire of 1507 and that it was dedicated to the solar disk and the use of warfare to gain sacrificial victims. Hassig and Umberger have analyzed the work in detail and both conclude that it is a memorial of the moving of the New Fire ceremony from one year to the next, using the form of a symbolic throne, also known as a *momoztli*. The momoztli was a form that was developed as a representational seat for Tezcatlipoca. In this instance, the deity is represented by the ruler Moteuczoma II.[51] The glyphs of 2 Reed, 1 Death, and 1 Flint are all associated with the New Fire ceremony, already seen on the stone sculpture of the reed bundle. All the other details of the piece also strongly suggest that the move occurred not in 1454–1455 but nearer to 1506–1507.[52] In particular, the work seems to proclaim that the New Fire ceremony was part of the legacy of Moteuczoma II. The presence of the two oversize date glyphs of 1 Rabbit and 2 Reed are indicators of the shift that occurred under the reign of Moteuczoma II, especially since the 2 Reed glyph is bound with a rope while the 1 Rabbit glyph is not.

One of the most imposing of pieces indicating that the New Fire ceremony took place in 2 Reed and associating it with Moteuczoma II is the bas-relief of the huey tlahtoani carved into the face of the rocky outcropping of Chapultepec near where the Mexica first settled in the Central Basin of Mexico and near the sacrifice of Izquitlan in the Swiftness of Huitzilopochtli. It is the only remaining image of a series carved of the huey tlahtoque of the Mexica. Unfortunately, the image has suffered from the ravages of time. Extirpation campaigns, conquering armies, and vandals have defaced portions of the image of Moteuczoma II and destroyed the other rulers' images completely. Nonetheless, there are some written descriptions from the colonial period that can assist in deciphering the traces left in the rock. The bas-relief depicts Moteuczoma II facing forward, dressed in the garb of Xipe Totec, the god of regeneration (see fig. 13).[53] He holds a *chicahuaztli* (staff of the god) in his right hand. His left hand holds a shield, darts, and a banner. On his left elbow is the *quetzalmachoncatl* (quetzal armband), a distinctive feature of the two leaders named Moteuczoma.[54]

The image of the ruler is surrounded by a series of glyphs. These must be reconstructed visually from the remnants and traces left on the stone. Several are fairly clear. On the upper left is the date glyph of 2 Reed, and it implies the New Fire ceremony since the knotted cord over the glyph can just be seen. Below it are the three symbols already seen on the Teocalli de la Guerra Sagrada: the crown and nose or lip plug associated with Moteuczoma's personal name and the symbol of the sacred war, the atl tlachinolli glyph. The glyphs on the right side,

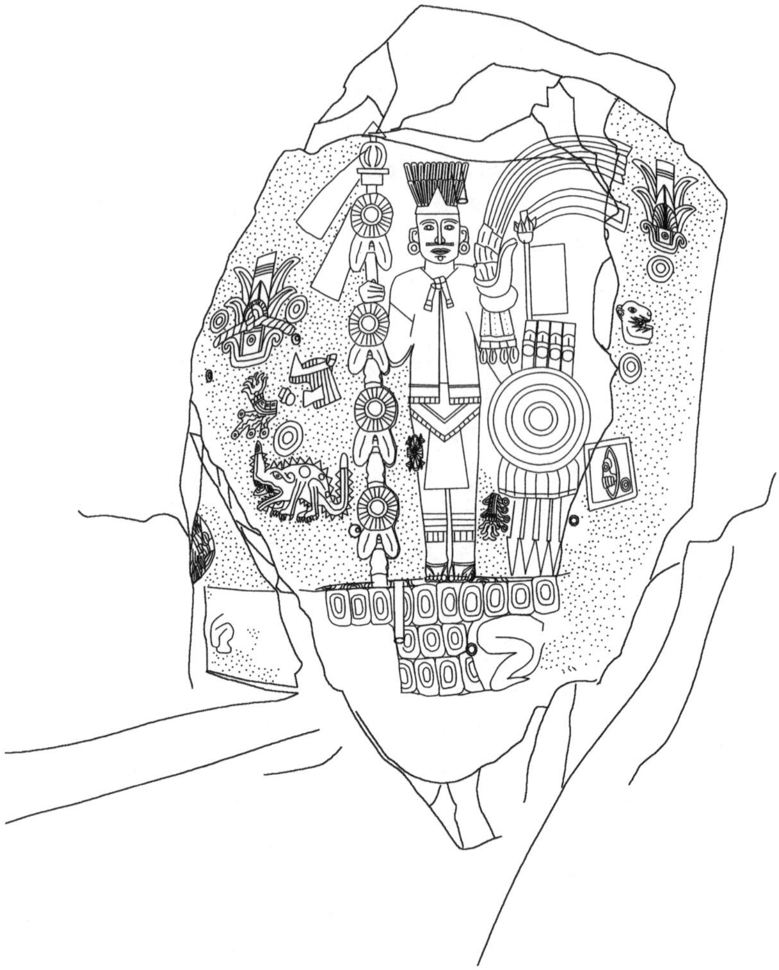

Fig. 13. Moteuczoma Xocoyotzin, bas-relief, Chapultepec Park, Mexico City. Drawing by Patrick Hajovsky.

to Moteuczoma's left, are much more difficult to envision and are possibly date glyphs relating to his birthday and perhaps 1 Flint, which could relate to several important events in Mexica history, including the departure from Aztlan.[55] For the purposes of this study, however, this commemorative sculpture seems to record the performance of the New Fire ceremony in the reign of Moteuczoma II and the ceremony's association with the sacred war.

At Dumbarton Oaks, in Washington, D.C., there is a large sculpture of a coiled snake, identified as a xiuhcoatl, which is associated with Huitzilopochtli. Like

Fig. 14. 2 Reed glyph and Moteuczoma Xocoyotzin personal glyph, Xiuhcoatl, Dumbarton Oaks. © Dumbarton Oaks, Pre-Columbian Collection, Washington, D.C.

many Mexica sculptures, not only is the surface finely carved, the base of the piece, hidden from view, also has carving on it (see fig. 14). The decoration is simple: a large square cartouche with the glyph for 2 Reed and the tied cord explaining the New Fire ceremony. On top of the date glyph is the personal name of Moteuczoma II in glyphs: the crown, a nose or lip plug, and an elaborate speech scroll. This speech glyph, while similar in some ways to the atl tlachinolli glyph already seen, is truly a horseshoe-shaped speech glyph, graphically depicting the speech of the person. In this instance, it has been interpreted as a smoke, fire, or mist speech glyph, all of which are frequently associated with rulers.[56] In this specific instance, it is probably part of the rebus depiction of Moteuczoma's name, representing the verb *zoma*, "to frown in anger/scowl/ be angry."[57] The crown glyph depicts the *-teuc-* (from the Nahuatl *teuchtli* or lord) portion of the name.[58] Again, this carving associates Moteuczoma II with the New Fire ceremony of 2 Reed in a very intimate and, in this particular instance, hidden manner, as if it is

Fig. 15. Moteuczoma Xocoyotzin and his personal glyph, Hackmack Box, Museum fur Volkerkunde, Hamburg. Drawing by Emily Umberger.

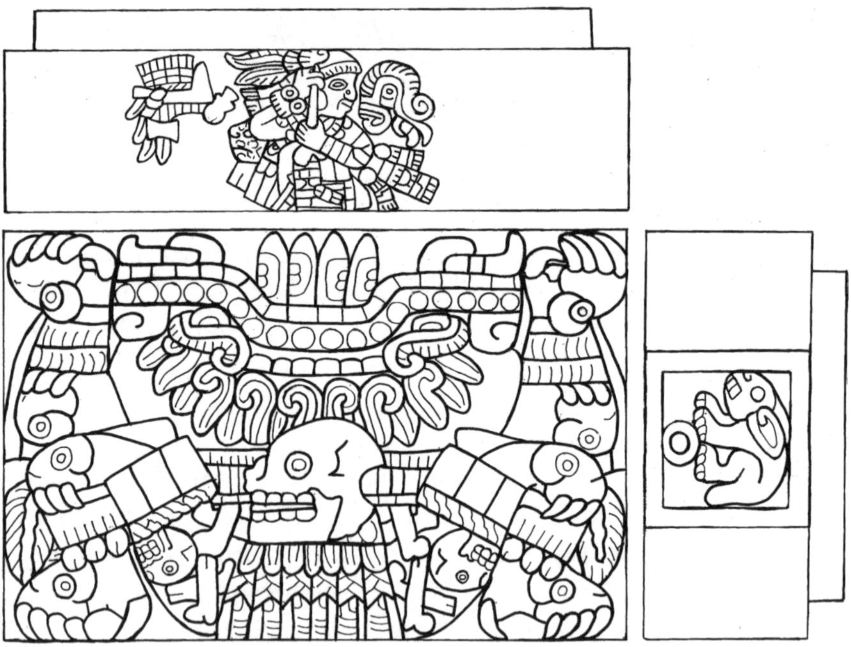

Fig. 16. Tlalteuctli, Hackmack Box, Museum fur Volkerkunde, Hamburg. Drawing by Emily Umberger, with permission.

Fig. 17. Tlalteuctli, Teocalli de la Guerra Sagrada, Museo Nacional de Antropología, Mexico. Drawing by Emily Umberger.

meant to communicate only with supernatural beings who might perceive the carvings that are out of sight.

The Hackmack Box, one of several stone boxes that were buried as containers for offerings, also has the same three elements for the personal name of Moteuczoma, although the steaming speech glyph comes out of the figure's mouth, to the right, while on the left are the nose/lip plug and crown (see fig. 15). Of all the glyphs on the piece, none represents 2 Reed, although 1 Rabbit does appear, but it is not tied with a rope and thus does not depict a New Fire ceremony. It could suggest that the year 1 Rabbit was being ignored. The important carving on the bottom of the box depicts Tlalteuctli, the Earth Monster (see fig. 16). Interestingly Tlaltecuhtli also appears on the top level of the Teocalli de la Guerra Sagrada (see fig. 17). Others have suggested that the xiuhcoatl of Dumbarton Oaks also represents the Earth Monster (see fig. 18) because of the distinctive claws on the surface of the snake.[59] The depiction of the Earth Monster on each of these pieces reinforces the importance of the New Fire ceremony in the continuation of the natural cycle, wherein things are born, live, die, and then are reengendered in the earth. A massive Tlaltecuhtli was also found in the Templo Mayor complex, in the forecourt just beyond the Coyolxauqui stone. This symbolizes that Tlaltecuhtli received the flesh of the victims while Huitzilopochtli received their hearts. Both were fed through the warriors captured in the Sacred War, the Flower War, also described as *in teoatl in tlachinolli* (the divine water, the fire, or the divine war).[60]

There were three reforms involving the New Fire ceremony. It was moved from the spring to Panquetzaliztli in the fall, from 1 Rabbit to 2 Reed, and from

Fig. 18. Xiuhcoatl—Tlaltecuhtli, Dumbarton Oaks. © Dumbarton Oaks, Pre-Columbian Collection, Washington, D.C.

the Templo Mayor to the Cerro de la Estrella. Only one move was intimately linked to the celebration of Panquetzaliztli: the shift from spring to late fall. At this point, there is no reason to believe that all the changes occurred at the same time. An analysis of the move from 1 Rabbit to 2 Reed may help to place the other reforms in historical context. The shift from the Templo Mayor to the top of Huixachtecatl undoubtedly occurred in order to make the ceremony one that could be witnessed by nearly all the residents of the Central Basin of Mexico, not just the residents of Tenochtitlan. That move would certainly help to emphasize Mexica dominance of not just of the Triple Alliance but the entire Central Basin.

In all likelihood, the move of the New Fire into Panquetzaliztli was not implemented until the 1507 celebration under the leadership of Moteuczoma II, as is argued above. Nonetheless, the change might have been disseminated fairly widely since the illustration of Panquetzaliztli in the *Primeros memoriales* includes one figure standing in the lower middle, holding the symbolic fiery torch associated with the ceremony (see plate 6). The figure, however, is not definitive. It could suggest coincidence with the New Fire or merely the burning of papers that preceded the sacrifices. Many argue that shift from 1 Rabbit to 2 Reed occurred in 1454, a year following a period of extreme weather that, in turn, caused serious droughts and widespread food shortages. Because the Nahua believed, to a certain extent, that history was cyclical, in order to break out of the pattern and to prevent similar droughts in later cycles, they felt that the start of the next epoch should be delayed a year. Conversely, we might also argue that the Mexica were so weakened by drought and pestilence that the demands of the New Fire were simply more than they could handle. When a drought began as the region approached the New Fire of 1506 or 1507, then, the wisdom of the move was confirmed.

Traditional sources outline the vicissitudes of the weather in the Central Basin of Mexico in the mid-fifteenth century during the reign of Moteuczoma I. Nigel Davies, drawing on several original accounts, describes them, noting a plague of locusts in 1446. This all but destroyed the crops, leading to shortages in the subsequent year. Then in 1449 the Central Basin of Mexico suffered extensive flooding. Heavy rains caused the lake to rise, inundating Tenochtitlan. The leader of Tetzcoco, Nezahualcoyotl, supervised the construction of a dike to protect Tenochtitlan from flooding. Also during this period, large numbers of laborers were drafted to assist in the enlargement of the Templo Mayor, causing its own set of social dislocations. Starting in about 1450, a string of bad harvests began, largely associated with drought but also exacerbated by frosts, heavy mountain snows, and other climatic anomalies. By 1454, the scheduled year for the binding of the year and New Fire ceremonies, famine had struck the Triple Alliance. Adults sold themselves and their children into slavery in order to purchase food; laborers were put on half rations. Even though the Triple Alliance had been organized to collect tribute from a wide area and then redistribute it preferentially to the residents of alliance cities, the weather patterns were so unusual that even tribute collections could not make up the shortfall. At the same time, some regions, like the Veracruz Coast, had abundant foodstuffs. Then in 1455 the rains and prosperity returned to the Central Basin of Mexico.[61] Because of the sequence of events, scholars conclude that the New Fire was moved from the "unlucky" year of 1 Rabbit to the subsequent year of 2 Reed, when the famine broke.[62]

Yet, in recent years, scholars have debated this position. In particular, Ross Hassig argues quite forcefully that the shift in the New Fire ceremony must have occurred after the 1454 celebration and that it was inaugurated in the 1507 ceremony. While allowing that the 1454 ceremony may have simply been ignored, he places the change at a point later in the century, after other policies had begun.

One of these was the practice of requiring tribute payments in one of the four designated months, including Panquetzaliztli. If the New Fire was held at its traditional time, unless they were specifically bidden to attend, no one from outside the Central Basin of Mexico would have witnessed the event, thus losing a prime opportunity to display Mexica power. While Huixachtecatl was reportedly the site for the ceremony in 1454, the temple itself was not constructed until later, but it was certainly completed by the 1507 ceremony. Hassig posits that a simple ceremony occurred at the Templo Mayor in 1454, followed by another in 1455 on the mountaintop, possibly inaugurating the new year count.[63] To complicate matters even more, there are indications that not all the communities of the Central Basin of Mexico used the same calendar at this moment. The year count of a document from Cuauhtitlan manifests confusion. For the year 1 Rabbit, glossed by the colonial editor as corresponding to 1454, the work describes the famine as if it began in that year and ended in 3 Flint (1456). Yet the work also lists a New Fire ceremony in 1455, which would put it in the second year of the famine.[64] The placing of events in historical time has as much to do with writers remembering later events and counting backward as it does to the absolute correspondence with an abstract notion of the flow of time.[65]

Recent archeological discoveries have undermined the argument in support of a sixteenth-century move of the New Fire ceremony to 2 Reed. A series of discoveries in the forecourt of the Templo Mayor between 2004 and 2013 have uncovered one set of bas-relief stones that strongly associate the celebration of the New Fire in 1455 during the reign of Moteuczoma I (Ilhuicamina). The assemblage includes stones that mark the year 2 Reed as well as depictions of a sacrificial victim carrying a banner and elements associated with the New Fire ceremony. These stones have been dated to the reign of Moteuczoma I.[66]

Consequently, while scholars, and perhaps some Mexica, looked to 1454 to explain the shift in the New Fire ceremony, in all likelihood, all three elements (year, month, and location) were shifted late in Aztec times, during the reign of Moteuczoma II, as part of a complete reform rather than as separate events altering the year, the month, and the location at different times. The conditions of the Aztec empire had reached a critical state by the time of Moteuczoma II (known as Xocoyotzin, "the Younger"). As the empire expanded, it became increasingly difficult to secure the captives and tributes that undergirded the system. While the Flower Wars originally augmented the number of captives needed for the sacrificial cycle, by the early sixteenth century, they had become ever more important. A significant financial outlay was required for far off provinces to bring tribute to Tenochtitlan. Thus, structurally, we can see that the empire was under some significant strain.

The younger Moteuczoma was elected as huey tlahtoani in 1502, following the death of Ahuitzotl. His reign lasted until the arrival of the Spanish, who eventually took him captive and in whose control he died. During his rule, three major issues demanded his attention. As noted, the empire had begun to reach its natural limits, imposed by communication and distance. Nonetheless, Moteuczoma II is credited with a significant number of conquests. Some of the conquests were of states that had been freely associated with the Aztecs, whom they had by then conquered, and other states that had been under Aztec control but had revolted and were once again subjugated. Thus, his conquests represented more of a filling in of the map rather than an expansion of the limits of the empire.[67]

Second, the Aztecs under Moteuczoma II were unable or unwilling to defeat several adversaries, some within the core region of the empire, others on the outer limits. In particular, the Aztecs either could not or would not finally defeat their neighbors, the Tlaxcalteca. Two other neighbors also played a game of shifting allegiances between the Tlaxcalteca and the Mexica: Chollolan and Huejotzinco. To the west, the Purépecha (Tarascan) Kingdom had successfully repelled the Mexica's repeated efforts at conquest. In the south, the two small regions known as Yopezingo and Tototepec similarly retained their independence, although larger Mixtec states had fallen to the Aztecs. In the north, the kingdom of Metztitlan stubbornly refused conquest. Thus, while Moteuczoma II could look with pride on some important conquests, several states remained outside Aztec control in spite of significant efforts to conquer them.[68]

Lastly, the Mexica found themselves near the ecological limits of their environment. Additional population growth could not be supported by the current agricultural basis, even augmented by tribute. With stagnant or near-stagnant tribute remittances and declined agricultural production, any small disturbance in productivity could wreak havoc on the economy. This occurred in 1505 when famine broke out due to flooding and other unexpected weather incidents.[69]

Moteuczoma II responded to these pressures in a manner that tended to change the structure of society and the nature of rulership. Prior to his time, the nobility had been merely one of several social categories within the larger Mexica culture. Leadership for society at large had tended to come from within the ranks of the warriors, merchants, and priests, regardless of social station, reflecting merit and accomplishments more than birth and heritage. Moteuczoma II increasingly relied on noble warriors as his closest advisors and less on commoners who might have risen through the ranks of either the priesthood or the military. This policy disadvantaged the merchants in particular. Merchants were also induced to lessen their conspicuous displays of wealth as well as pay greater sums to the state, especially in the form of support for public ceremonies, and work directly for the state both in ambassadorial roles and in tribute collection and distribution.[70] Nonetheless, within the limits imposed by the state, the merchants remained one of the most powerful groups within the Mexica state, especially since they provided the state with a significant portion of the wealth available for direct use by the ruler.[71]

The status of the merchants under Moteuczoma II, however, was not completely clear-cut. Several scholars have held that the merchants were definitively relegated to a secondary position, making way for leading warriors and members of the nobility. The emperor had reimposed their tribute obligations and required them to be modest in public, not flaunting their wealth. In return, they would be privately accorded positions of social importance and access to the ranks of the nobility.[72] Others argued that while this was all true, in reality, the merchants continued to be important voices in the palaces, exercising political power in the councils of state. Moreover, rather than being increasingly subject to the state, their power was on the increase prior to the arrival of the Spanish.[73]

Lastly, during the reign of Moteuczoma II, two more reforms occurred. One was that tribute payments from the outlying kingdoms and states, which had gone through a series of changes over several decades, were now due at four fixed times during the year. This gave the Aztecs an opportunity to put on mammoth and costly ceremonies to cow and impress visiting dignitaries. The system of imperial expansion and tribute collection was, ironically, a pyramid scheme in many ways. In a pyramid scheme, the entrance fees of the second and subsequent rounds of participants pay the early investors. As long as new investors are recruited, the existing investors feel that they are getting a solid return. Similarly, the Aztec military and nobility could continue to reap benefits from tribute as long as the empire continued to grow. More warriors joined the military as leadership was extended deeper and deeper into the nobility, and thus more people had to be rewarded. Residual amounts of tribute also needed to be distributed among the populace. But the system only worked if expansion continued. Thus, by the rule of Moteuczoma II, it was necessary to enforce Mexica authority more forcefully to keep the flow of tribute coming and to maintain enthusiasm about further expansion. Moreover, having to impress foreign states required more and more sacrifices, which in turn required more warfare from which to collect the potential sacrificial victims.

Under Moteuczoma II, the date for the New Fire ceremony was moved from the beginning of the solar year, between Atl cahualo and Izcalli, to the end of Panquetzaliztli. As is seen above, this change had the effect of, once again, driving home the point that Huitzilopochtli was the supreme god and an embodiment of the sun. It would have occurred under the rule of Moteuczoma II when, Graulich argues, the xiuhpohualli aligned itself so that the final rituals of Panquetzaliztli roughly coincided with the winter solstice, but certainly by 1507.[74] Thus, although the shift of the New Fire ceremony potentially had its roots in the rule of Moteuczoma I (Ilhuicamina), it actually dates to that of his homologue, Moteuczoma II (Xocoyotzin). The strongest evidence of this shift is found in the *Codex Telleriano-Remensis*. That document records that because of a two-hundred-year history of difficulties in the year 1 Rabbit, Moteuczoma shifted the date to the year 2 Reed after making propitiatory sacrifices in the earlier year. Furthermore, the annotators comment that the year was also when the temple at Huixachtepetl was completed.[75] The impressive sculptures such as the Teocalli de la Guerra Sagrada, the Moteuczoma bas-relief at Chapultepec, and the Dumbarton Oaks xiuhcoatl provide physical records of this accomplishment.

The third element of reform of the New Fire ceremony was the movement of the actual ritual from the Templo Mayor to a new sanctuary located on Huixachtepetl. The consensus, as noted, has been that this move might have occurred as early as 1454–55, but the new sanctuary was most certainly used in 1507.[76]

The New Fire ceremony also highlighted the participation of runners. After the fire priest had kindled the new flame in the chest cavity of the sacrificial victim, special messengers carried the fire from Huixachtepetl first to the Templo Mayor and then to all the neighborhoods of Mexico-Tenochtitlan. Each calpolli and altepetl would have a special runner to bring the fire from the Templo Mayor. Thus, runners played a central role in the distribution of the fire and the rekindling of hearths and sacrificial fires throughout the Central Basin of Mexico. Of course, running was also central to the celebration of Panquetzaliztli. Under the Mexica, one of the central rituals of the feast was Swiftness of Huitzilopochtli from the Templo Mayor, to Tlatelolco, Chapultepec, Tlacopan, Coyohuacan, and then back to the Templo Mayor. In this way, the caste of runners was celebrated and highlighted when the two rituals coincided once every fifty-two years. Just as Huitzilopochtli was placed in a superior position by having the New Fire ceremony occur in Panquetzaliztli, runners were elevated as a result of their ritual obligations.

Final Observations

In the century of Mexica expansion prior to the arrival of the Spanish, three important moments led to significant changes in the Panquetzaliztli ceremonies. In 1427, with independence from the Tepaneca of Azcapotzalco, the Mexica began to deftly insert their national god into the generally accepted Nahua pantheon of deities, giving him attributes of others, principally of Tezcatlipoca and Tonatiuh. What had been a series of rituals to prepare warriors and society at large for the forthcoming season of warfare became an extravaganza celebrating Huitzilopochtli's birth, his apotheosis as a solar deity, the Mexica's migration, and their adoption by Huitzilopochtli as his chosen people. Many scholars have posited that the destruction of the books under Itzcoatl had to do with the Mexica wishing to erase their past as a tribute-paying entity rather than an imperial capital that received tribute. Others have posited that the Mexica wished to elevate Huitzilopochtli, and so the old legends and stories needed to be erased. But neither of these efforts would have been successful at the time because everyone living in 1427 knew that the Mexica were rude, recently arrived barbarians from the north; they also knew that Huitzilopochtli was a new and poorly understood god. The major changes that occurred had more to do with politics and economics. Itzcoatl and Tlacaelel wanted to change the very political constitution of the Mexica. They wanted to move from their existing political organization, where the elders and representatives of the calpolli were the ultimate decision makers, to a more closed system, where the ruler (huey tlahtoani) and his close advisers had more authority. The military was elevated to be included in decision making. As the military succeeded in conquering new territories and those territories paid tribute, the empire was sound, profitable, and growing. This was more of a constitutional change than a religious reform or a simple book burning. This new model was then integrated into the ritual calendar, the imperial sculpture and artwork, and the structure of the government. Thus, Huitzilopochtli, as a representative of the Mexica's culture, hopes, and desires, came to be given a place of preeminence in all things, but this was especially reflected in the rituals of the solar calendar.[77]

As the new system developed, the Mexica became the prime movers of the Triple Alliance. Their partners, Tlacopan and Tetzcoco, represented older political units in the Central Basin. Tetzcoco was the senior partner in terms of gravitas but perhaps not in military might, having also been subjected to Tepaneca rule. Tlacopan was clearly the weakest of the three, having been a secondary Tepaneca capital.[78] The Mexica were able to dominate the alliance due, in no small part, to their success in the market. The Mexica pochtecah of Tlatelolco constituted an important weapon for the newly created alliance by sending their members into distant regions for trade as well as for diplomacy and intelligence gathering. Thus, the Mexica came to rely on more than military prowess for their success. Economic and diplomatic advances also assisted the progress of the empire. Under Axayacatl, it became clear that the two polities, Tenochtitlan and Tlatelolco, might have distinct goals in foreign affairs. At that point, the Tenochca moved to take over Tlatelolco to bring the merchants and their skills and contacts directly under the authority of the huey tlahtoani of the Triple Alliance. A special relationship was then developed. This eventually became manifest in the central role that merchants played in the most important month of festivals in Mexica life, Panquetzaliztli, which was dedicated to their tribal god, Huitzilopochtli.

By the time Moteuczoma II (Xocoyotzin) gained the throne, the Triple Alliance had been in existence for nearly seventy years and was beginning to show its age. The success of the state was, in many ways, dependent on expansion. More resources were needed to supply larger populations. But not all conquests had been successful. Some conquered areas had thrown off Aztec control. Moteuczoma then instituted a series of reforms that had a great impact on Mexica life.

Perhaps one of the most important reforms was to formalize the system whereby subject states were required to pay tribute four times a year, during festivals that were highly orchestrated to provide a maximum show of power and ruthlessness. Not only was the tribute collected, but increasingly, the leaders of the other states were required to attend. At the same time, Moteuczoma also redoubled Aztec pressure on states that had revolted, bringing them forcefully back into the Aztec sphere. Nonetheless, several states remained stubbornly outside the empire. The Flower Wars provided an alternative for supplying sacrificial victims to the celebrations in Tenochtitlan. To put it crassly, the Aztecs would have their victims, whether through conquest or ritual battle. If all else failed, slaves could be purchased to satisfy the needs of the ceremonies. Thanks to the merchants, the state had the financial wherewithal to make this happen. Moteuczoma walked a thin line with regard to the merchants. While he could not allow them to be perceived as a privileged class, he needed them for the purposes of the empire. Thus, their position in the state was confirmed again, and they took roles of importance in the celebration of Panquetzaliztli.

Linked to the use of the monthly celebrations as a means of cowing opponents, a series of calendar reforms were put in place during Moteuczoma's reign. The largest of these was to decouple the New Fire ceremony from the end of the solar year and to place it in conjunction with Panquetzaliztli. At the same time, the year in which the celebration was to occur was definitively changed from 1 Rabbit to 2 Reed. By adding the New Fire ceremony to the larger celebration of Panquetzaliztli, the Mexica had an opportunity to enhance what was already the largest and most spectacular monthly festival. Since the celebration only occurred every fifty-two years, it would not become a constant and continual burden but could serve as an enhancement in those years when it was celebrated. The correspondence of the New Fire with Panquetzaliztli also underscored the importance of Huitzilopochtli as the prime deity.

Looking at this series of changes, we can also trace the course of Mexica expansion and eventual crisis. The first phase of Mexica history saw the reinvention of the polity and the creation of the Triple Alliance. Tribute exacted from subject peoples enriched the Mexica and their partners. Warfare and sacrifice became twin pillars consolidating Mexica hegemony, and they used both to intimidate potential opponents and to keep possibly wayward subject populations under control. The merchant class played an important role in all this. They served as spies, both among subject peoples and outside the Aztec sphere of influence, investigating possible new conquests. The merchants also assisted in the distribution of goods from tribute and other sources as well. Yet, when an altepetl became too much of a threat, it was conquered by Tenochtitlan and became more closely incorporated. At this point, merchants and trade became an alter ego of warriors and warfare, and merchants began to take on an important role in the Panquetzaliztli celebrations.

As the empire expanded ever farther, Tenochtitlan also grew, and there was a never-ending need for both tribute and sacrificial victims. But the logistics of the empire were skewed. The concentration of nonagricultural population was in the capital. The frontiers provided products as well as manpower, tribute, and war captives for sacrifice. Between campaigns, however, sacrificial victims were still needed. The institution of the Flower War had emerged early in the history of the Triple Alliance as a means of supplying victims. Slave trading also increased to fill the gap. By the time of Moteuczoma II, the empire was at a critical state. Because conquests were increasingly farther afield, logistical issues became more acute. Some energy was spent in reconquering already subjected populaces, but the Aztecs also encountered certain populations against whom they simply had little military success: the Purépecha of the west, Tlaxcala in the east, Metztitlan in the north, and various regions in the far south.[79]

The vision of Panquetzaliztli that can be gleaned from traditional sources is a snapshot of the ceremonies at the end of their development. The rituals manifest the vestiges of bygone days. Through their analysis, we can begin to understand the impact that historical events had on their development. Panquetzaliztli, as it appeared at the end of the Mexica era, manifested changes from three different epochs. The political reforms of Itzcoatl, Moteuczoma I, and Tlacaelel asserted the primacy of Huitzilopochtli and the policy of governance through warfare and tribute. The Tlatelolca war of Axayacatl subsumed the merchant class into the larger Tenochca Mexica polity to an even greater degree than it had initially, and eventually it led to the merchants' active participation in the rituals of the festival. The political reforms of Moteuczoma II shifted the New Fire ceremony to Panquetzaliztli in order to place an even stronger emphasis on both the supremacy of Huitzilopochtli and the use of terror and awe in statecraft.

The thread connecting all these ceremonies and statecraft is the ritual of running. The two signature festivals of the Mexica, the New Fire and Panquetzaliztli, both featured running and runners as key elements. One commemorated their migration from Aztlan, the very event that told of their history and triumph. It also incorporated the reenactment of the birth and the triumph of their god. The other ceremony assured the continuation of the cosmos, the transit of the sun, and the continued fertility of their world. The New Fire ceremony also inextricably linked Huitzilopochtli with the cosmos, not simply with the rising sun but with the whole action of the universe. This triumph was then communicated through runners, who spread the news throughout the Central Basin of Mexico and beyond. Thus, the very essence of the Mexica and their god was intimately linked to running. The empire was knit together by runners and porters, who sent messages to and from the farthest reaches of the empire, and tlamama, who carried the burdens back and forth. Running was the mechanism whereby the Mexica chose to demonstrate and announce their reign and power.

NOTES

Introduction

1. The term for city-state is *altepetl* (sing.) or *altepeme* (pl.). It is a diphrase, two words that together signify a third concept. *Atl* means "water" while *tepetl* means "hill," but together they mean "city," or "city-state."

2. In Spanish, the ruler is known as "Moctezuma," which is phonetically closer to the Nahuatl. In some colonial documents, the name was rendered as "Moteucçoma." Part of the problem is that Nahuatl has a consonant that is rendered in English with the digraph *kw*. English and Spanish speakers have little difficulty pronouncing this consonant when it is followed by a vowel, such as in the word "quick." But when it is syllable final and/or followed by a consonant, it is difficult.

3. In Spanish, rules of emphasis would place the natural accent on the last syllable, since the word ends in a consonant. Thus, in Spanish, the word "Náhuatl" requires the use of a graphic accent since the stress falls on the first syllable.

4. An extremely useful discussion of the physical and ritual geography of Tenochtitlan is Mundy, *The Death of Aztec Tenochtitlan.*

5. Barrera Rodríguez, "The *Huei Tzompantli* of Tenochtitlan."

6. "Atlacuihuayan" is the least similar to the Spanish-imposed forms. Although his analysis of the Nahuatl is probably incorrect, Robelo does mention it: Robelo, *Diccionario de aztequismos,* 325.

7. In this instance, "vague" implies that the calendar does not have a clearly established rule to compensate for the fact that the actual solar year is just over 365 days through the adding of leap days, also known as intercalary days.

8. The issue of whether or not the Nahua calendar had leap days is considered more fully in chapter 5.

9. Sahagún, *Florentine Codex,* 2:1–34.

10. One needs to compare several sources to determine a definitive list. Sahagún, *Florentine Codex,* 2:1–34; Caso, *Los calendarios prehispánicos,* 33–39; Caso, "Calendrical Systems of Central Mexico," 339–43.

11. The numbering of the months depends on which of the eighteen is considered the starting point. Most colonial observers list Panquetzaliztli as the fifteenth while some modern scholars list it as the sixteenth. For example, Motolinia and the Tovar Calendar place it at fourteen. Tovar, *Tovar Calendar,* 32–33.

12. Berdan, "The Imperial Tribute Roll of the Codex Mendoza," in Berdan and Anawalt, *The Codex Mendoza,* 1: 56, 63; Hassig, *Time, History, and Belief,* 80. The others were Tlacaxipehualiztli, Etzcualiztli, and Ochpaniztli.

13. There is very little agreement on the exact correlation between the Mexica calendar and the European. Every observer reports a slightly different date. This might have to do with different communities using calendars that ran slightly off from one another. Most evidence from the sixteenth century points to Panquetzaliztli running from about November 20 until about December 10. One widely respected late sixteenth-century author, however, had the month running from December 4 until December 23. The Gregorian reform of the Julian calendar can explain part of this discrepancy. After 1582, November 5 became November 15, so December 10 became December 20. Chimalpahin Quauhtlehuanitzin, *Codex Chimalpahin*, 2:126. For the fullest discussion, see Prem, *Manual de la antigua cronología*; although now somewhat dated, see also Caso, *Los calendarios prehispánicos*, 35–64.

14. Sahagún, *Historia general*, 130.

15. Hassig, *Time, History, and Belief*, 111–15.

16. DiCesare, *Sweeping the Way*.

17. Graulich, *Fiestas de los pueblos indígenas*.

18. Sahagún, *Florentine Codex*, 2:66–77.

19. Sahagún, 2:118–26.

20. Anderson, "Sahagún's 'Doctrinal Encyclopedia,'" 109–22; Klor de Alva, "Sahagún's Misguided Introduction," 83–92.

21. León-Portilla, *Bernardino de Sahagún*, 205–13, sees the missionary as an early practitioner of the modern ethnographic method of participant observer, using standard questionnaires as part of his interviewing method. On the other hand, Browne, *Sahagún and the Transition to Modernity*, sees Sahagún situated at the collision of the late-medieval tradition of Scholasticism with (but not yet part of) the modern world that would lead to the Age of Reason.

22. For biographies of Sahagún, see León-Portilla, *Bernardino de Sahagún*; Browne, *Sahagún and the Transition to Modernity*; Bustamante García, *Fray Bernardino de Sahagún*.

23. Browne, 208–13 passim.

24. Miguel León-Portilla has been an advocate of the view of Sahagún as an early cultural anthropologist. León-Portilla, *Bernardino de Sahagún*. Walden Browne has argued forcefully that Sahagún was fully immersed in the medieval world and was only partially beginning to manifest a modern perspective. Browne, *Sahagún*.

25. Sahagún, *Primeros memoriales*, 3–4. Unless otherwise stated, references to Sahagún's *Primeros memoriales* are for the 1997 Sullivan edition.

26. Anderson, "Los 'Primeros Memoriales' y el *Codice Florentino*," 90–91.

27. Dibble, "Los manuscritos de Tlatelolco y México," 27–64; Bustamante García, *Fray Bernardino de Sahagún*, 247–305; Cline and d'Olwer, "Sahagún and His Works," 190–92; Rios Castaño, "From the 'Memoriales con escolios,'" 214–28.

28. Browne, *Sahagún*, 190–92.

29. The best biography of Durán is found in the introduction to Durán, *Book of the Gods*, 3–47, by editors Horcasitas and Heyden, see especially 47–40 for his sources and methods.

30. Durán, 34–47.

31. Steck, *Motolinia's History*, 1–70. This is a particularly favorable biography of Motolinia, written by a fellow Franciscan. See also Ramírez, *Fray Toribio de Motolinia*.

32. Burrus, "Religious Chroniclers and Historians," 144–45.

33. Alcina Franch, "Juan de Torquemada, 1564–1624," 256–75; León-Portilla, "Biografía de Fray Juan de Torquemada," 13–55.

34. Graulich, *Fiestas de los pueblos*, 202–6.

35. This is not unlike the relationship of the Jewish people with their deity. This relationship might have struck a chord in the friars who copied down the earliest versions of this myth, perhaps emphasizing the exceptionalism of the Mexica to be a parallel to the Jews.

36. Sahagún, *Florentine Codex*, 3:1–5. Several modern scholars have posited that some of the nativity myths of Huitzilopochtli are, in reality, recollections of the celebrations of Panquetzaliztli: Gillespie, *The Aztec Kings*, 211–13; Brotherston, "Sacred Sand," 307.

37. Brotherston, "Huitzilopochtli," 163; Molina, *Vocabulario*, 111; Sahagún, *Florentine Codex*, 3:5, "Caiac nex in ita."

38. Baquedano and Graulich, "Decapitation among the Aztecs," 166.

39. Read, *Time and Sacrifice*, 74–76; Milbrath, "Decapitated Lunar Goddesses," 186–88.

40. Seler, "Some Remarks on the Natural Bases of Mexican Myths," in *Collected Works*, 4:157; Lesur, "El dios Huitzilopochtli," 184–87. Karl Taube has associated the xiuhcoatl with a meteor in "The Turquoise Hearth," 288–301.

41. Sahagún, *Florentine Codex*, 2:175. When discussing the temple of Huitzilopochtli, Sahagún refers to it as "Coatepec."

42. An important version of the Mexica migration is found in a document called the *Tira de Peregrinación*, or the *Codex Boturini*.

43. Garibay, *Teogonía*, 43.

44. Davies, *The Aztecs*, 172–73.

45. One of the epithets for Huitzilopochtli was Tetzauhuitl (the Terror or Scandal). Tetzauhteotl is the combination of Tetzauhuitl and *teotl*, for "god" or "divinity."

46. Castillo, *Historia de la venida de los mexicanos*, 52, 110–11; Olivier, *Mockeries and Metamorphoses*, 31.

47. Uchmany, "Huitzilopochtli," 213–27.

48. Sahagún, *Historia general*, book 12, chaps. 2–4, 6 (pp. 724–27, 728).

49. The "Spanish league" at the time was a somewhat flexible measurement of length. The range was between 4.2 and 5.5 kilometers, or about 2.6 to 3.5 miles.

50. Torquemada, *Monarquía Indiana*, 4:320–21 (book 14, chap. 1); Hassig, *Trade, Tribute, and Transportation*, 32.

51. Molina, *Vocabulario*, folio 113v; Torquemada, 4:320–21.

52. Sahagún, *Florentine Codex*, 8:72–73.

53. Torquemada, *Monarquía Indiana*, 4:320–21 (book 14, chap. 1), calls the club a *macana*, which is a Taino word adopted by the Spanish in the Antilles early in the colonial period and then applied elsewhere. Clavijero, *Historia Antigua de México*, 211–12 (book 7, chap. 12).

54. Sahagún, *Florentine Codex*, 7:29–30; Read, *Time and Sacrifice*, 124–27; Carrasco, *City of Sacrifice*, 96–112. The exact timing of the celebration is subject to debate and will be considered in chapter 5.

55. Clavijero, *Historia Antigua de México*, 212 (book 7, chap. 12).

56. The verb "to carry something" is *mama*. The particle *tla-* is a direct object pronoun signifying "something." Thus, *tlamama* means "he/she/it carries something." In the colonial

period, this word appeared in several different variants including *tlameme, tameme,* and *tamama.* The plural form is *tlamamahqueh.* See Hassig, *Trade, Tribute, and Transportation,* 28. Karttunen, *An Analytical Dictionary of Nahuatl,* 134.

57. Hassig, *Trade, Tribute, and Transportation,* 32. In all likelihood, the interval also represented the distance a porter could be expected to cover in one day.

58. Nicholson, "The Significance of the 'Looped Cord' Year Symbol," 135–48.

59. Hassig, *Trade, Tribute, and Transportation,* 28.

60. Hassig, 36; Castillo, *Estructura económica,* 110–13.

61. The singular form for these words is *pochtecatl* and *oztomecatl.* The plural is formed through dropping the *-tl* and replacing it with a glottal stop, represented in the ACK system with the letter *h.*

62. Hassig, *Trade, Tribute, and Transportation,* 123–26; Hirth, *The Aztec Economic World,* 242–43.

63. *Tira de Peregrinación,* folio 2; Tezozomoc, *Crónica mexicayotl,* 19. Alvarado Tezozomoc gives the leaders names as Iztac Mixcoatzin, Apanecatl, Tetzcoatl, and Chimalma. All are designated as teomama.

64. Tezozomoc, *Crónica mexicayotl,* 16.

65. Sahagún, *Florentine Codex,* book 7, chaps. 7, 21; Read, *Time and Sacrifice,* 92.

CHAPTER 1. Panquetzaliztli outside Tenochtitlan

1. Nicholson, "Representing the *Veintena* Ceremonies," 99–100.

2. One reason why *teixiptla* appears less frequently is that "his, her, or its" ixiptla (that is, an object possessed by a specific person) would be *iixiptla.* But the two *i*'s generally get fused in writing. *Ixiptla* is part of a class of nouns in Nahuatl that must be possessed by someone, as with body parts and kinship terms. A hand must be someone's hand. Hvidtfeldt, *Teotl and *Ixiptlatli,* 78–79, holds that the base word has a glottal stop at the end of the stem. Using the ACK system, the word would be written *ixiptlahtli.* Others hold that the base word does not and thus would be *ixiptlatl.* The glottal stop is a consonant in Nahuatl. While it is present in spoken English, it lacks a graphic character. In the ACK convention in Nahuatl, the stop is nowadays written with the letter *h.* For Bassett's discussion of the notion of teixiptla, see Bassett, *Fate of Earthly Things,* 132–35.

3. Motolinia, *Memoriales,* 53. "Panquezalistle. Esta fiesta era el nacimiento de Uchilobus de la virgin, y hacían a Uchilobus de semillas, y todos cuantos habían habido en la guerra los mataban, y todos los comían, y a uno le vestían de color azul y pintada la cara de azul con cada dos rayas de amarillo y le mataban en la piedra de Mutizuma, y ofrecían unos bollos de semillas, y no comían dende el sol salía hasta que estaba puesto, y duraba un día."

4. A gladiatorial or sacrificial stone that is associated with Moteuczoma I was recently discovered under the former palace of the Archbishops of Mexico, which is known as the Stone of Montezuma, or the Temalacatl of Moteuczoma. Matos Moctezuma and López Luján, *Escultura Monumental Mexica,* 318–26.

5. Motolinia, *Memoriales,* 60–61. The term *mamalti* is a generic term for "captives." Molina, *Vocabulario,* folio 52r. It is probably the plural form of the other word for war captive: *malli.* Reduplication of the *ma-* and the addition of the plural *-tin* would result in *mamaltin.*

6. Motolinia, 60–61.

7. Motolinia, 72.

8. Motolinia, 72.

9. Sahagún, *Primeros memoriales*, 75.

10. Unfortunately, the distribution of the broken body of the god along with the mildly intoxicating beverage has many similarities to the Christian Eucharist and thus might be an interpretation inserted by Sahagún that was not necessarily fully present in the original sources.

11. Sahagún, *Primeros memoriales*, 86–87.

12. Sahagún, 65, 86. The name Chonchayotl is an odd one. On the surface, there is no clear meaning. It might however be a version of Tzonchayotl, which would mean something like "Chayote Head." Frances Karttunen, personal communication. A chayote is a Mesoamerican edible gourd that is light green, pear shaped, and covered with stubble, not unlike the wild hair of Chonchayotl.

13. Sahagún, 64–65.

14. Sahagún, 221.

15. Sahagún, 93–94.

16. Sahagún, *Florentine Codex*, 9:60.

17. Sahagún, *Primeros memoriales*, 94n4. As the headdress, then, it harkens back to the brothers of Huitzilopochtli, the Four Hundred Huitznahua, who also used it as their insignia. Also, the bells that he wears on his legs might be an oblique reference to his sister, Coyolxauqui, "Bells on Her Cheeks." The word *anecuyotl* should probably be written *aneucyotl* in that the *-cu-* is a digraph to represent the sound of *kw*. But in this setting, it should be *-uc-*, which is the proper form in syllable final position.

18. Heyden, "Dryness Before the Rains," 198.

19. This term could also be reasonably translated as "snake penis."

20. Sahagún, *Florentine Codex*, book 6, chaps. 28–29.

21. Boone, *Incarnations of the Aztec Supernatural*, 29, 38; Baquedano and Graulich, "Decapitation among the Aztecs," 165–66.

22. Carrasco, *City of Sacrifice*, 24–25. The other diphrase for war is *in atl in tlachinolli* (the water the fire).

23. Sahagún, *Primeros memoriales*, 136–37; Garibay, *Veinte himnos*, 77–82.

24. Sahagún, 94–95. Material in brackets appears in the translation.

25. This word should be *teocuitlapanitl*, as written here, meaning "golden banner." As it is written in the text, *tecuitlapanitl*, it means "rock scum banner."

26. Sahagún, *Primeros memoriales*, 113n99. Of the six artists identified as participating in the illustration of the *Primeros memoriales*, the same person who painted the image of Huitzilopochtli also executed the one of Painal (35).

27. Sahagún, *Florentine Codex*, 1:1.

28. Sahagún, 1:1.

29. "General History of the Things of New Spain by Fray Bernardino de Sahagún: The Florentine Codex," World Digital Library, Library of Congress, https://www.wdl.org/en /item/10096/view/1/31/.

30. See also Magaloni Kerpel, *The Colors of the New World*, 9–13.

31. Molina, *Vocabulario,* folio 45v. See also folio 95v, "Teixipltlatini."

32. Sahagún, *Florentine Codex,* 1:1–2. For an illuminating discussion of the relationship between the drawn image, the description, and the notion of ixiptla, see Magaloni Kerpel, *The Colors of the New World,* 10–12.

33. "General History," https://www.wdl.org/en/item/10096/view/1/31/.

34. Magaloni Kerpel, *The Colors of the New World,* 43.

35. Magaloni Kerpel, 46–47.

36. Sahagún, *Florentine Codex,* 1:2.

37. Translation by Schwaller. If the Nahuatl had referred to both objects, it would have read "Quimtocaia."

38. Magaloni Kerpel, *The Colors of the New World,* 45–47.

39. List modified from Nicholson, "The Iconography," 245; Boone, *Incarnations,* 5–8.

40. Sahagún, *Primeros memoriales: Facsimile Edition,* folio 252v.

41. A comparison of this to the *Codex Borbonicus* is found in Couch, *The Festival Cycle of the Aztec Codex Borbonicus,* 78–79.

42. The bag is also the symbol for 8,000 in the Nahua numbering system.

43. Hvidtfeldt, *Teotl and *Ixiptlatli,* 138–39.

44. Indeed, *xiuhcoatl* could be translated as "blue-green (leaf) snake" or metaphorically as "annual snake," but it is usually translated as "fire snake."

45. Nahuatl does not distinguish between green and blue; consequently, the term is normally translated as "blue-green."

46. Admittedly, this sets up the possibility of circular logic: finding in the *Codex Borgia* what we expect, based on Sahagún, rather than exploring its own intrinsic meaning in its own unique cultural context.

47. *Veintena* comes from the Spanish word *veinte* for twenty. This is in contrast with the cycle of thirteen images that appears in the ritual calendar (tonalpohualli) and called *trecenas* from the Spanish word for thirteen, *trece.*

48. Milbrath, *Heaven and Earth in Ancient Mexico,* 30.

49. Milbrath, plates 18, 30; see also plate 12.

50. Drawing on Toribio de Benavente (Motolinia), Kruell posits that in many cities Panquetzaliztli was dedicated to the cult of Tezcatlipoca, not Huitzilopochtli, Kruell, "Panquetzaliztli," 87.

51. Batalla Rosado, *El códice Borgia,* 435–37; Anders, Jansen, and Reyes García, *Los tiempos del cielo,* 241. Nowotny, *Tlacuilolli,* 33–34, 266–68, 275, merely describes it as a ritual fire boring. Boone, *Cycles of Time,* 207–9, likens it to the New Fire. After having first embraced this notion, Milbrath, *Heaven and Earth,* 123n20, has rejected it because of a lack of evidence of a New Fire ceremony in Tlaxcala.

52. Milbrath.

53. Don,

54. Dibble, "The Boban Calendar Wheel," 171–82.

55. Tovar, *The Tovar Calendar,* 12–13.

56. Anawalt, *Indian Clothing,* 24–25.

57. In most of the descriptions of the vague solar year, Panquetzaliztli is considered the fifteenth month.

58. Tovar, *The Tovar Calendar*, 32–33, plate 12.

59. Tovar, *Origen de los mexicanos*, 10–13; Glass, "A Census of Native American Pictorial Manuscripts," 223–25.

CHAPTER 2. Panquetzaliztli Celebrations in Mexico-Tenochtitlan

1. The ceremonies are succinctly described by Hirth, *Aztec Economic World*, 229–35; Brundage, *Jade Steps*, 222–26; González Torres, *El sacrificio humano*, 202–8; Berdan, "Economies of Mexica Religious Performance," 140; and others.

2. The descriptions of the Panquetzaliztli ceremonies that follow are taken from Sahagún, *Florentine Codex*, 2:145–47. There is another brief synopsis of the rituals found in chapter 15, (2:27–28), but it is written only in Spanish. An analysis of that section is found later in this chapter.

3. Sahagún, 2:141–50.

4. Sahagún, 9:45–67. González Torres, *El sacrificio humano*, 229–37, outlines the participation of the merchants in the ceremonies.

5. The discussions of the calendar's functioning and its correlation with the Christian system go far beyond the limits of this book. The major contribution of the mid-twentieth century was Caso, *Los calendarios*. Much of that same material has been reevaluated by Prem, *Manual de la cronología*.

6. Browne, *Sahagún and the Transition to Modernity*, 198 passim.

7. The description of the Panquetzaliztli ceremonies that follow are taken from Sahagún, *Florentine Codex*, book 2, chap. 34 (pp. 141–44, 145–51).

8. Sahagún's intent is unclear in this statement. He writes that the priests fasted for eighty days, beginning on the *last* day of Ochpaniztli. On the surface, it would seem that it would have only been a sixty-day fast. But adding the twenty days that they might fast through the month of Panquetzaliztli itself, we reach eighty. In his descriptions of the month, Sahagún seems to frequently count backward. Thus, what we might consider the fifteenth day of the month, he would call the fifth. Sahagún, 2:142.

9. This title means "the person from Tlaxotlan," which happens to be one of the waypoints on the marathon that the bearer of the Huitzilopochtli image runs. The hymn can be found in Sahagún, *Primeros memoriales*, 130–31. See also Sahagún, *Veinte himno*, 29–39. An early analysis was provided by Seler, "Uitzilopochtli, the Talking Hummingbird," in *Collected Works*, 5:98; Seler, "The Religious Songs of the Ancient Mexicans," in *Collected Works*, 3:232–35.

10. Brotherston, "Huitzilopochtli and What Was Made of Him," 159.

11. A Tlaxotec is a person from Tlaxotlan.

12. Sahagún, *Florentine Codex*, 2:221–22.

13. Sahagún, *Primeros memoriales*, 130–31.

14. Sahagún, *Florentine Codex*, 2:221.

15. For example, in Chimalpahin's description of the Aztec migration, he refers to the god as "*yn tetzahuitl huitzilopochtli*," translated by Schroeder as "the portent Huitzilopochtli." Chimalpahin Quauhtlehuanitzin, *Codex Chimalpahin*, 1:70–71; Olivier, *Mockeries and Metamorphoses*, 31.

16. Molina, *Vocabulario*, 111. "*Cosa escancalosa, o espantosa, o cosa de aguero.*"

17. Sahagún, *Florentine Codex*, 3:5. "Auh in Vitzilobuchtli: no mitoaia tetzavitl, iehica ca çan jvitl, in temoc otztic in jnan in coacue: caic nez in ita."

18. *Codex Mendoza*, folios 70v–71r.

19. Sahagún, *Florentine Codex*, 12:1. "How there were seen the signs, the omens of evil"; "*in mottac in machiotl yoã in tetzauitl.*"

20. Sahagún, *Veinte himno*, 36–37.

21. Sahagún, 35–36; Olivier, *Mockeries and Metamorphoses*, 232–40.

22. Molina, *Vocabulario*, 120.

23. Sahagún, *Veinte himno*, 37.

24. Later, the descriptions mention a snake dance, wherein dancers closely follow one another, as a snake slithers, through the city. This might be the dance depicted in the *Primeros memoriales*. It is not clear whether that is the dance occurring here.

25. Sahagún, *Florentine Codex*, 2:141. From *ahuiani* for "prostitute."

26. Sahagún, *Historia general*, 142.

27. Sahagún, *Historia general*, 143, par. 10; Sahagún, *Florentine Codex*, 2:142.

28. The descriptions in the next section are taken from Sahagún, *Florentine Codex*, 9:45–49.

29. Hassig, *Aztec Warfare*, 119–21, 128–30.

30. Townsend, "'What in the World Have You Done To Me,'" 362, contains a recent, good summary of Aztec slave owning. Hassig, *Trade, Tribute, and Transportation*, 112–13, discusses the slave market. Clendinnen, *Aztecs*, 98–101.

31. Townsend, 360–61; Carrasco, *City of Sacrifice*, 206.

32. Sahagún, *Florentine Codex*, 9:46.

33. The description of the sacrifices made to Huitzilopochtli come from Durán, *Book of the Gods*, 92–94; Hassig, *Aztec Warfare*, 7–13.

34. Sahagún, *Florentine Codex*, 9:46.

35. Sahagún, 9:46. Hassig posits that the merchant-bathers were just one type of merchant. Hassig, *Trade, Tribute, and Transportation*, 117. It is worth noting that in Nahuatl, while the merchants are called "those who customarily bathe people," the victims are called "the (nonhuman) bathed ones." The *te-* prefix denotes a human object, while the *tla-* prefix is used for nonhuman objects. Sahagún also used variants on the term; "those who would bathe" were *tealtiz*.

36. Hirth, *Aztec Economic World*, 229–30,

37. Sahagún, *Florentine Codex*, 9:47. The original Nahuatl reads *onmatl* (two measures). The *matl* was about 1.5 meters or 5 feet, or the average distance between two outstretched hands. Williams and Jorge y Jorge, "Aztec Arithmetic Revisited," 74. A fathom was approximately 6 feet or about 1.8 meters. Dibble and Anderson chose to translate *onmatl* as "fathom" because they are relatively similar.

38. For the categories of merchants, see Hassig, *Trade, Tribute, and Transportation*, 117.

39. Sahagún, *Florentine Codex*, 9:48. Some of the prices mentioned are twenty small capes for the tomatoes and one small cape for a boat filled with water. The highest-quality cape was called *tototlaqualtequachtli* (bird-food cape).

40. Sahagún, *Florentine Codex*, 9:45–49, lists the following cities as having representatives at Tochtepec: Tenochtitlan, Tlatelolco, Huexotla, Coatlichan, Chalco, Xochimilco,

Huitzilopochco, Mixcoac, Azcapotzalco, Quautitlan, and Otumba. There is some confusion about precisely where Tochtepec may have been located. There was a small altepetl by that name in what is today the State of Puebla, between Puebla City and Tecamachalco. There was a district either in Tlatelolco or somewhere in the Central Basin of Mexico that was also called Tochtepec. It is a bit surprising, but following the Sahagún narrative in book 9, the merchant-bathers would decamp for Tochtepec, toward the Gulf Coast, just for a series of ceremonies aimed at gaining the support of the leaders of the merchant's guild. See also Hassig, *Trade, Tribute, and Transportation*, 123–24. Van Zantwijk, "Las organizaciones," 5; Van Zantwijk, *The Aztec Arrangement*, 134. The consensus holds that the Tochtepec described in the *Florentine Codex* was indeed the one located several hundred miles to the southeast of Mexico-Tenochtitlan. Hirth, *Aztec Economic World*, 232–33; Gerhard, *Guide to the Historical Geography*, 300–305; Carrasco, *The Tenochca Empire*, 331–43.

41. The following section deals with the ritual performances at Tochtepec. Sahagún, *Florentine Codex*, 9:51–53; Van Zantwijk, *Aztec Arrangement*, 166–70; Hirth, *The Aztec Economic World*, 232–33.

42. Yacateuctli (Nose Lord) was the patron deity of the long-distance merchants, who were known as the vanguard merchants. While sometimes thought of as an aspect of Quetzalcoatl, he is probably closer to the trickster god Tezcatlipoca. O'Mack, "Yacateuctli and Ehecatl-Quetzalcoatl," 1–33.

43. The sacrifice of quail through beheading was fairly ubiquitous in preconquest Mexico. But, in keeping with the confusion of Huitzilopochtli and Tezcatlipoca in Panquetzaliztli, the beheading of quail was frequently associated with Tezcatlipoca. Baquedano and Graulich, "Decapitation among the Aztecs," 173.

44. As will be seen, the victims were only beheaded after they had been sacrificed through the removal of their hearts. In his description of the sacrifices themselves, Sahagún does not mention the beheadings.

45. Sahagún, *Florentine Codex*, 9:51–53.

46. The following section is taken from Sahagún, 9:55–57 (chap. 12).

47. Sahagún, 9:55. The functions of the Quappoyaualtzin appear in Hirth, *Aztec Economic World*, 210. The Huetzcatocatzin (Honored Laugh Follower) and Zanatzin (Honored Thrush) were two of the four leaders of the merchant's guild perhaps also with military obligations. The one leader missing from this text was the Huey Ozomatzin. Máynez, *El calepino*, 118, 372.

48. Sahagún, 9:56.

49. Burkhart, *The Slippery Earth*, 181–82.

50. Máynez, *El calepino*, 288–89.

51. Máynez, 257, translates the term as "bathing offering papers"; "Tetehualtia."

52. All four of these words appear in the third-person singular. Thus, these words would mean something like "one confesses," "one acquires something," "one bathes paper offerings," and "one kills something or someone." The last three are built on agentive verbs.

53. One might be somewhat suspicious of Christian intrusion in the Nahuatl here, since the term for the god here, "Our Lord," was the one adopted by the missionaries as a term for the Christian god, *totecuio*. It does mean "our lord," but the context is questionable.

54. Sahagún, *Florentine Codex*, 9:55–57.

55. Sahagún, 9:59–61.

56. Sahagún, 9:59.

57. Sahagún, 9:59.

58. Durán, *Book of the Gods*, 232. Durán notes that all victims, but especially those who represented the gods, were ritually bathed.

59. Anderson, "The Institution of Slave Bathing," 82.

60. Dibble and Anderson conclude that Sahagún meant the eleventh, although he wrote, "when the ninth day arrived." Sahagún, *Florentine Codex*, 2:141. The reason must be because the "ninth" day is followed, in the description, by the "fifth day," thus each of these is a reference to how many days remained in the month rather than how far into the month they occurred. Sahagún, *Florentine Codex*, 9:60.

61. Durán, *History of the Indies*, 232.

62. López Luján and González López, "Tierra, agua y fuego," 39.

63. Sahagún, *Florentine Codex*, 2:141–42.

64. We assume that the merchants and warriors took charge of bathing the slaves because, throughout the section, Sahagún uses the term "merchant" and "bather" almost interchangeably.

65. See also Sahagún, *Historia*, 143, par. 12.

66. Anderson, "The Institution of Slave Bathing," 82.

67. Compare this with the descriptions of Huitzilopochtli in Sahagún, *Primeros memoriales*, 93–94.

68. Sahagún, *Historia*, 142–43.

69. Sahagún, 143.

70. Sahagún, *Florentine Codex*, 2:142.

71. Sahagún, 9:60.

72. Sahagún, 9:59–61.

73. Sahagún, 2:142. The fact that they returned home in the company of their wives implies that they had jointly participated in, or that the wives had at least witnessed, the bathing ceremony.

74. Sahagún indicates, the "fifth day" before the end of the month.

75. Sahagún, *Florentine Codex*, 2:142; Mazzetto, "Las *ayauhcalli* en el ciclo de las veintenas," 151.

76. Sahagún, 2:142; Mazzetto, 152.

77. Sahagún, 9:47.

78. This word might be translated as "to bend the snake/to snake bend." Cf. Molina, *Vocabulario*, folio 65, "necuiloa."

79. Sahagún, *Florentine Codex*, 2:143.

80. Sahagún, *Primeros memoriales*, 65.

81. Graulich, "Miccailhuitl," 60–61.

82. Sahagún calls this the twentieth (*tlacempoalti*), but the running ritual occurs on the twentieth, and last, day, and clearly the events described here occurred on the day before that.

83. Sahagún, *Florentine Codex*, 9:63.

84. Sahagún, 2:143.

85. It is odd that the sacrificial victims might visit relatives, since, in general, they were war captives or other slaves. This comment would imply that some of the victims were individuals who might have entered slavery voluntarily only to be sacrificed. Clendinnen holds that nearly all sacrificial victims except infants who were offered to Tlaloc and "god impersonators" were foreigners. Yet she and others describe the washing rituals practiced in Panquetzaliztli as necessary to cleanse the stain of delinquent Mexica who had entered into slavery. She holds that the kinship referred to here is ritual. Clendinnen, *Aztecs*, 99–102. Sahagún, *Historia general*, 144, also notes that the victims went to visit the homes of relatives, "*parientes*."

86. Sahagún, *Florentine Codex*, 2:144.

87. Dibble and Anderson chose not to translate *xalaquia*. It is composed to two morphemes: *xal* from *xalli* (sand) and *aquia* (to enter), offering a tentative meaning of "to enter sand," with the sense of something difficult to walk through. Charles Dibble has studied this ceremony and believes that the victims were bathed in sand as part of the purification process in anticipation of sacrifice the next day. It was linked to bathing in water and with drinking a substance known as "obsidian knife blade wash water," which will be seen later. Dibble, "The Xalaquia Ceremony," 197–202.

88. Heyden, "Sand in Ritual and in History," 192–93. As noted, Clendinnen sees the bathing as a two-part process that ritually prepared unclean slaves for immolation. The bathing in the lake removed the stain of slavery; the later face washing then prepared them for sacrifice. Clendinnen, *Aztecs*, 99.

89. Dibble, "The Xalaquia Ceremony," 199–201; Johansson, "Estudio comparative de la gestación," 104–9. The term "Coaxalpan" also refers to one of the places through which the Centzon Huitznahua passed as they attacked the newborn Huitzilopochtli. López Austin and López Luján, *Monte sagrado—Templo mayor*, 307–9; Graulich, *Fiestas de los pueblos*, 2; Hvidtfeldt, *Teotl and *Ixiptlatli*, 112.

90. López Luján and González López, "Tierra, agua, y fuego," 40–41; Brotherston, "Sacred Sand," 306–7; López Austin and López Luján, 304–9.

91. This ritual was discussed earlier. Sahagún, *Florentine Codex*, 9:63.

92. Dibble, "The Xalaquia Ceremony," 197–202; Anderson, "The Institution of Slave-Bathing," 83–84. *Teoctli* can easily be confused with the word for "lord or noble," which is *teuctli*. The former is a combination of the word for a deity, *teo-tl*, and the word for pulque, *oc-tli*.

93. Sahagún, *Florentine Codex*, 2:144.

94. Sahagún, 9:63.

95. The next two paragraphs are taken from Sahagún, 9:63–64.

96. Sahagún, 9:63.

97. Sahagún, 9:64.

98. Sahagún, *Florentine Codex*, 2:144; Sahagún, *Historia*, 144, par 22.

99. Sahagún, *Historia*, 144, par 25. "Esto se hacía en todas las casas del pueblo."

CHAPTER 3. The Final Day of Panquetzaliztli

1. For a fuller description of the concept of ixiptla, see chapter 1.

2. Durán, *Book of the Gods*, 458.

3. In Nahuatl there is no difference between *i* and *y*. Thus, in some instances, authors prefer "Paynal" while others use "Painal." It has been standardized as "Painal" in this book.

4. Sahagún offers different details on the nature of the image. In book 2, chapter 34, he notes belatedly that the image was made of amaranth. In book 2, appendix, "Temple of Uitzilopochtli," he insists that there were two amaranth dough images but that the image of the Swiftness of Huitzilopochtli was only made of sticks. Sahagún, *Florentine Codex*, 2:145–46; cf. 2:175.

5. Bassett, *Fate of Earthly Things*, 130–31; Hvidtfeldt, *Teotl and *Ixiptlatli*, 128, 138–39. For a detailed discussion of the category of this priest, the tlamacazqui, see Contel and Dabrowska, "'Mas nosotros que somos dioses,'" 32–35.

6. Sahagún, *Florentine Codex*, 2:175, indicates there might even have been as many as three images.

7. Sahagún, 2:70–72. Toxcatl occurred in the late spring and featured a teixiptla of Tezcatlipoca in the form of a man who was chosen to impersonate the god. But in the latter days of the month, two figurines were central to the events of the ceremony. This similarity to Panquetzaliztli confused early observers, particularly among the conquistadors who witnessed the Toxcatl celebration.

8. Sahagún, 2:175–76; Bassett, *Fate of Earthly Things*, 130–31.

9. Durán, *Book of the Gods*, 83–84. Because of similarities with practices involving Christian nuns, one must be wary of the details provided by Durán.

10. The following description is based on Durán, 86–89.

11. Boone, *Incarnations of the Aztec Supernatural*, 35–36; Mazzetto, "¿Miel o sangre?" Others note that since the tzoalli was made from toasted and ground amaranth, it differs significantly from alegría, although the modern Mexican Spanish word for amaranth is *alegría*. Reyes Equiguas, "El huauhtli," 81.

12. While Sahagún's description of the running ceremony begins at *Florentine Codex*, 2:145, he does not mention that the figure is made of amaranth dough until 2:146.

13. Sahagún, 3:5–6

14. Bassett, *Fate of Earthly Things*, 132; Sahagún, 2:175. "Auh in muchioaia, in tlacatia Vitzilobuchtli ixiptla: vmpa in itocaiocan Itepeioc" (And when the image of Uitzilopochtli was made when it took human form, it was there at Itepeyoc). Here, the verb *tlacati* can mean "to take human form" or "to become animate."

15. At least one dough image was sent to Europe in the sixteenth century; there are records of it being given by Francesco de Medici to Albrecht V. Keating and Markey, "'Indian' Objects," 292.

16. Durán, *Book of the Gods*, 80.

17. Durán, 86.

18. Sahagún, *Florentine Codex*, 1:1; Torquemada, *Monarquía Indiana*, 3:76.

19. These accouterments are very reminiscent of the supernaturals and culture heroes described by Boone, *Cycles of Tome*, 207, especially among the Mixtec, who used them to drill new fire and thus to found a new community.

20. Sahagún, *Primeros memoriales*, 94–95. The suggestion that Painal was similar to Mercury helps to demonstrate that one must be judicious in using Sahagún because of intrusive material.

21. Durán, *Book of the Gods*, 458.

22. Sahagún, *Florentine Codex*, 3:5–6. This has led to confusion about the number of figurines.

23. Durán, *Book of the Gods*, 86–87.

24. Durán, 458.

25. Sahagún, *Florentine Codex*, 3:27.

26. Olivier, *Mockeries and Metamorphoses*, 155–56.

27. Karttunen, *Analytical Dictionary*, 253.

28. The day is conjectural, counting backward from the known ceremony of Painal that occurred on the twentieth of the month.

29. This name is suggestive of Huitzilopochtli, since it seems to be *I* + *opoch*, which could be translated as something like "his/her/its left." Karttunen, *Analytical Dictionary*, 179.

30. Boone, *Incarnations of the Aztec Supernatural*, 37.

31. Sahagún, *Florentine Codex*, 2:71–72.

32. Sahagún, 3:7.

33. Sahagún, 3:7–8.

34. Durán, *Book of the Gods*, 86.

35. Durán, 86–87.

36. Sahagún, *Florentine Codex*, 2: 145, 175.

37. Sahagún, 2:145. "Njmã ie ic oaltemo in teucalticpac in paynal in jcpac Vitzilobuchtli."

38. Sahagún, 2:179. "Niman ie ic oalquiça, in paynaltzin."

39. Sahagún, 9:64–66; Torquemada, *Monarquía Indiana*, 3:405.

40. Sahagún, *Historia general*, 31. If, in fact, the person carrying the god was the priest identified as Topiltzin Quetzalcoatl, his sacrifice would have been highly unusual since priests were not usually sacrificed. On the other hand, the bearer may have been an impersonator dressed to represent the god Topiltzin Quetzalcoatl.

41. As noted earlier, this might be a conflation of the ceremony in Toxcatl, where two dough images participated.

42. Torquemada, *Monarquía Indiana*, 3:404–5.

43. Robelo, *Diccionario de aztequismos*, 265. Karttunen notes that the absolutive form is *pamitl* but that, when possessed, the stem converts to *pan-*. The stem also seems to appear from time to time as *pantli*, which is also the word for "wall." Karttunen, *Analytical Dictionary*, 186.

44. Sahagún, *Historia general*, 144–45.

45. Torquemada, *Monarquía Indiana*, 3:405.

46. Sahagún, *Florentine Codex*, 3:186.

47. Sahagún, *Historia general*, 144, par. 26.

48. Torquemada, *Monarquía Indiana*, 3:405.

49. Hassig, *Aztec Warfare*, 121.

50. Davies, *The Aztecs*, 129–32.

51. Torquemada, *Monarquía Indiana*, 3:405.

52. In modern Mexico City, there is a place called Nonoalco located in the Colonia Tlatelolco, Delegación Cuauhtemoc, just to the west of the Plaza of Three Cultures. Colonial

documents refer to an islet located just to the northwest of Tlatelolco. Sahagún, *Primeros memoriales*, 142n20. See also Rojas, *Tenochtitlan*, 45, 47.

53. Chimalpahin Quauhtlehuanitzin, *Codex Chimalpahin*, 2:81; Tezozomoc, *Crónica mexicayotl*, 32.

54. Sahagún, *Historia general*, 144, par. 27.

55. Sahagún uses an alternate orthography of this name: "Quauitl icac." Revised Nahuatl orthography would write this name as "Cuahuitl Icac," which will be used throughout.

56. Sahagún, *Florentine Codex*, 2:145.

57. The birth myth of Huitzilopochtli will be explored further in a later section. Sahagún, *Florentine Codex*, 3:2–3; Robelo, "Diccionario de mitologia nahoa," 280–81.

58. Sahagún, *Florentine Codex*, 2:145; Sahagún, *Historia general*, 145. The critical word is *vi*, which is a Sahagún spelling of a word normally rendered as *huih*, a plural form for the verb "to go," i.e., "they went." Hvidtfeldt concurs, noting that from Nonoalco until Acachinanco, Sahagún refers to "runners," not a single runner. Hvidtfeldt, *Teotl and *Ixiptlatli*, 129.

59. González Aparicio, *Plano reconstructive*, 53–55.

60. Sahagún, *Florentine Codex*, 2:176.

61. Sahagún, *Florentine Codex*, 2:145; Sahagún, *Historia*, 145, par. 28.

62. Sahagún, *Florentine Codex*, 9:64.

63. Sahagún, 12:66; *Hunt-Cortes Digest* 2, no. 1 (January–March 1905): 72; Lockhart, *We People Here*, 261. Interestingly, three of the stops on the ceremonial route were also sites of major Spanish troop concentrations in the final assault on Tenochtitlan: Nonoalco, Mazatzintamalco, and Acachinanco.

64. Durán, *Book of the Gods*, 458.

65. Motolinia, *Memoriales*, 61.

66. Pasztory, *Aztec Art*, 127–29.

67. The Santa Cruz map from the mid-sixteenth century shows a river flowing on the south side of Chapultepec, roughly where Constituyentes now runs. The map was previously available online from the Uppsala University Library. An adequate version can be found at "Tenochtitlán, 1521," World Digital Library, Library of Congress, https://www.wdl.org/en/item/503/. See also the published version, Linné, *El Valle y la Ciudad de Mexico en 1550*.

68. The name of this place corresponds to one of the original seven calpolli (kinship groups) of the Mexica in their migration from Aztlan. It was one of the original barrios of Tenochtitlan, located near Chapultepec. Sahagún, *Primeros memoriales*, 91n72; see also Carrasco, *The Tenochca Empire of Ancient Mexico*, 94.

69. Sahagún, *Primeros memoriales*, 91–92.

70. Davies, *The Aztecs*, 25–28; Chimalpahin Quauhtlehuanitzin, *Codex Chimalpahin*, 1: 81, 109; Tezozomoc, *Crónica mexicayotl*, 32, 74. Interestingly, the establishment of the community occurred after building a temple to Huitzilopochtli and a ball court, both places used for ritual sacrifice in the celebration.

71. Sahagún includes Tepetocan in all three of his descriptions of the route. Sahagún, *Florentine Codex*, 2: 145, 176; 9:64.

72. At this point in the narrative, Hvidtfeldt argues that the narration shifts from referring to plural "runners" to a singular "runner." Hvidtfeldt, *Teotl and *Ixiptlatli*, 129.

73. Sahagún, *Primeros memoriales,* 68n44. Sullivan posits that it is a subbarrio south of Tenochtitlan and east of the Iztapalapa causeway. There was a Mazatlan in the Tlacopan district, but located to the north and west of the altepetl in what is now the State of Mexico, and so it seems unlikely to correspond to this Mazatlan, which clearly is not far from Coyohuacan. Carrasco, *The Tenochca Empire,* 180, 183, 188. There is a street located north of Coyoacan and to the east of the old causeway in modern Mexico City called Tetepilco.

74. Sahagún, *Historia general,* 145, par. 30.

75. Sahagún, *Florentine Codex,* 9:64.

76. Sahagún, 12:86–89.

77. González Aparicio, *Plano reconstructive,* 58; Mazzetto, "Las *ayauhcalli,*" 161.

78. Bernal Díaz del Castillo, *La historia verdadera,* 1:255–56. In this particular edition, the place-name is rendered as "Acacingo." On the famous Santa Cruz map, the spot is marked with a cross. The cross on the southern outskirts of Tenochtitlan marked, according to Tezozomoc, "*Acachinanco donde se puso la primera cruz, que ahora esta por la parte de Coyoacan, camino real que ahora entra en Mexico.*" Tezozomoc, *Crónica mexicayotl,* 500; González Aparicio, *Plano reconstructive,* 58–59.

79. Sahagún, *Florentine Codex,* 12:88–89; Lockhart, *We People Here,* 261.

80. Sahagún, 2:176.

81. Chimalpahin Quauhtlehuanitzin, *Codex Chimalpahin,* 1:109; Tezozomoc, *Crónica mexicayotl,* 74. Coatlan, Huitznahuac, and Izquitlan were all listed as original calpolli of Tenochtitlan. Dibble and Anderson have identified one of the places called Coatlan as part of Tlatelolco, which would not be a reasonable place for the action described here. Sahagún, 12:117n18.

82. Rovira Morgado, "*Huitznáhuac,*" 51–52.

83. There is some confusion because there was a calpolli called Huitznahuac ("South" or "Next to the Spines"), so it is not clear whether the adversaries were residents of the neighborhood of Huitznahuac or were captured warriors imitating the minor deities called the Huitznahua. It was one of the neighborhoods mostly closely associated with Huitzilopochtli. Van Zantwijk, "Los seis barrios sirvientes de Huitzilopochtli," 177–85. Curiously, Brundage, *The Jade Steps,* 142–43, implies that the ritual battle occurred in the ball court.

84. Sahagún, *Florentine Codex,* 9:64.

85. Sahagún, *Historia general,* 145, par. 31. "Los esclavos que habían de morir, un bando eran de Huitznahua y de otro bando, otros esclavos, y de la parte de Huitznahua ayudaban los soldados de Huitznahua."

86. Sahagún, *Florentine Codex,* 2:146.

87. Sahagún, 9:64.

88. Tezcatlipoca was known for this vision device, which might have also included his obsidian mirror from which he received his name. Olivier, *Mockeries and Metamorphoses,* 60; Vesque, "'El instrument para ver,'" 113–24.

89. Sahagún, *Historia general,* 145. "Dos plumajes redondos como rodelas, y tenían el medio agujerado; eran aquellas como mazas que llevaban delante de aquel dios puestas en unas astas, como astas de lanzas."

90. Durán, *Book of the Gods,* 458–59.

91. Sahagún, *Florentine Codex*, 12:88.

92. Durán, *Book of the Gods*, 458–59.

93. Sahagún, *Florentine Codex*, 2:147.

94. Torquemada, *Monarquía Indiana*, 3:418

95. Torquemada, 3:405.

96. Durán, *Book of the Gods*, 87–88.

97. Durán, 88.

98. Durán, 89. This also smacks of Christian theology applied to Mexica practice.

99. The description of the sacrifices made to Huitzilopochtli comes from Durán, 90–94.

100. Durán, 458.

101. Sahagún, *Florentine Codex*, 9:65.

102. Sahagún, 9:65.

103. Sahagún, 9:65; 2:147.

104. Sahagún, 9:65–66.

105. Sahagún, 9:66; 2:148.

106. Sahagún, 2:148.

107. López Luján and the Templo Mayor archeologists have discovered the remains of at least one child who may well have been sacrificed during a Panquetzaliztli ritual. López Luján et al., "Huitzilopochtli y el sacrificio de niños," 388–89.

108. Sahagún, *Florentine Codex*, 9:66.

109. The second word means "sacrificial streamers" and is the base for the name of the ceremony *teteualtia*.

110. Sahagún, *Historia*, 145, par. 39.

111. Sahagún, *Florentine Codex*, 9:66–67.

112. Durán, *Book of the Gods*, 90.

113. Durán, 88–89.

114. Durán, 91–94. This admonition resembles Christian practice of not eating immediately before or after consuming the Eucharist.

115. Sahagún, *Florentine Codex*, 1:19–20; González Torres, *El sacrificio humano*, 228–29.

116. Sahagún, 9:66–67.

117. Van Zantwijk, *The Aztec Arrangement*, 166–70.

118. Sahagún, *Historia general*, 146; Hvidtfeldt, *Teotl and *Ixiptlatli*, 132.

119. The word *mitl* could signify either an arrow or a dart. See also, Hvidtfeldt, *Teotl and *Ixiptlatli*, 126–27.

120. Sahagún, *Florentine Codex*, 3:6. Sahagún seems to make a distinction between *tlaxilacalli* and *calpolli*, which are frequently thought of as essentially synonymous. He seems to indicate that the tlaxilacalli was a larger district within the altepetl while the calpolli might be a smaller neighborhood within a tlaxilacalli. Other research indicates quite the contrary, that the calpolli was the larger unit and the tlaxilacalli the smaller, block-oriented unit. Clendinnen, *Aztecs*, 21; Lockhart, *Nahuas after the Conquest*, 16–17.

121. Sahagún, 3:5–6.

122. Clendinnen, *Aztecs*, 52, suggests that during penance, people refrained from washing their hair.

123. Sahagún, *Florentine Codex*, 3:8–9.

124. Sahagún, 2:148–50.

125. Clendinnen, *Aztecs*, 48.

126. Sahagún, *Florentine Codex*, 2:148. The Nahuatl expressed each of these actions in a single, very complex word. For example "shaved their heads like servants" is *quinquatexoloxima*.

127. Sahagún, *Historia*, 146, par. 46. "Dábanlos porrazos y trasquilábanlos, arrastraban y acoceábanlos y arrojábanlos por allí muy maltrados." We can appreciate the difficulty of translating, since English and Spanish do not closely align in these expressions.

128. Sahagún lists the following: all who worked, served, cared for the tobacco, cared for the chocolate, carried the water, carried serving vessels, served and made tamales, and served and made pulque as well as everyone in the neighborhood. Sahagún, *Florentine Codex*, 2:148–49.

129. Sahagún, *Florentine Codex*, 2:148–49.

130. Sahagún, 2:150.

131. One early advocate of this interpretation was Eduard Seler, who published a study in 1892 on Huitzilopochtli, Seler, *Collected Works*, 5:96–98. This interpretation continues to be reinforced by more modern scholars. Graulich, *Fiestas de los pueblos*, 202–3; Mazzetto, *Lieux de culte*, 603. Brotherston, "Sacred Sand," 307, even suggests that the myths might be descriptions of the celebrations rather than vice versa.

CHAPTER 4. **Other Ceremonies and Other Sources**

1. The following description is based upon Sahagún, *Florentine Codex*, 9:87–88.

2. In Nahua belief, individuals had spirit guides called *nahualli*. The word can also refer to the priest who transforms himself into an animal spirit.

3. Sahagún, *Florentine Codex*, 9:87–88.

4. Boone, *Incarnations*, 32; Torquemada, *Monarquía Indiana*, 3:390.

5. Olivier, *Mockeries and Metamorphoses*, 44.

6. Sahagún, *Florentine Codex*, 2:66–68.

7. There is still a hill named Tepetzingo in what was Lake Tetzcoco, to the west of Chiconcuac and to the east of Ecatepec. In preconquest times, this hill would have been a small island in the lake. There is another Tepetzingo in the modern-day State of Hidalgo, not too far from Tepepulco, but it would not have been in the lake.

8. Sahagún, *Florentine Codex*, 2:70–71.

9. Carrasco, "The Sacrifice of Tezcatlipoca," 36.

10. Sahagún, *Florentine Codex*, 2:70–73; 12:51–54.

11. Sahagún, 2:72–73.

12. Torquemada, *Monarquía Indiana*, 3:380–81 (libro X, cap. XVI); Sahagún, 2:71–72.

13. Torquemada, 3:381–82; Sahagún, 2:72–73.

14. Martínez, *Documentos cortesianos*, 1:207.

15. Olivier, *Mockeries and Metamorphoses*, 226. Boone, *Incarnations*, 34, believes that Sahagún conflates Panquetzaliztli and Toxcatl since no other chronicler recalls the dough figurine during the conquest episode.

16. Sahagún, *Florentine Codex*, 2:111–17

17. The *yauhtli* (*Tagetes lucida*) is also known as "unscented marigold" or "Mexican marigold."

18. The god was also known as Huehueteotl (Old God).

19. Sahagún, *Florentine Codex*, 2:115; Hvidtfeldt, *Teotl and *Ixiptlatli*, 90.

20. Sahagún, 2:111–17.

21. Sahagún, 2:164.

22. Sahagún, 2:120–21.

23. Now known as Iztaccihuatl (White Woman).

24. *Codex Mendoza*, folio 56v, 171–73; Sahagún, *Florentine Codex*, 2:122–23; Carrasco, "The Sacrifice of Women in the Florentine Codex," 216–17.

25. Sahagún, 2:125.

26. DiCesare, *Sweeping the Way*, 98–99.

27. Sahagún, *Florentine Codex*, 2:157.

28. Sahagún, 2:162–64.

29. As will be seen in future chapters, it is possible that this ceremony was in imitation of Panquetzaliztli since the nemontemi represented the end of an annual cycle. In the larger fifty-two year cycle, the New Fire ceremony had migrated to Panquetzaliztli.

30. Sahagún, *Florentine Codex*, 2:164–66; Castillo, "El bisesto Nahuatl," 76–104, in particular 76–92.

31. Sahagún, 2:190, 211

32. Berdan, "Ports of Trade," 188.

33. Sahagún, *Florentine Codex*, 2: 44, 81, 131, 153.

34. Sahagún, 2:137–38.

35. Sahagún, 2:162–63.

36. Sahagún, 2:103–4.

37. Sahagún, 2:162–63.

38. Sahagún, 2:127.

39. Sahagún, 2:139.

40. Robertson, *Mexican Manuscript Painting*, 178; Boone, *Incantations*, 32–33.

41. This might represent the long breechclout described by Sahagún as a special gift for the disguised merchants. Sahagún, *Florentine Codex*, 9:55.

42. Sahagún, 2:148–49.

43. Olivier, *Mockeries and Metamorphoses*, 28–32, 35–42.

44. Selected from the longer list in Olivier, 54–55.

45. *Codex Telleriano-Remensis*, 127–30.

46. Olivier, *Mockeries and Metamorphoses*, 54–55.

47. *Codex Telleriano-Remensis*, folio 5r, 147–48.

48. *Codex Telleriano-Remensis*, 125.

49. Other sources indicate that the god was celebrated four times each year. Carrasco, "The Sacrifice of Tezcatlipoca," 40.

50. Olivier, *Mockeries and Metamorphoses*, 231–40.

51. *Codex Telleriano-Remensis*, 148, 256.

52. *Codex Telleriano-Remensis*, folio 5r, 148, 255–56.

53. "Codex Vaticanus 3738 A," Foundation for the Advancement of Mesoamerican Studies, www.famsi.org/research/loubat/Vaticanus%203738/page_49v.jpg. The *Codex Vaticanus A* is also known as the *Codex Vaticanus 3738* or the *Codex Rios*. It is held in the Vatican Library and is attributed to the Dominican friar Pedro de los Rios. The Vaticanus is so closely related to the *Telleriano-Remensis* that Quiñones-Keber includes the comments from the Vaticanus in her work: *Codex Telleriano-Remensis*, 148.

54. Boone, *Incarnations of the Aztec Supernatural*, 40.

55. Nuttall, *The Book of the Life of the Ancient Mexicans*, vol. 1, folio 42v–43r.

56. Torquemada, *Monarquía Indiana*, 3:427; Hassig, *Aztec Warfare*, 54.

CHAPTER 5. The Transformation of Panquetzaliztli

1. Sahagún, *Florentine Codex*, 2:42, 47, and so on. One should be careful in looking at the translation offered by Dibble and Anderson. In their first edition of this particular volume, they do not translate the Nahuatl in this way. The word in question is *nextlaoaliztli*. In their first edition they translate it as "blood sacrifice." Later it is translated as "the feast and debt-payment." The second translation is much closer to the Nahuatl, where the root morpheme refers to reciprocity. At the same time, Molina glosses *nextlaualli* as "blood sacrifice offered to the idols." Molina, *Vocabulario*, folio 71v.

2. Hassig argues that while this may be true on one level, in reality the religion was used by rulers for political and imperial purposes. Hassig, *Time, History, and Belief*, 102.

3. Anderson, "Los 'Primeros memoriales,'" 56.

4. Hassig, *Time, History, and Belief*, 80. The others were Tlacaxipehualiztli, Etzcualiztli, and Ochpaniztli.

5. This was suggested by Brundage, *The Jade Steps*, 13, nearly thirty years ago, but without further explanation or exploration.

6. Sahagún, *Florentine Codex*, 2:141.

7. Durán, *Book of the Gods*, 459.

8. Graulich, *Fiestas de los pueblos*, 193–94.

9. Sahagún, *Primeros memoriales*, 74.

10. Karttunen, *An Analytical Dictionary*, 3.

11. Motolinia, *Memoriales*, 62.

12. Sahagún, *Historia general*, 130.

13. *Codex Telleriano-Remensis*, e.g., folios 40r–v.

14. Sahagún, *Primeros memoriales*, 64–65.

15. Sahagún, *Florentine Codex*, 2:27.

16. Sahagún, *Historia general*, 143.

17. Sahagún, *Florentine Codex*, 2:143.

18. Durán, *Book of the Gods*, 459.

19. Sahagún, *Florentine Codex*, 2:142–43.

20. Sahagún, *Primeros memoriales*, 65.

21. Sahagún, *Florentine Codex*, 3:148.

22. Sahagún, *Primeros memoriales*, 65.

23. Durán, *Book of the Gods*, 460.

24. Sahagún, *Primeros memoriales*, 65.

25. Durán, *Book of the Gods*, 95.

26. Sahagún, *Primeros memoriales*, 65.

27. Sahagún, *Florentine Codex*, 2:149–50.

28. Graulich, *Fiestas de los pueblos*, 219; Olivier, *Mockeries and Metamorphoses*, 94.

29. Graulich, 202–6.

30. This is not unlike the relationship of the Jewish people with their deity. From the King James Bible: "And I will take you to me for a people, and I will be to you a God" (Exodus 6:7). This relationship might have struck a chord in the friars who copied down the earliest versions of this myth, perhaps emphasizing the exceptionalism of the Mexica to be a parallel to the Jews.

31. Brotherston, "Huitzilopochtli," 163; Molina, *Vocabulario*, 111; Sahagún, *Florentine Codex*, 3:5. "*Caiac nex in ita*."

32. Sahagún, 3:1–5. Several modern scholars have posited that some of the nativity myths of Huitzilopochtli are, in reality, recollections of the celebrations of Panquetzaliztli. Gillespie, *The Aztec Kings*, 211–13; Brotherston, "Sacred Sand," 307.

33. Baquedano and Graulich, "Decapitation among the Aztecs," 166. The down balls also appear on his shield, the tehuehuelli.

34. Read, *Time and Sacrifice*, 74–76. Milbrath, "Decapitated Lunar Goddesses," 186–88.

35. Seler, "Some Remarks on the Natural Bases of Mexican Myths," in *Collected Works*, 4:157; Lesur, "El dios Huitzilopochtli," 184–87. Karl Taube has associated the xiuhcoatl with a meteor. Taube, "The Turquoise Hearth," 288–301.

36. Sahagún, *Florentine Codex*, 2:175. When discussing the temple of Huitzilopochtli, Sahagún refers to it as Coatepec.

37. Van Zantwijk, *Aztec Arrangement*, 256.

38. Aveni et al., "Myth, Environment, and the Orientation of Templo Mayor of Tenochtitlan," 303. We must note that in order for this to be feasible, the Aztecs needed to have intercalary days, that is, days inserted into the 365-day solar year to keep it aligned with the movement of the sun.

39. Aveni et al., 304.

40. Carrasco, "Myth, Cosmic Terror, and the Templo Mayor," 137.

41. Aveni et al., "Myth, Environment, and the Orientation," 295–304.

42. Nicholson, "Religion in Pre-Hispanic Central Mexico," 401.

43. An important version of the Mexica migration is found in a document called the *Tira de Peregrinación* or the *Codex Boturini*.

44. Garibay, *Teogonía*, 43.

45. Davies, *The Aztecs*, 172–73.

46. As noted, one of the epithets for Huitzilopochtli was Tetzahuitl. The fishnet cape worn by Huitzilopochtli in many illustrations might refer to this older fisher deity.

47. Castillo, *Historia de la venida de los mexicanos*, 52, 110–11; Olivier, *Mockeries and Metamorphoses*, 31. "Huitzilipoch" is not easily translated. The *-poch* suffix could be related to a child or to smoke.

48. Uchmany, "Huitzilopochtli," 213–27.

49. Matos Moctezuma, "Templo Mayor: History and Interpretation," 48–49.

50. Carrasco, "Myth, Cosmic Terror and the Templo Mayor," 135–36.

51. Castañeda de la Paz, "La *Tira de peregrinación*," 186–98. In the text as Castañeda reads it, one of the divine personages is *amimitl*, possibly translated as "water arrow"—or better, "water arrows," since the *mi-* is reduplicated, showing plurality—who is identified as an avatar of Mixcoatl. The interpretation offered by Castañeda has not yet received much support from scholars. Important here is the notion that the Mexica abandoned their original deity for Huitzilopochtli.

52. Castañeda de la Paz, 186–98. Castañeda also points out that Mixcoatl and Chimalma were the parents of Quetzalcoatl. The priest in Aztlan was identified as Mixcoatl, the name of the deity he served, while the female figure is depicted as Chimalma. Chimalma was also one of the four leaders of the Aztecs on their migration.

53. Uchmany, "Huitzilopochtli," 229.

54. Brundage, *The Fifth Sun*, 138.

55. Matos Moctezuma, "Symbolism of the Templo Mayor," 200–201; Carrasco, *City of Sacrifice*, 64.

56. Heyden, "Caves, Gods, and Myths," 14–17.

57. In the battle at Huitznahuac, the slaves and warrior victims would represent Huitzilopochtli, fighting his brothers the Huitznahua, then as the victims proceed to the Templo Mayor, they each become a teixiptla of the deity. The bathing rituals have prepared them to become god impersonators, an event which occurred as they moved toward their ultimate sacrifice.

58. Matos Moctezuma, "Symbolism of the Templo Mayor," 200.

59. Seler, "Some Remarks on the Natural Bases of Mexican Myths," in *Collected Works*, 4:159.

60. Seler, 4:160–61. This interpretation was based on the origin legend found in the writings of Tezozomoc, *Crónica mexicayotl*, 32–35; Matos Moctezuma, "Symbolism of the Templo Mayor," 200.

61. Davies, *The Aztecs*, 14. The New Fire ceremonies celebrated the closing of a fifty-two year period.

62. Brundage, *The Fifth Sun*, 147. He indicates that four persons were sacrificed here.

63. Sahagún, *Florentine Codex*, 7:7–8.

64. Sahagún, 3:2–3.

65. Hvidtfeldt, *Teotl and *Ixiptlatli*, 135, claims that the last term refers to the "foremost terrace of the temple." See also López Austin and López Luján, *Monte Sagrado—Templo Mayor*, 304–9.

66. Davies, *The Aztecs*, 76–77.

67. Compare this with the variations discussed by Graulich, *Myths of Ancient Mexico*, 226–30; Brundage, *The Fifth Sun*, 139. Boone, "Migration Histories," 121–51, argues that the migration story is, itself, a ritual performance, recapitulating and manifesting the entire sweep of Mexica cultural history. Navarette Linares, *Los orígenes*, compares all the migration stories of the people of the Central Basin of Mexico to create a larger perspective. González Torres, *El sacrificio humano*, 205–8, suggests that even more than a symbolic representation of the migration, it also depicts the early conquests of the Mexica after their embrace of Huitzilopochtli.

68. Boone, 123.

69. Brundage, *The Fifth Sun*, 139.

70. Edgerton, *Theaters of Conversion*, 62. He also notes that the calendar frame to the depiction of the founding of Tenochtitlan in the *Codex Mendoza* must be read in a counterclockwise manner from the year 2 House to the year 13 Reed.

71. Sahagún, *Florentine Codex*, 2:42.

72. Mundy, *The Death of Aztec Tenochtitlan*, 23.

73. Sahagún, *Florentine Codex*, 2:42–44; Sahagún, *Historia general*, 98–99; Arnold, *Eating Landscape*, 130–34.

74. Aveni, "Mapping the Ritual Landscape," 58–73.

75. Sahagún, *Florentine Codex*, 2:53–54.

76. Sahagún, 2:70–71.

77. Sahagún, 2:120–21.

78. Sahagún, 2:122.

79. Sahagún, 2:125–26.

80. Durán, *Book of the Gods*, 235–36.

81. Durán, 229.

82. Graulich, *Fiestas de los pueblos*, 208–9. An early analysis of the confusion between the two gods is offered by Seler, "Uitzilopochtli, the Talking Hummingbird," in *Collected Works*, 5:96–97.

83. Brotherston, "Huitzilopochtli," 159; Olivier, *Mockeries and Metamorphoses*, 28, 271.

84. Garibay, *Teogonía*, 23–24; Nicholson, "Religion," 397–98.

85. Nicholson, "7, Fifty-two year bundle stone (*xiuhmolpilli*)," 43–45, esp. 45; Hunt, *The Transformation of the Hummingbird*, 164–65.

86. Johansson, "Tezcatlipoca o Quetzalcoatl," 179–99. This is a general overview of the relationship of the two gods, focusing ultimately on the notion that the Aztecs believed that the Spanish were emissaries of Quetzalcoatl.

87. Olivier, *Mockeries and Metamorphoses*, 256–57. Olivier expands on this rivalry in his article: "Enemy Brothers or Divine Twins?," 59–82.

88. Alva Ixtlilxochitl, *Obras históricas*, 1: 273, 324.

89. López Austin, *The Myth of Quetzalcoatl*, 25–28.

90. Graulich, *Fiestas de los pueblos*, 191–92.

91. *Centzon*, in Nahuatl, means "four hundred" and also simply implies a large number of items. Graulich, "Dualities in Cacaxtla," 104; Graulich, "Mexico City's 'Templo Mayor' Revisited," 27.

92. Olivier, *Mockeries and Metamorphoses*, 168.

93. Olivier, "El symbolism sacrificial," 453, considers that symbols of the sacrificial victims represent the Mimixcoa. Olivier considers the figures seen especially on folios 38v and 39r of the *Codex Telleriano Remensis* to be Mimixcoa. Graulich, *Myths of Ancient Mexico*, 163–64.

94. Graulich, "The Metaphor of the Day," 49; Graulich, "Miccailhuitl," 50; Kruell, "Panquetzaliztli," 81–93.

95. Umberger, "Tezcatlipoca and Huitzilopochtli," 84–87.

96. Brundage, *The Fifth Sun*, 150; Conrad and Demarest, *Religion and Empire*, 28.

97. Olivier, *Mockeries and Metamorphoses*, 26–32; Sullivan, "The Rhetorical Orations or *huehuetlatolli*," 86.

98. Durán, *The History of the Indies*, 44n3.

99. Conrad and Demarest, *Religion and Empire*, 38.

100. Nicholson, "Religion," 426.

101. Olivier, *Mockeries and Metamorphoses*, 26–29.

102. Alva Ixtlilxochitl, *Obras históricas*, 1:324, 402 passim; Durán, *The History of the Indies*, 44n3.

103. Sahagún, *Florentine Codex*, 7:4–7.

104. Brotherston, "Huitzilopochtli," 159. See also Sahagún, *Primeros memoriales*, 93–95.

105. Sahagún, *Florentine Codex*, 3:4. *"Auh ce pitzaoac in jcxi yiopochcopa, qujpotonj in jxocpal."*

106. Sahagún, 9:53.

107. Baquedano and Graulich, "Decapitation among the Aztecs," 173.

108. Graulich, *Fiestas de los pueblos*, 206–7.

109. Graulich, 216–17.

110. Hassig, *Aztec Warfare*, 54.

111. Hassig, *Trade, Tribute and Transportation*, 119–21.

112. Sahagún, *Florentine Codex*, 9:32; Hassig, 119–21; Conrad and Demarest, *Religion and Empire*, 66; Katz, *Situación social y económica*, 69.

113. Hassig, *Aztec Warfare*, 162–63.

114. Conrad and Demarest, *Religion and Empire*, 50–51.

115. Hassig, *Trade, Tribute, and Transportation*, 117; Hirth, *Aztec Economic World*, 208–13.

116. For a full discussion of the structure, membership, and organization of merchant groups, see Hirth, *Aztec Economic World*, 192–94. He argues that there were significant differences between these merchant groups and guilds and those of medieval Europe.

117. Van Zantwijk, "Las organizaciones social económica," 7–8; Van Zantwijk, *Aztec Arrangement*, 144–50; Katz, *Situación social y económica*, 73–75; Hirth, *Aztec Economic World*, 223–28. The pursuit of ever-higher rank within the merchant guild through ceremonial participation and the expenditure of large sums of money, as described by Van Zantwijk, has a modern parallel with the *cargo* system first studied in the highlands of Chiapas. See Cancian, *Economics and Prestige in a Maya Community*.

118. Berdan, "Ports of Trade in Mesoamerica," 189.

119. Katz, *Situación social y económica*, 75.

120. Katz, 78.

121. Durán, *Book of the Gods*, 415–17; Sahagún, *Florentine Codex*, 2: 3–4, 47–56.

122. Durán, 430–33; Sahagún, 2: 11–12, 78–90.

123. Durán, 447–49; Sahagún, 2: 19–20, 118–26. For a fuller analysis of the month, see DiCesare, *Sweeping the Way*.

124. Hassig, *Aztec Warfare*, 54.

125. Hassig, 262.

126. Carrasco, *City of Sacrifice*, 81–87.

127. Durán, *The History of the Indies*, 334–35, 336.

128. Durán, 407–8. The other festivals included Huey Tecuilhuitl (the "Feast of the Lords) and the Feast of Revelations, during which hallucinogenic mushrooms were consumed.

129. León-Portilla, *Aztec Thought and Culture*, 160–61.

130. Durán, *History of the Indies*, 206

131. Battock, "Acerca de las pinturas," 113, offers a good summary of much of the discussion regarding the burning of the books and histories over the last century.

CHAPTER 6. Looking at History through Panquetzaliztli

1. Schroeder, *Tlacaelel Remembered*, 62–75; Durán, *History of the Indies*, 71–95.

2. Sahagún, *Florentine Codex*, 10:191. The reference in Sahagún relates to the period when the Mexica were wandering in the wilderness, and so it is quite possible that the Itzcoatl mentioned was not the tlahtoani of Tenochtitlan but some other historic Mexica with the same name. León-Portilla, "Itzcoatl," 122–26; León-Portilla, *Aztec Thought*, 155–56; León-Portilla, *Los antiguos*, 90–93; Brotherston, "Huitzilopochtli," 162; Marcus, *Mesoamerican Writing Systems*, 146–49; Battock, "Acerca de las pinturas," 113.

3. Nicholson, "Religion," 397–99; Hassig, *Time, History and Belief*, 63–65. One should note that thirteen was also a propitious number in that the ritual calendar had thirteen numbers associated with twenty images. There is also evidence that the Mexica believed that there were thirteen heavens.

4. Hassig, *Time, History, and Belief*, 67–69.

5. León-Portilla, *Aztec Thought*, 161–62.

6. Durán, *History of the Indies*, 74; Schroeder, *Remembering Tlacaelel*, 63.

7. León-Portilla, *Aztec Thought*, 163. The exact lines quoted can also be found in Durán, 232; Schroeder, 75. For a brief but clear discussion of the Flower War, see Hassig, *Aztec Warfare*, 128–30 passim.

8. Brotherston, "Huitzilopochtli," 159.

9. A brief survey of this comes from Umberger, "Tezcatlipoca and Huitzilopochtli," 83–87.

10. In recent years, there have been three careful analyses of this war: Umberger, "Metaphorical Underpinnings"; Klein, "Fighting with Femininity"; Graulich, "Más sobre la Coyolxauhqui." See also Durán's account of the election and war, Durán, *History of the Indies*, 62. For older takes on the events, see Brundage, *A Rain of Darts*, 179–91; Davies, *The Aztecs*, 124–26.

11. See Umberger.

12. Umberger, 12.

13. Durán, *History of the Indies*, 249–50.

14. Durán, 260–61; Davies, *The Aztecs*, 129–30.

15. Umberger, "The Metaphorical Underpinnings," 21.

16. Durán, *History of the Indies*, 262; Hirth, *The Aztec Economic World*, 215–18; Katz, *Situación social y económica*, 78; Katz, *The Ancient American Civilizations*, 186–87.

17. Davies, *The Aztecs*, 131–32; Katz, 186–87.

18. Acosta Saignes, "Los pochteca," 22; Umberger, "The Metaphorical Underpinnings of Aztec History," 26.

19. Umberger, 11–29; Durán, *History of the Indies*, 260–61.

20. *Codex Mendoza*, 4:25.

21. Hirth, *The Aztec Economic World*, 235–36.

22. *Codex Mendoza*, 2:112–14; Kelly and Palerm, *The Tajín Totonac*, 268–69, 291–95.

23. Gerhard, *A Guide to the Historical Geography*, 300–305.

24. The Hopi also have a New Fire ceremony roughly corresponding to the winter solstice. Waters, *The Book of the Hopi*, 138–41. Many other North American groups also had ceremonies involving the creation of a new fire. See Furst, "The Aztec New Fire Ritual," 30–32.

25. Hassig, *Time, History, and Belief*, 15–16. In opposition, Graulich, "The Metaphor of the Day," 49, 50–59, holds that the calendar moved through the seasons. In C.E. 680, for example, Panquetzaliztli would have been in late June and early July. Graulich developed his ideas more fully by 1999 (*Ritos aztecas*, 63–69), when he unequivocally rejects the idea of added days. His analysis of the New Fire ceremony occurs on 220–24. The most respected archeoastronomer, Antony Aveni, holds that there were occasional adjustments to the calendar to keep it in line with the actual solar movement: Aveni, Calnek, and Hartung, "Myth, Environment, and the Orientation of the Templo Mayor of Tenochtitlan," 289–91. Perhaps most convincing is Victor Castillo, "El bisesto Nahuatl," 76–104, in particular 76–92, who argues that in the *Florentine Codex*, there is evidence of the addition of a day to the month of Izcalli every four years, which would be roughly sufficient to keep the calendar aligned with the seasons; Sahagún, *Florentine Codex*, 2:162–64. One of the first attempts was made by Seler, "Corrections to the Length of the Year," in *Collected Works*, 4:91–103. Graulich, *Fiestas de los pueblos*, 214, who generally argues against leap days, notes that around 1500 there was an effort to reestablish a tie between the months of the solar year and the movement of the sun. This coincides roughly with the rise to power of Moteuczoma II in 1502. Krupp, "The 'Blinding of the Years,'" 11, argues that the transit of the Pleiades might actually have assisted in the alignment of the calendar and prompted the addition of leap days. The whole issue is outlined in Olivier, *Mockeries and Metamorphoses*, 203–4.

26. The description that follows is taken from Sahagún, *Florentine Codex*, 7:25–31. For a detailed analysis of the ceremony and its deeper meaning, see Read, *Time and Sacrifice in the Aztec Cosmos*.

27. Sahagún, 7: 25–26, 31–32.

28. Van Zantwijk, "Las organizaciones social-económicas," 5.

29. Sahagún, *Florentine Codex*, 7:27.

30. Durán, *Book of the Gods*, 469–70; Sahagún, 7:27–28.

31. Sahagún, 7:25–28.

32. Sahagún, 7:29–30; Carrasco, *City of Sacrifice*, 98.

33. Sahagún, 7:30–31.

34. Carrasco, *City of Sacrifice*, 102–3, envisions a far more complex series of alignments.

35. Hassig, *Time, History, and Belief*, 38–39.

36. Hassig, 38–47, argues that only the last New Fire ceremony, in 1507, occurred in the new year of 2 Reed. Read, *Time and Sacrifice*, 1–43, details the symbolism and nature of the shift from 1 Rabbit to 2 Reed.

37. Couch, *The Festival Cycle of the Aztec Codex Borbonicus*, 78–79.

38. Pharo, *The Ritual Practice of Time*, 245–50.

39. Hassig, *Time, History and Belief*, 45, 85–89; Read, *Time and Sacrifice*, 103.

40. Broda, "La fiesta del fuego Nuevo," 294, sees the zenith of the Pleiades as also linked to the nadir of the sun.

41. Unlike the Maya calendar, the Mexica calendar did not have a zero day, a distinct starting point from which all other dates were counted. The Maya solar year wandered through the seasons since its count was tied to a single starting point. The Mexica could link their solar calendar to the seasons. Consequently, as long as the tonalpohualli and xiuhpohualli remained in alignment, extra days could be added, and some feasts moved from one point in the cycle to another. Hassig, *Time, History, and Belief*, 135–36.

42. Milbrath, *Heaven and Earth*, plates 18, 30; Boone, *Cycles of Time and Meaning*, 207–9.

43. As noted earlier, the *Codex Borgia* in all likelihood came from the Puebla-Tlaxcala Valley. Milbrath, *Heaven and Earth*, 1.

44. Anders, Jansen, and Reyes García, *El libro del ciuacoatl*, 33–40.

45. Patrick Johansson, "El desliz cronológico," 78, reports this as an interpretation found in the *Codex Vaticanus A*.

46. Tichy, "Order and Relationship," 233–34, and others argue that the New Fire ceremony must have inaugurated the month of Panquetzaliztli, and the useless days, the nemontemi, would fall right before the start of the month. Pharo, *The Ritual Practice of Time*, 248–49, suggests that once every fifty-two years, the nemontemi were placed after the major sacrifices of Panquetzaliztli, followed by the New Fire ceremony. Umberger, "Events Commemorated by Date Plaques," 442–44, argues that in reality, the nemontemi and the New Fire were two distinct ceremonies that were normally celebrated in conjunction with one another but could, theoretically, be split. Johansson, "El desliz cronológico," has a very curious view that the nemontemi were saved up and then used en mass every four or more years.

47. Seler, *Collected Works*, 3:172–4. On 175–76, Seler also notes that the deity Tlacahuepan, known as the Younger Brother, was shared by both Tezcatlipoca and Huitzilopochtli. With the latter, he was an alternative identify for Painal. See also Caso, *Los calendarios prehispánicos*, 132–40. Umberger, "Aztec Sculptures," 123–24, argues that these two dates might mark a fifty-two-day period in the middle of which was the actual 2 Reed day in the 2 Reed year in which the sacrifice occurred.

48. Pharo, *The Ritual Practice of Time*, 310 passim, provides a very detailed summary of the main arguments in favor of each possibility. The evidence for 1507 relies on an entry in the *Codex Telleriano-Remensis*, 274.

49. Graulich, *Fiestas de los pueblos*, 221. Tena, *El calendario mexica*, 92–93, holds that the change might have occurred shortly after the founding of Tenochtitlan or in 1350–51. López Luján, "Cuando la gente 'Se uno-aconejó,'" outlines the archeological evidence for abnormal climate conditions in the middle of the fifteenth century.

50. There is a general absence of sculptures or pictorial manuscripts that clearly tie any other ruler to a New Fire ceremony in 2 Reed. Pharo, *The Ritual Practice of Time*, 315–22.

51. A momoztli was envisioned as a seat or throne for Tezcatlipoca. These were erected at crossroads or other symbolically important places. Noguera, "Funciones del momoztli."

52. Hassig, *Time, History and Belief*, 104–6; Umberger, "Events Commemorated by Date Plaques," 442–44; Umberger, "Aztec Sculptures," 173–92; Pharo, *The Ritual Practice of Time*, 315–18; Hajovsky, *On the Lips of Others*, 109–13. Klein, "Ideology of Autosacrifice," 338–49, differs in her interpretation of some of the decoration but affirms the notion that the structure symbolized the shift from 1 Rabbit to 2 Reed.

53. Figure 13 is a reconstruction of the probable appearance of the Chapultepec bas-relief based on currently available information, but it is subject to change as further information becomes available. Hajovsky, 120–25.

54. Gillespie, *The Aztec Kings*, 124–25.

55. Hajovsky, *On the Lips of Others*, 118–25; Umberger, "Aztec Sculptures," 147–51; Nicholson, "The Chapultepec Cliff Sculpture," 394–417.

56. Townsend, *State and Cosmos*, 58–59.

57. Karttunen, *Analytical Dictionary*, 348.

58. Gordon Whittaker, email, July 5, 2017. "I regard the horseshoe as the glyph for (MO) ZOMA 'be angry,' while the crown is the well-known glyph for TECUH(TLI)/TEUC(TLI) 'lord.' The whole composition reads as MO/TECUH/ZOMA (MO-TEUC-ZOMA), in my opinion. The horseshoe is in reality an elaborate speech or breath scroll, and the spiny frill lining it appears to represent the heat radiating from the speech or breath." Whittaker also considers the middle object to be a lip plug or labret.

59. Hajovsky, *On the Lips of Others*, 97–98.

60. Matos Moctezuma, "Tlaltecuhtli," 19–20; Sahagún, *Florentine Codex*, 6:11–12.

61. Davies, *The Aztecs*, 91–94. See also Durán, *History of the Indies*, 238–41.

62. This argument is outlined by Hassig, *Time, History, and Belief*, 84–86.

63. Hassig, 90–97.

64. *History and Mythology of the Aztecs*, 107.

65. Hassig, *Time, History, and Belief*, 113–15.

66. López Luján and González López, "Tierra, agua y fuego," 24–34.

67. Hassig, *Aztec Warfare*, 219–35; Katz, *Ancient American Civilizations*, 237–38; Davies, *The Aztecs*, 221.

68. Hassig, 190–93, 208–11, 225–27, 233–34; Graulich, *Montezuma*, 54; Davies, *The Aztecs*, 219–21.

69. Mundy, *The Death of Aztec* Tenochtitlan, 67–71, discusses the ongoing battle the Mexica had with water; Van Zantwijk, *The Aztec Arrangement*, 280–86; Katz, *Ancient American Civilizations*, 238; Davies, *The Aztecs*, 221.

70. Hassig, *Aztec Warfare*, 220–22; Vázquez Chamorro, "Las reformas," 207–11; Davies, 214–16; Katz, 238–41; León-Portilla, *Los antiguos mexicanos*, 104–5.

71. Hirth, *The Aztec Economic World*, 208–23; Vázquez Chamorro, "Las reformas," 217–18.

72. Hajovsky, *On the Lips of Others*, 86; Hassig, *Aztec Warfare*, 220–23; Katz, *Ancient American Civilizations*, 217.

73. Hirth, *The Aztec Economic World*, 210–11; Vázquez Chamorro, "Las reformas," 210; Davies, *The Aztecs*, 139.

74. Graulich, *Fiestas de los pueblos*, 214. Graulich holds that the Aztecs lacked a method for inserting leap days, thus allowing the xiuhpoalli to wander, not connected to the seasons. He posits that under Moteuczoma, Panquetzaliztli had aligned with the solstice, since the year had begun at the spring equinox. Graulich, *Montezuma*, 123. Many other scholars do not concur with Graulich on the issue of leap days.

75. *Codex Telleriano-Remensis*, 274.

76. Hassig, *Time, History, and Belief*, 90–97; Jansen and Pérez Jiménez, *Time and the Ancestors*, 402–8; Tena, *El calendario mexica*, 98.

77. Nicholson, "Religion in Pre-Hispanic Central Mexico," 425–26; Davies, *The Aztecs*, 187–90; Hassig, *Aztec Warfare*, 17–26, 263–66; Hirth, *The Aztec Economic World*, 48–57; Conrad and Demarest, *Religion and Empire*, 37–45.

78. Carrasco, *The Tenochca Empire*, 43–44.

79. Blanton, "A Consideration of Causality," 219–25.

BIBLIOGRAPHY

Acosta Saignes, Miguel. *Los pochteca: ubicación de los mercaderes en la estructura social tenochca.* Mexico: Escuela Nacional de Antropología, 1945.

Acuña Delgado, Angel. "Funciones y definición conceptual de la carrera Rarámuri en la Sierra Tarahumara." *Nueva Antropología* 19 (January–April 2005): 149–71.

Aguilera, Carmen. "The 'Templo Mayor' as a Dual Symbol of the Passing of Time." In *Mesoamerican Dualism/Dualismo Mesoamericano,* edited by Rudolf Zantwijk, 74–93. Utrecht: RUU-ISOR, 1990.

Alcina Franch, José. "Juan de Torquemada, 1564–1624." In *Guide to Ethnohistorical Sources, Part 2,* edited by Howard F. Cline and John B. Glass, 256–75. Handbook of Middle American Indians 13, edited by Robert Wauchope. Austin: University of Texas Press, 1973.

Alva Ixtlilxochitl, Fernando de. *Obras históricas.* Edited by Edmundo O'Gorman. 2 vols. Mexico: Universidad Nacional Autónoma de México, 1975–77.

Alvardo Tezozomoc, Hernando. *Cronica Mexicana.* Edited by Manuel Orozco y Berra. Mexico: Irineo Paz, 1878.

Anawalt, Patricia Rieff. *Indian Clothing before Cortés: Mesoamerican Costumes from the Codices.* Norman: University of Oklahoma Press, 1981.

Anders, Ferdinand, Maarten Jansen, and Luis Reyes García. *El libro del ciuacoatl: Homenaje para el año del Fuego Nuevo, libro explicativo del llamado Códice Borbónico.* Mexico: Fondo de Cultura Económico, 1991.

———. *Los tiempos del cielo y de la oscuridad: Oráculos y liturgia, libro explicativo del llamado Códice Borgia.* Mexico: Fondo de Cultura Económico, 1993.

Anderson, Arthur J. O., "The Institution of Slave-Bathing." *Indiana* (Ibero-American Institute, Berlin) 7 (1982): 81–92.

———. "Los 'Primeros Memoriales' y el *Codice Florentino.*" *Estudios de Cultura Náhuatl* 24 (1994): 49–91.

———. "Sahagún's 'Doctrinal Encyclopedia.'" *Estudios de Cultura Nahuatl* 16 (1983): 109–22.

Arnold, Philip, P. *Eating Landscape: Aztec and European Occupation of Tlalocan.* Niwot: University Press of Colorado, 1999.

Aveni, Anthony F. "Mapping the Ritual Landscape: Debt Payment to Tlaloc during the Month of Atlcahualo." In *Aztec Ceremonial Landscapes,* edited by David Carrasco, 58–73. Louisville: University Press of Colorado, 1999.

Aveni, Anthony F., and Edward E. Calnek. "Astronomical Considerations in the Aztec Expression of History, Eclipse Data." *Ancient Mesoamerica* 10 (1999): 87–98.

Aveni, Anthony F., Edward E. Calnek, and H. Hartung. "Myth, Environment, and the

Orientation of the Templo Mayor of Tenochtitlan." *American Antiquity* 53 (April 1988): 287–309.

Báez-Jorge, Félix. "Planos simbólicos del Templo Mayor." *Estudios de Cultura Nahuatl* 19 (1989): 311–20.

Baird, Ellen T. *The Drawings of Sahagún's "Primeros memoriales": Structure and Style.* Norman: University of Oklahoma Press, 1993.

Baquedano, Elizabeth, ed. *Tezcatlipoca: Trickster and Supreme Deity.* Boulder: University Press of Colorado, 2014.

Baquedano, Elizabeth, and Michel Graulich. "Decapitation among the Aztecs: Mythology, Agriculture and Politics, and Hunting." *Estudios de Cultura Nahuatl* 23 (1993): 163–78.

Barrera Rodríguez, Rául. "The *Huei Tzompantli* of Tenochtitlan." Paper presented at "The Foundation of Heaven: The Great Temple of Tenochtitlan, Symposium in Honor of Eduardo Matos Moctezuma," April 2017.

Bartl, Renate, Barbara Göbel, and Hanns J. Prem. "Los calendarios aztecas de Sahagún." *Estudios de Cultura Nahuatl* 19 (1989): 13–82.

Bassett, Molly H. *The Fate of Earthly Things: Aztec Gods and God-Bodies.* Austin: University of Texas Press, 2015.

Batalla Rosado, Juan José. *El códice Borgia: Una guía para un viaje alucinante por el inframundo.* Madrid: Testimonio Compañía Editorial, 2008.

———. "Los códices mesoamericanos: Métodos de estudio." *Itinerarios* 8 (2008): 43–65.

Battock, Clementina. "Acerca de las pinturas que se quemaron y la reescritura de la historia en tiempos de Itzcoatl. Una revision desde la perspectiva simbólica." *Estudios de Cultura Nahuatl* 43 (2012): 95–113.

Beekman, Christopher S., and Alexander F. Christensen. "Controlling for Doubt and Uncertainty through Multiple Lines of Evidence: A New Look at the Mesoamerican Nahua Migrations." *Journal of Archeological Method and Theory* 10 (June 2003): 111–64.

Berdan, Frances F. "Economics of Mexica Religious Performance." In *Rethinking the Aztec Economy,* edited by Deborah L. Nichols, Frances F. Berdan, and Michael E. Smith, 130–55. Tucson: University of Arizona Press, 2017.

———. "The Imperial Tribute Roll of the Codex Mendoza." In *The Codex Mendoza,* edited by Frances F. Berdan and Patricia Rieff Anawalt, 1:55–79. Berkeley: University of California Press, 1992.

———. "Ports of Trade in Mesoamerica: A Reappraisal." In *Cultural Continuity in Mesoamerica,* edited by David L. Browman, 170–98. The Hague: Mouton, 1978.

Berdan, Frances F., Richard E. Blanton, Elizabeth Hill Boone, Michael E. Smith, and Emily Umberger. *Aztec Imperial Strategies.* Washington, D.C.: Dumbarton Oaks, 1996.

Berdan, Frances F., John K. Chance, Alan R. Sandstrom, Barbara L. Stark, James Taggart, and Emily Umberger. *Ethnic Identity in Nahua Mesoamerica: The View from Archeology, Art History, Ethnohistory, and Contemporary Ethnography.* Salt Lake City: University of Utah Press, 2008.

Blanton, Richard E. "A Consideration of Causality in the Growth of Empire: A Comparative Perspective." In *Aztec Imperial Strategies,* edited by Frances F. Berdan et al., 219–27. Washington, D.C.: Dumbarton Oaks, 1996.

Boone, Elizabeth Hill, ed. *The Aztec Templo Mayor.* Washington, D.C.: Dumbarton Oaks, 1987.

———. *Cycles of Time and Meaning in the Mexican Books of Fate*. Austin: University of Texas Press, 2007.

———. *Incarnations of the Aztec Supernatural: The Image of Huitzilopochtli in Mexico and Europe*. Philadelphia: American Philosophical Society, 1989.

———. "Migration Histories as Ritual Performance." In *Aztec Ceremonial Landscapes*, edited by David Carrasco, 121–51. Niwot: University Press of Colorado, 1991.

———. "The Petroglyphic Prayer on the Rim of the Sun Stone of Motecuhzoma Ilhuicamina." *Ancient Mesoamerica* 24 (2013): 225–41.

———. *Stories in Red and Black: Pictorial Histories of the Aztecs and Mixtecs*. Austin: University of Texas Press, 2000.

Boone, Elizabeth Hill, and Walter D. Mignolo, eds. *Writing Without Words: Alternative Literacies in Mesoamerica and the Andes*. Durham, NC: Duke University Press, 1994.

Bosch García, Carlos. *La esclavitud prehispánica entre los aztecas*. Mexico: Colegio de México, 1994.

Boturini Benaducci, Lorenzo. *Idea of a New General History of North America: An Account of Colonial Native Mexico*. Edited and translated by Stafford Poole. Norman: University of Oklahoma, 2015.

Broda, Johanna. "La fiesta del fuego nuevo, y el culto Azteca de los Pleyades." In *La antropología americanista en la actualidad: Homenaje a Rafael Girard*, 2:283–303. Mexico: Editores Mexicanos Unidos, 1980.

———. "Tlacaxipeualiztli: A Reconstruction of an Aztec Calendar Festival from 16th Century Sources." *Revista española de antropología Americana* 5 (1970): 197–273.

Broda, Johanna, David Carrasco, and Eduardo Matos Moctezuma. *The Great Temple of Tenochtitlan: Center and Periphery in the Aztec World*. Berkeley: University of California Press, 1987.

Brotherston, Gordon. "Huitzilopochtli and What Was Made of Him." In *Mesoamerican Archeology: New Approaches*, edited by Norman Hammond, 155–66. Austin: University of Texas Press, 1974.

———. "Sacred Sand in Mexican Picture-Writing and Later Literature." *Estudios de Cultura Nahuatl* 11 (1974): 303–9.

———. "The Year in the Mexican Codices: The Nature and Structure of the Eighteen Feasts." *Estudios de Cultura Nahuatl* 34 (2003): 67–97.

Brown, Betty Ann. "Seen but Not Heard: Women in Aztec Ritual." In *Text and Image in Pre-Columbian Art*, edited by Janet Berlo, 119–53. Oxford: British Archeological Reports Press, 1983.

Browne, Walden. *Sahagún and the Transition to Modernity*. Norman: University of Oklahoma Press, 2000.

Brumfiel, Elizabeth M. "Huitzilopochtli's Conquest: Aztec Ideology in the Archeological Record." *Cambridge Archeological Journal* 8 (1988): 3–13.

Brundage, Burr Cartwright. *The Fifth Sun*. Austin: University of Texas Press, 1979.

———. *The Jade Steps: A Ritual Life of the Aztecs*. Salt Lake City: University of Utah Press, 1985.

———. *A Rain of Darts: The Mexica Aztecs*. Austin: University of Texas Press, 1972.

Burkhart, Louise. *The Slippery Earth: Nahua-Christian Moral Dialogue in Sixteenth Century Mexico*. Tucson: University of Arizona Press, 1989.

Burrus, Ernest J. "Religious Chroniclers and Historians: A Summary with Annotated Bibliography." In *Guide to Ethnohistorical Sources, Part 2*, edited by Howard F. Cline and John

B. Glass, 138–85. Handbook of Middle American Indians 13, edited by Robert Wauchope. Austin: University of Texas Press, 1973.

Bustamante García, Jesús. *Fray Bernardino de Sahagún: una revisión crítica de los manuscritos y de su proceso de composición*. Mexico: Universidad Nacional Autónoma de México, 1990.

Cancian, Frank. *Economics and Prestige in a Maya Community: The Religious Cargo System in Zinacantan*. Stanford, Cal.: Stanford University Press, 1965.

Carrasco, David, ed. *Aztec Ceremonial Landscapes*. Niwot: University Press of Colorado, 1991.

———. *City of Sacrifice: The Aztec Empire and the Role of Violence in Civilization*. Boston: Beacon, 1999.

———. "Give Me Some Skin: The Charism of the Aztec Warrior." *History of Religions* 35 (1995): 1–26.

———. "Myth, Cosmic Terror, and the Templo Mayor." In *The Great Temple of Tenochtitlan: Center and Periphery in the Aztec World*, edited by Johanna Broda, David Carrasco, and Eduardo Matos Moctezuma, 124–69. Berkley: University of California Press.

———. "The Sacrifice of Tezcatlipoca: To Change Place." In *Aztec Ceremonial Landscapes*, edited by David Carrasco, 31–57. Niwot: University Press of Colorado, 1991.

———. "The Sacrifice of Women in the Florentine Codex: The Hearts of Plants and Players in War Games." In *Representing Aztec Ritual*, edited by Eloise Quiñones Keber, 197–226. Niwok: University Press of Colorado, 2002.

Carrasco, Pedro. *The Tenochca Empire of Ancient Mexico: The Triple Alliance of Tenochtitlan, Tetzcoco, and Tlacopan*. Norman: University of Oklahoma Press, 1999.

Caso, Alfonso. "Calendrical Systems of Central Mexico." In *Archaeolgy of Northern Mesoamerica*, edited by Gordon F. Ekholm and Ignacio Bernal, 333–48. Handbook of Middle American Indians 10, edited by Robert Wauchope. Austin: University of Texas Press, 1971.

———. *Los calendarios prehispánicos*. Mexico: Universidad Nacional Autónoma de México, 1967.

Castañeda de la Paz, María. "La *Tira de la peregrinación* y la ascendencia chichimeca de los tenochca." *Estudios de Cultura Nahuatl* 38 (2007): 183–212.

Castañeda de la Paz, María, and Sebastián van Doesburg. "Coatepec en las Fuentes del centro de México y su presencia en el valle de Coixtlahuaca." In *Pictografía y escritura alfabética en Oaxaca*, edited by Sebastián van Doesburg, 161–96. Oaxaca: Instituto Estatal de Educación Pública, 2008.

Castillo, Bernal Díaz del. *Historia verdadera de la conquista de la Nueva España*. Vol. 1. Mexico: Dastin, 2003.

Castillo, Cristóbal del. *Historia de la venida de los mexicanos y de otros pueblos e Historia de la conquista*. Mexico: Instituto Nacional de Antropología e Historia, 1991.

Castillo, Victor M. *Estructura económica de la sociedad mexica según las fuentes documentales*. Mexico: Universidad Nacional Autónoma de México, 1972.

Castillo Farreras, Victor Manuel. "El bisiesto Nahuatl." *Estudios de cultura Náhuatl* 9, no. 75 (1971): 75–104.

Chimalpahin Quauhtlehuanitzin, Domingo de San Antón Muñón. *Codex Chimalpahin*. Edited and translated by Arthur J. O. Anderson and Susan Schroeder. 2 vols. Norman: University of Oklahoma Press, 1997.

Chinchilla Mazariegos, Oswaldo. "La muerte de Moquihuix. Los mitos cosmogónicos mesoamericanos y la historia Azteca." *Estudios de Cultura Nahuatl* 42 (2011): 77–108.

Clavigero, Francesco Saverio. *Historia Antigua de México*. Mexico : Editorial Porrúa, 1971.

Clendinnen, Inga. *Aztecs*. Cambridge: Cambridge University Press, 1991.

———. *The Cost of Courage in Aztec Society: Essays on Mesoamerican Society and Culture*. Cambridge: Cambridge University Press, 2010.

Cline, Howard F., and Nicolau d'Olwer. "Sahagún and his Works." In *Guide to Ethnohistorical Sources, Part 2*, edited by Howard F. Cline, 186–207. Handbook of Middle American Indians 13, edited by Robert Wuachope. Austin: University of Texas Press, 1973.

Codex Mendoza. Edited by Frances F. Berdan and Patricia Rieff Anawalt. 4 vols. Berkeley: University of California Press, 1992.

Codex Telleriano-Remensis. Edited by Eloise Quiñones-Keber. Austin: University of Texas Press, 1995.

Conrad, Geoffrey W., and Arthur A. Demarest. *Religion and Empire: The Dynamics of Aztec and Inca Expansionism*. Cambridge: Cambridge University Press, 1984.

Contel, José, and Katarzyna Mikulska Dabrowska. "'Mas nosotros que somos dioses nunca moriremos.' Ensayo sobre *Tlamacazqui*: ¿Dios, sacerdote o qué otro demonio?" In *De dioses y hombres: Creencias y rituales mesoamericanos y sus supervivencias*, edited by Katarzyna Mikulska Dabrowska and José Contel, 23–65. Warsaw: University of Warsaw, Instituto de Estudios Ibéricos e Iberoamericanos, 2011.

Cortés, Rocio. "¿Dónde está Tlaloc? El Templo mayor mexica: Edificación real y simbólica del imperio en Fuentes escritas y materiales." *MLN* 118 (2003): 341–82.

Couch, N. C. Christopher. *The Festival Cycle of the Aztec Codex Borbonicus*. Oxford: BAR, 1985.

Davies, Nigel. *The Aztecs*. Norman: University of Oklahoma Press, 1980.

———. *The Toltec Heritage: From the Fall of Tula to the Rise of Tenochtitlan*. Norman: University of Oklahoma Press, 1980.

Dehouve, Daniele. "Las funciones rituales de los altos personajes mexicas." *Estudios de Cultura Nahuatl* 45 (2013): 37–68.

Díaz Alvarez, Ana. "*Tlalpohualli*, la cuenta de las cosas. Reflexiones en torno a la reconstrucción de los calendarios Nahuas." *Estudios de Cultura Nahuatl* 46 (2013): 159–97.

Dibble, Charles. "The Boban Calendar Wheel." *Estudios de Cultura Nahuatl* 20 (1990): 173–82.

———. "Los manuscritos de Tlatelolco y México y el Codice Florentino." *Estudios de Cultura Nahuatl* 29 (1999): 27–64.

———. "The *Xalaquia* Ceremony." *Estudios de Cultura Nahuatl* 14 (1980): 198–202.

DiCesare, Catherine R. *Sweeping the Way: Divine Transformation in the Aztec Festival of Ochpaniztli*. Boulder: University Press of Colorado, 2009.

Dodds Pennock, Caroline. *Bonds of Blood: Gender, Lifecycle and Sacrifice in Aztec Culture*. New York: Palgrave Macmillan, 2008.

Don, Patricia Lopes. *Bonfires of Culture: Franciscans, Indigenous Leaders, and the Inquisition in Early Mexico, 1524–1540*. Norman: University of Oklahoma Press, 2010.

Durán, Diego de. *Book of the Gods and Rites of the Ancient Calendar*. Edited and translated by Fernando Horcasitas and Doris Heyden. Norman: University of Oklahoma Press, 1971.

———. *The History of the Indies of New Spain*. Edited and translated by Doris Heyden. Norman: University of Oklahoma Press, 1994.

Durand-Forest, Jaqueline. "Practique divinatoire et cycle liturgique chez les anciens Mexicains." *Indiana* 10 (1985): 163–82.

Duverger, Christian. *La flor letal: Economía del sacrificio azteca.* Mexico: Fondo de Cultura Económico, 1983.

Edgerton, Samuel Y. *Theaters of Conversion: Religious Architecture and Indian Artisans in Colonial Mexico.* Albuquerque: University of New Mexico Press, 2001.

Elson, Christina M., and Michael E. Smith. "Archeological Deposits from the Aztec New Fire Ceremony." *Ancient Mesoamerica* 12 (2001): 157–74.

Furst, Jill Leslie McKeever. "The Aztec New Fire Ritual: A World Renewal Rite." *Journal of Latin American Lore* 18 (1992): 29–36.

Garibay, Angel María, ed. *Teogonía e historia de los mexicanos; Tres opúsculos del siglo XVI.* Mexico: Porrúa, 1979.

Gerhard, Peter. *A Guide to the Historical Geography.* Cambridge: Cambridge University Press, 1972.

Gillespie, Susan D. *The Aztec Kings: The Construction of Rulership in Mexica History.* Tucson: University of Arizona Press, 1989.

Glass, John B., with Donald Robertson. "A Census of Native American Pictorial Manuscripts." In *Guide to Ethnohistorical Sources,* edited by Howard F. Cline, 81–252. Handbook of Middle American Indians 14, edited by Robert Wauchope. Austin: University of Texas Press, 1975.

Glass, John B. *Sahagún: Reorganization of the Manuscrito de Tlatelolco, 1566–1569.* Lincoln Center, Mass.: Conemex Associates, 1978.

González Aparicio, Luis. *Plano reconstructive de la region de Tenochtitlan.* Mexico: Instituto Nacional de Antropología e Historia, 1973.

González Torres, Yolotl. "El gran ausente: Huitzilopochtli, su representación metafórica." *Arqueología Mexicana* 22 (May–December 1996): 70–72.

———. *El sacrificio humano entre los mexicas.* Mexico: Fondo de Cultura Económico, 1985.

Graulich, Michel. "Aztec Human Sacrifice as Expiation." *History of Religions* 39 (2000): 352–71.

———. "Double Immolations in Ancient Mexican Sacrificial Ritual." *History of Religions* 27 (1988): 393–404.

———. "Dualities in Cacaxtla." In *Mesoamerican Dualism/Dualismo Mesoamericano,* edited by Rudolf Van Zantwijk, 94–118. Utrecht: RUU-ISOR, 1990.

———. *Fiestas de los pueblos indígenas: Ritos aztecas, las fiestas de las veintenas.* Mexico: Instituto Nacional Indigenista, 1999.

———. "Las fiestas del año solar en el Códice Borbónico." *Itinerarios* 8 (2008): 185–94.

———. "Más sobre la Coyolxauhqui y las mujeres desnudas de Tlatelolco." *Estudios de Cultura Nahuatl* 31 (2000): 77–94.

———. "The Metaphor of the Day in Ancient Mexican Myth and Ritual." *Current Anthropology* 22 (February 1981): 45–60.

———. "Mexico City's 'Templo Mayor' Revisited." In *Ancient America: Contributions to New World Archeology,* edited by Nicholas Saunders, 19–32. Oxford: Oxbow, 1992.

———. "Miccailhuitl: The Aztec Festivals of the Deceased." *Numen* 36 (June 1989): 43–71.

———. *Montezuma ou l'apogée et la chute de l'empire aztèque.* Lille: Librairie Arthème Fayard, 1994.

———. *Myths of Ancient Mexico.* Translated by Bernard R. Ortiz de Montellano and Thelma Ortiz de Montellano. Norman: University of Oklahoma Press, 1997.

———. "Myths of Paradise Lost in Pre-Hispanic Central Mexico." *Current Anthropology* 24 (1983): 575–88.

———. "Quetzalcoatl-Ehecatl, the Bringer of Life." In *Ancient America: Contributions to New World Archeology*, edited by Nicholas Saunders, 33–38. Oxford: Oxbow, 1992.

———. *Ritos aztecas: Las fiestas de las veintenas.* Mexico: Instituto Nacional Indigenista, 1999.

Graulich, Michel, and Guillaume Olivier. "¿Deidades insaciables? La comida de los dioses en el México antiguo." *Estudios de Cultura Nahuatl* 34 (2004): 121–55.

Grigsby, Thomas L., and Carmen Cook de Leonard. "Xilonen in Tepoztlán: A Comparison of Tepoztecan and Aztec Agrarian Ritual Schedules." *Ethnohistory* 39 (1992): 108–47.

Grimstead, Deanna N. "Ethnographic and Modeled Costs of Long Distance, Big-Game Hunting." *American Antiquity* 75 (Jan. 2010): 61–80.

Gutiérrez de MacGregor, María Teresa, and Jorge González Sánchez. "De Aztlan a Tenochtitlan: cartografía actual de los lugares señalados en la Tira de la Peregrinación." *Journal of Latin American Geography* 10 (2011): 35–51.

Hajovsky, Patrick Thomas. *On the Lips of Others: Moteuczoma's Fame in Aztec Monuments and Rituals.* Austin: University of Texas Press, 2015.

Hassig, Russ. *Aztec Warfare: Imperial Expansion and Political Control.* Norman: University of Oklahoma Press, 1988.

———. *Time, History, and Belief in Aztec and Colonial Mexico.* Austin: University of Texas Press, 2001.

———. *Trade, Tribute, and Transportation: The Sixteenth-Century Political Economy of the Valley of Mexico.* Norman: University of Oklahoma Press, 1985.

Heyden, Doris. "Caves, Gods, and Myths: Worldview and Planning in Teotihuacan." In *Mesoamerican Sites and Worldviews*, edited by Elizabeth Benson, 1–39. Washington, D.C.: Dumbarton Oaks, 1981.

———. "Dryness Before the Rains: Toxcatl and Tezcatlipoca." In *To Change Place: Aztec Ceremonial Landscapes*, edited by David Carrasco, 188–202. Niwot: University Press of Colorado, 1991.

———. "El árbol en el mito y el símbolo." *Estudios de Cultura Nahuatl* 23 (1993): 201–19.

———. "Sand in Ritual and in History." In *Representing Aztec Ritual: Performance, Text, and Image in the Work of Sahagún*, edited by Eloise Quiñones-Keber, 173–96. Boulder: University Press of Colorado, 2002.

———. "Tezcatlipoca en el mundo Nahuatl." *Estudios de Cultura Nahuatl* 19 (1989): 83–93.

Hirth, Kenneth G. *The Aztec Economic World: Merchants and Markets in Ancient Mesoamerica.* Cambridge: Cambridge University Press, 2016.

History and Mythology of the Aztecs: The Codex Chimalpopoca. Translated by John Bierhorst. Tucson: University of Arizona Press, 1992.

"Histoyre du Mechique, manuscript français du XVIe siècle." Edited by E. de Jonghe. *Journal de la Sociètè des Americanistes*, n.s., 2 (1905): 1–41.

Hunt, Eva. *The Transformation of the Hummingbird: Cultural Roots of a Zinacantecan Mythical Poem.* Ithaca, N.Y.: Cornell University Press, 1977.

Hvidtfeldt, Arild. *Teotl and *Ixiptlatli: Some Central Conceptions in Ancient Mexican Religion.* Copenhagen: Muksgaard, 1958.

Ingham, John M. "Human Sacrifice at Tenochtitlan." *Comparative Studies in Society and History* 26 (July 1964): 379–400.

———. "Time and Space in Ancient Mexico: The Symbolic Dimensions of Clanship." *Man*, n.s., 6 (1971): 615–29.

Irigoyen-Rascón, Fructuoso. *Tarahumara Medicine: Ethnobotany and Healing among the Rarámuri of Mexico.* Norman: University of Oklahoma Press, 2015.

James, Susan E. "Some Aspects of the Aztec Religion in the Hopi Kachina Cult." *Journal of the Southwest* 42 (2000): 897–926.

Jansen, Maarten, and Gabina Aurora Pérez Jiménez. "Renaming the Mexican Codices." *Ancient Mesoamerica* 15 (2004): 267–71.

———. *Time and the Ancestors: Aztec and Mixtec Ritual Art.* Leiden: Brill, 2017.

Jiménez Moreno, Wigiberto. "De Tezcatlipoca a Huitzilopochtli." *Actes du 42 Congreso International des Americanistes* 6 (1979): 27–34.

Johansson, Patrick. "El desliz cronológico de los meses en el calendario náhuatl *cempoallapohualli.*" *Estudios de Cultura Nahuatl* 52 (2016): 75–117.

———. "Estudio comparative de la gestión y del nacimiento de Huitzilopochtli en un relato verbal, una variante pictográfica y un 'texto' arquitectónico." *Estudios de Cultura Nahuatl* 30 (1999): 71–111.

———. "La gestación mítica de México-Tenochtitlan." *Estudios de Cultura Nahuatl* 25 (1995): 95–130.

———. "Tezcatlipoca o Quetzalcoatl: Una disyuntiva mítico-existencial precolombina." *Estudios de Cultura Nahuatl* 23 (1993): 179–99.

Karttunen, Frances E. *An Analytical Dictionary of Nahuatl.* Norman: University of Oklahoma Press, 1992.

Katz, Friedrich. *Ancient American Civilizations.* New York: Praeger, 1972.

———. *Situación social y económica de los aztecas durante los sivlos XV y XVI.* Mexico: Universidad Nacional Autónoma de México, 1966.

Keating, Jessica, and Lia Markey. "'Indian' Objects in Medici and Austrian Hapsburg Inventories." *Journal of the History of Collections* 23 (2011): 283–300.

Kelly, Isabel, and Angel Palerm. *The Tajín Totonac: Part 1, History, Subsistence, Shelter, and Technology.* Washington, D.C.: Smithsonian Institution, Institute of Social Anthropology, 1952.

Klein, Cecelia F. "Fighting with Femininity: Gender and War in Aztec Mexico." *Estudios de Cultura Nahuatl* 24 (1994): 219–53.

———. "The Ideology of Autosacrifice at the Templo Mayor." In *The Aztec Templo Mayor,* edited by Elizabeth Hill Boone, 293–370. Washington, D.C.: Dumbarton Oaks, 1987.

———. "The Devil and the Skirt" *Ancient Mesoamerica* 11 (2000): 1–26.

Klor de Alva, J. Jorge. "Sahagún's Misguided Introduction to Ethnography and the Failure of the *Coloquios* Project." In *The Work of Bernardino de Sahagún: Pioneer Ethnographer of Sixteenth-Century Aztec Mexico,* edited by Jorge Klor de Alva, H. B. Nicholson, and Eloise Quiñones-Keber, 83–92. Albany, N.Y.: Institute for Mesoamerican Studies, University at Albany, 1988.

Klor de Alva, J. Jorge, H. B. Nicholson, and Eloise Quiñones Keber, eds. *The Work of Bernardino de Sahagún: Pioneer Ethnographer of Sixteenth-Century Aztec Mexico.* Albany, N.Y.: Institute for Mesoamerican Studies, University at Albany, 1988.

Kruell, Gabriel Kenrick. "Panquetzaliztli: El nacimiento de Huitzilopochtli y la caída de Tezcatlipoca." *Estudios Mesoamericanos* 10 (January–June 2011): 81–93.

Krupp, Edwin C. "The 'Binding of the Years,' the Pleiades, and the Nadir Sun." *Archaeoastronomy* 5 (1982): 9–13.

Kummels, Ingrid. "Reflecting Diversity: Variants of the Legendary Footraces of the Rarámuri in Northern Mexico." *Ethnos* 66 (2001): 73–98.

León-Portilla, Miguel, *Aztec Thought and Culture*. Norman: University of Oklahoma Press, 1963.

———. *Bernardino de Sahagún: First Anthropologist*. Norman: University of Oklahoma Press, 2012.

———. *Bernardino de Sahagún pionero de la antropología*. Mexico: Universidad Naciona Autónoma de México and Colegio Nacional, 1999.

———. "Biografía de Fray Juan de Torquemada." In *Monarquía Indiana*, by Juan de Torquemada, edited by Miguel León-Portillo, 7:13–55. Mexico: Universidad Nacional Autónoma de México, 1975–1983.

———. "Itzcoatl: Creador de una cosmovision." In *Siete ensayos sobre cultura náhuatl*. Mexico: Universidad Nacional Autónoma de México, 1958.

———. *Los antiguos mexicanos a través de sus crónicas y cantares*. Mexico: Fondo de Cultura Económico, 1961.

Lesur, Yolotl G. de. "El dios Huitzilopochtli en la peregrinación mexica de Aztlan a Tula." *Anales del Institute Nacional de Antropologia e Historia* 19 (1966 [1968]): 175–90.

Limón Olvera, Silvia. *El fuego sagrado. Simbolismo y realidad entre los nahuas*. Mexico: Universidad Nacional Autónoma de México, 2012.

Linné, Sigvald. *El Valle y la Ciudad de Mexico en 1550: Relación histórica fundada sobre un mapa geográfico, que se conserva en la biblioteca de la Universidad de Uppsala, Suecia*. Stockholm: Folkens museum Etnografiska, 1988.

Lockhart, James, ed. and trans. *We People Here: Nahuatl Accounts of the Conquest of Mexico*. Berkeley: University of California Press, 1993.

———. *The Nahuas after the Conquest: Indians of Central Mexico, Sixteenth through Eighteenth Centuries*. Stanford, Cal.: Stanford University Press, 1992.

Loftin, John D. "A Hopi-Anglo Discourse on Myth and History." *Journal of the American Academy of Religion* 63 (1995): 677–93.

———. "Supplication and Participation: The Distance and Relation of the Sacred in Hopi Prayer Rites." *Anthropos* 81 (1986): 177–201.

Lombardo de Ruiz, Sonia. *Desarrollo urbano de México-Tenochtitlan según las Fuentes históricas*. Mexico: Instituto Nacional de Antropología e Historia, 1973.

López Austin, Alfredo. *The Human Body and Ideology: Concepts of the Ancient Nahuas*. 2 vols. Salt Lake City: University of Utah Press, 1988.

———. *The Myth of Quetzalcoatl: Religion, Rulership, and History in the Nahua World*. Translated by Russ Davidson with Guilhem Olivier. Boulder: University Press of Colorado, 2015.

López Austin, Alfredo, and Leonardo López Luján. *Monte Sagrado—Templo Mayor*. Mexico: Universidad Nacional Autónoma de México, 2009.

López Luján, Leonardo. "Cuando la gente 'Se uno-aconejó': La gran sequía de 1454 en la cuenca de México." *Arqueología Mexicana* 25, no. 149 (January–February 2018): 36–45.

López Luján, Leonardo, Ximena Chávez Balderas, Norma Valentín, and Aurora Montúfar. "Huitzilopochtli y el sacrificio de niños en el Templo Mayor de Tenochtitlan." In *El sacrificio humano en la tradición religiosa mesoamericana*, edited by Leonardo López Luján and Guilhem Olivier, 367–94. Mexico: Instituto Nacional de Antropología e Historia and Universidad Nacional Autónoma de México, 2010.

López Luján, Leonardo, and Angel González López. "Tierra, agua y fuego al pie del Templo Mayor de Tenochtitlan: un conjunto de bajorrelieves de la época de Motecuhzoma Ilhuicamina." *Estudios de Cultura Nahuatl* 47 (2014): 7–51.

López Luján, Leonardo, and Alfredo López Austin. "Los mexicas en Tula y Tula en Mexico-Tenochtitlan." *Estudios de Cultura Nahuatl* 38 (2007): 33–83.

López Luján, Leonardo, and Guilhem Olivier, eds. *El sacrificio humano en la tradición religiosa mesoamericana.* Mexico: Instituto Nacional de Antropología e Historia and Universidad Nacional Autónoma de México, 2010.

Magaloni Kerpel, Diana. *The Colors of the New World: Artists, Materials, and the Creation of the Florentine Codex.* Los Angeles: Getty Research Institute, 2014.

Marcus, Joyce. *Mesoamerican Writing Systems: Propaganda, Myth, and History in Four Ancient Civilizations.* Princeton, N.J.: Princeton University Press, 1992.

Martínez, José Luis, ed. *Documentos cortesianos.* 4 vols. Mexico: Fondo de Cultura Económica, 1993.

Matos Moctezuma, Eduardo. "Las seis Coyolxauqui: Variaciones sobre un mismo tema." *Estudios de Cultura Nahuatl* 21 (1991): 16–29.

———. "Symbolism of the Templo Mayor." In *The Aztec Templo Mayor,* edited by Elizabeth Hill Boone, 185–209. Washington, D.C.: Dumbarton Oaks, 1987.

———. "Templo Mayor: History and Interpretation." In *Moctezuma's Mexico: Visions of the Aztec World,* edited by David Carrasco and Eduardo Matos Moctezuma, 3–98. Boulder: University Press of Colorado, 2003.

———. "Tlaltecuhtli: Señor de la tierra." *Estudios de Cultura Nahuatl* 27 (1997): 15–40.

Matos Moctezuma, Eduardo, and Leonardo López Luján. *Escultura monumental mexica.* Mexico: Fondo de Cultura Económico, 2012.

Máynez, Pilar. *El calepino de Sahagún: Un acercamiento.* Mexico: Universidad Nacional Autónoma de México and Fondo de Cultura Económico, 2002.

Mazzetto, Elena. "Las *ayauhcalli* en el ciclo de las veintenas de; año solar." *Estudios de Cultura Nahuatl* 48 (2014): 135–75.

———. *Lieux de culte e parcours cérémoniels dans les fêtes des vingtaines a Mexico—Tenochtitlan.* London: British Archeological Reports, 2014.

———. "¿Miel o sangre?: Nuevas problemáticas acerca de la elaboración de las efigies de tzoalli de las divinidades nahuas." *Estudios de Cultura Náhuatl* 53 (2018).

McDougall, Christopher. *Born to Run: A Hidden Tribe, Superathletes, and the Greatest Race the World Has Never Seen.* New York: Vintage, 2009.

Milbrath, Susan. "Decapitated Lunar Goddesses in Aztec Art, Myth, and Ritual." *Ancient Mesoamerica* 8 (1997): 185–206.

———. *Heaven and Earth in Ancient Mexico: Astronomy and Seasonal Cycles in the Codex Borgia.* Austin: University of Texas Press, 2013.

Minneci, Mónica. "Antithesis and Complementarity: Tezcatlipoca and Quetzalcoatl in Creation Myths." *Estudios de Cultura Nahuatl* 30 (1999): 153–64.

Molina, Alonso de. *Vocabulario en lengua castellana y Mexicana y Mexicana y castellana.* Preliminary Study by Miguel León-Portilla. Mexico: Editorial Porrúa, 1970.

Motolinia [Toribio de Benavente]. *Memoriales o Libro de las cosas de la Nueva España y de los naturales de ella.* Edited by Edmundo O'Gorman. Mexico: Universidad Nacional Autónoma de México, 1971.

Mundy, Barbara E. *The Death of Aztec Tenochtitlan, the Life of Mexico City.* Austin: University of Texas Press, 2015.

Navarrete Linares, Francisco. *Los orígenes de los pueblos indígenas del valle de Mexico: Los altepetl y sus origenes.* Mexico: Universidad Nacional Autónoma de México, 2011.

Neumann, Franke J. "A Sacred Material in Aztec Ritual." *History of Religions* 13 (1973): 149–59.

Nichols, Deborah L., Frances F. Berdan, and Michael E. Smith, eds. *Rethinking the Aztec Economy.* Tucson: University of Arizona Press, 2017.

Nicholson, H. B. "The Chapultepec Cliff Sculpture of Motecuhzoma Xocoyotzin." *El México antiguo* 9 (1961): 379–444.

———. "The Iconography of the Deity Representations in Fray Bernardino de Sahagún's *Primeros Memoriales*: Huitzilopochtli and Chlachiuhtlicue." In *The Work of Bernardino de Sahagún,* edited by Jorge Klor de Alva, H. B. Nicholson, and Eloise Quiñones-Keber, 229–53. Albany, N.Y.: Institute for Mesoamerican Studies, 1988.

———. "Religion in Pre-Hispanic Central Mexico." In *Archaeology of Northern Mesoamerica,* edited by Gordon F. Ekholm and Ignacio Bernal, 395–446. Handbook of Middle American Indians 10, edited by Robert Wauchope. Austin: University of Texas Press, 1971.

———. "Representing the *Veintena* Ceremonies in the *Primeros Memoriales.*" In *Representing Aztec Ritual,* edited by Eloise Quiñones-Keber, 63–106. Boulder: University Press of Colorado, 2002.

———. "The Significance of the 'Looped Cord' Year Symbol in Pre-Hispanic Mexico: An Hypothesis." *Estudios de Cultura Nahuatl* 6 (1966): 135–48.

Nicholson, H. B., and Eloise Quiñones-Keber. *Art of Aztec Mexico: Treasures of Tenochtitlan.* Washington, D.C.: National Gallery of Art, 1983.

Noguera, Eduardo. "Las funciones del momoztli." *Anales de Antropología* 10 (1973): 111–22.

Nowotny, Karl Anton. *Tlacuilolli: Style and Contents of the Mexican Pictorial Manuscripts with a Catalog of the Borgia Group.* Norman: University of Oklahoma Press, 2005.

Nuttall, Zelia. *The Book of the Life of the Ancient Mexicans.* Berkeley: University of California Press, 1983.

Offner, Jerome A. "Archival Reports of Poor Crop Yields in the Early Postconquest Texcocan Heartland and Their Implications for Studies of Aztec Population." *American Antiquity* 45 (1980): 848–56.

Olivier, Guilhem. "El symbolism sacrificial de los Mimixcoa: Cacería, Guerra, sacrificio e identidad entre los Mexicas." In *El sacrificio humano en la tradición religiosa mesoamericana,* edited by Leonardo López Luján and Guilhem Olivier, 453–82. Mexico: Instituto Nacional de Antropología e Historia and Universidad Nacional Autónoma de México, 2010.

———. "Enemy Brothers or Divine Twins?" In *Tezcatlipoca: Trickster and Supreme Deity,* edited by Elizabeth Baquedano, 59–82. Boulder: University Press of Colorado, 2014.

———. *Mockeries and Metamorphoses of an Aztec God: Tezcatlipoca—"Lord of the Smoking Mirror."* Translated by Michel Besson. Boulder: University Press of Colorado, 2003.

O'Mack, Scott. "Yacateuctli and Ehecatl-Quetzalcoatl: Earth-Divers in Aztec Central Mexico." *Ethnohistory* 38 (1991): 1–33.

Palka, Joel W. "Left/Right Symbolism and the Body in Ancient Maya Iconography and Culture." *Latin American Antiquity* 13 (December 2002): 419–43.

Pasztory, Esther. *Aztec Art.* Norman: University of Oklahoma Press, 1983.

Pennington, Campbell W. "La Carrera de bola entre los tarahumaras de Mexico." *América Indígena* 30 (1970): 15–40.

———. *The Tarahumar of Mexico: Their Environment and Material Culture.* Salt Lake City: University of Utah Press, 1963.

Pharo, Lars Kirkhusmo. *The Ritual Practice of Time: Philosophy and Sociopolitics of Mesoamerican Calendars.* Leiden: Brill, 2014.

Prem, Hanns J. *Manual de la antigua cronología Mexicana.* Mexico: Centro de Investigaciones y Estudios Superiores en Antropología Social and Miguel Angel Porrúa, 2008.

Quiñones-Keber, Eloise, ed. *Representing Aztec Ritual: Performance, Text, and Image in the Work of Sahagún.* Boulder: University Press of Colorado, 2002.

Raat, W. Dirk, and George R. Janecek. *Mexico's Sierra Tarahumara: A Photohistory of the People of the Edge.* Norman: University of Oklahoma Press, 1996.

Ramírez, José Fernando. *Fray Toribio de Motolinia y otros estudios.* Mexico: Editorial Porrúa, 1957.

Read, Kay. "The Motion of Cosmic Forces in Mexica Rulership." *History of Religions* 34 (1994): 39–69.

———. *Time and Sacrifice in the Aztec Cosmos.* Bloomington: Indiana University Press, 1998.

Reyes Equiguas, Salvador. "EL huauhtli en la cultura náhuatl." Master's thesis, Universidad Nacional Autónoma de Mexico, 2006.

Rios Castaño, Victoria. "From the 'Memoriales con escolios' to the Florentine Codex: Sahagún and His Nahua Assistant' Co-Authorship of the Spanish Translation." *Journal of Iberian and Latin American Research* 20 (2014): 214–28.

Robelo, Cecilio A. *Diccionario de aztequismos.* Mexico: Fuente Cultural, 1948.

———. "Diccionario de la mitología nahoa." *Anales del Museo Nacional de Mexico,* n.s., 3 (1906): 97–116, 191–96, 237–44, 479–84.

Robertson, Donald. *Mexican Manuscript Paining of the Early Colonial Period: The Metropolitan Schools.* Norman: University of Oklahoma Press, 1959.

———. "The Sixteenth-Century Mexican Encyclopedia." *Cahiers d'histoire mondiale* 9 (1966): 617–27.

Rojas, Jose Luis de. *Tenochtitlan: Capital of the Aztec Empire.* Gainesville: University Press of Florida, 2012.

Rovira Morgado, Rossend. "*Huitznáhuac*: Ritual politico y administración segmentaria en el centro de la parcialidad de Teopan (México-Tenochtitlan)." *Estudios de Cultura Nahuatl* 41 (2010): 41–64.

Ruz Barrio, Miguel A. "Codices matritenses de fray Bernardino de Sahagún: studio codicológico del manuscrito de la Real Academic de Historia." *Revista Española de Antropología de América* 40 (2010): 198–208.

Sahagún, Bernardino de. *Florentine Codex.* Edited and translated by Arthur J. O. Anderson and Charles Dibble. 13 vols. Salt Lake City: University of Utah Press, 1950–82.

———. *Historia general de las cosas de la Nueva España.* Edited by Angel María Garibay. Mexico: Editorial Porrúa, 1975.

———. *Primeros memoriales: Facsimile Edition.* Norman: University of Oklahoma Press, 1993.

———. *Primeros memoriales: Paleography of Nahuatl Text and English Translation.* Edited by Thelma Sullivan. Norman: University of Oklahoma Press, 1997.

———. *Veinte Himno sacros de los nahuas.* Edited by Angel María Garibay. Mexico: Universidad Nacional Autónoma de México, 1958.

———. *Vida económica en Tenochtitlan.* Edited by Angel María Garibay. Mexico: Universidad Nacional Autónoma de México, 1961.

Sandstrom, Alan R. "The Cave-Pyramid Complex among the Contemporary Nahua of Northern Veracruz." In *In the Maw of the Earth Monster: Mesoamerican Ritual Cave Use,* edited by James E. Brady and Keith M. Prufer, 33–68. Austin: University of Texas Press, 2005.

Schroeder, Susan. "The First American Valentine: Nahua Courtship and Other Aspects of Family Structuring in Mesoamerica." *Journal of Family History* 23 (1998): 341–54.

———. *Tlacaelel Remembered mastermind of the Aztec Empire.* Norman: University of Oklahoma Press, 2016.

Seeman Conzatti, Emilia. *Usos del papel en el calendario ritual mexica.* Mexico: Instituto Nacional de Antropología e Historia, 1990.

Seler, Eduard. *Collected Works in Mesoamerican Linguistics and Archeology.* 6 vols. Culver City: Labyrinthos, 1991–97.

Smith, Michael E. "The Aztlan Migrations of the Nahuatl Chronicles: Myth or History?" *Ethnohistory* 31 (Summer 1984): 153–86.

Steck, Francis Borgia. *Motolinia's History of the Indians of New Spain.* Washington, D.C.: Academy of American Franciscan History, 1951.

Sullivan, Thelma D. "The Rhetorical Orations or *huehuetlatolli.*" In *Sixteenth Century Mexico: The Works of Sahagún,* edited by Munroe S. Edmunson, 79–109. Albuquerque: University of New Mexico Press, 1976.

Taube, Karl. "The Symbolism of Turquoise in Ancient Mesoamerica." In *Turquoise in Mexico and North America: Science, Conservation, Culture and Collections,* edited by J. C. H. King et al., 117–34. London: Archetype Publications, 2012.

———. "The Turquoise Hearth: Fire, Self Sacrifice, and the Central Mexican Cult of War." In *Mesoamerica's Classic Heritage: From Teotihuacan to the Great Aztec Temple,* edited by David Carrasco et al., 269–340. Niwot: University Press of Colorado, 2000.

Tena, Rafael. *El calendario mexica y la cronografía.* Mexico: Instituto Nacional de Antropología e Historia, 1987.

Tezozomoc, Fernando Alvarado. *Crónica mexicayotl.* Translated by Adrián León. Mexico: Universidad Nacional Autónoma de México, 1949.

Tichy, Franz. "Order and Relationship of Space and Time in Mesoamerica." In *Mesoamerican Sites and Worldviews,* edited by E. P. Benson, 217–45. Washington, D.C.: Dumbarton Oaks, 1981.

Tira de Peregrinación o Códice Boturini : inehnemi aztekatin (su caminar de los aztecas). México : Instituto Nacional de Antropología e Historia, 2000.

Torquemada, Juan de. *Monarquía Indiana.* Edited by Miguel León-Portilla. 7 vols. Mexico: Universidad Nacional Autónoma de México, 1975–1983.

Tovar, Juan de. *Origen de los mexicanos.* Barcelona: Linkgua Ediciones, 2009.

———. *The Tovar Calendar An Illustrated Mexican Manuscript Ca. 1585.* Edited by George Kubler and Charles Gibson. New Haven, Conn.: The Academy, 1951.

Townsend, Camilla. "'What in the World Have You Done to Me, My Lover?': Sex, Servitude, and Politics among the Pre-Conquest Nahuas as Seen in the *Cantares Mexicanos.*" *The Americas* 62 (2006): 349–89.

Uchmany, Eva Alexandra. "Huitzilopochtli, dios de la historia de los Azteca-mexitin." *Estudios de Cultura Nahuatl* 13 (1978): 213–37.

Uchmany, Eva Alexandra. "Las carácteristicas de un dios tutelar mesoamericano: Huitzilopochtli." *Actes du XLIIe Congrès International des Américanistes* 6 (1976): 49–62.

Umberger, Emily Good. "Aztec Sculptures, Hieroglyphs, and History." Ph.D. diss., Columbia University, 1981.

———. "El trono de Moctezuma." *Estudios de Cultura Nahuatl* 17 (1984): 63–83.

———. "Events Commemorated by Date Plaques at the Templo Mayor: Further Thoughts on the Solar Metaphor." In *The Aztec Templo Mayor,* edited by Elizabeth Hill Boone, 442–44. Washington, D.C.: Dumbarton Oaks, 1987.

———. "Metaphorical Underpinnings of Aztec War: The Case of the 1473 Civil War." *Ancient Mesoamerica* 18 (2007): 11–29.

———. "Notions of Aztec History: The Case of the Great Temple Dedication," *RES: Anthropology and Aesthetics* 42 (2002): 86–108.

———. "Tezcatlipoca and Huitzilopochtli: Political Dimensions of Aztec Deities." In *Tezcatlipoca: Trickster and Supreme Deity,* edited by Elizabeth Baquedano, 83–112. Boulder: University Press of Colorado, 2014.

Van Zantwijk, Rudolf. *The Aztec Arrangement: The Social History of Pre-Spanish Mexico.* Norman: University of Oklahoma Press, 1985.

———. "El parentesco y la afiliación étnica de Huitzilopochtli." *Actes du 42 Congreso International des Americanistes* 6 (1979): 63–68.

———. "The Great Temple of Tenochtitlan: Model of Aztec Cosmovision." In *Sites and World-Views,* edited by Elizabeth P. Benson, 71–86. Washington, D.C.: Dumbarton Oaks, 1981.

———, ed. *Mesoamerican Dualism/Dualismo Mesoamericano.* Utrecht: RUU-ISOR, 1990.

———. "Las organizaciones social-económicas y religiosas de los mercaderes gremiales aztecas." *Boletín de Estudios Latinoamericanos* 10 (1970): 1–20.

———. "Los seis barrios sirvientes de Huitzilopochtli." *Estudios de Cultura Nahuatl* 6 (1966): 177–85.

Vázquez Chamorro, Germán. "Las reformas socio-económicas de Motecuhtzoma II." *Revista española de antropología Americana* 11 (1981): 207–17.

Vesque, Martine. "'El instrument para ver' o *tlachieloni.*" *Trace* 71 (January 2017): 111–37.

Waters, Frank. *The Book of the Hopi.* New York: Penguin, 1963.

Williams, Barbara J., and María del Carmen Jorge y Jorge. "Aztec Arithmetic Revisited: Land-Area Algorithms and Acolhua Congruence Arithmetic." *Science* 320 (April 2008): 72–77.

Zingg, Robert. *Behind the Mexican Mountains.* Austin: University of Texas Press, 2001.

INDEX

References to illustrations are in *italic* type.